TORAH

OF THE EARTH

EXPLORING

4,000 Years of

ECOLOGY in

Jewish Thought

VOL. 2

ZIONISM:
One Land, Two Peoples

ECO-JUDAISM:
One Earth, Many Peoples

EDITED BY
ARTHUR WASKOW

For People of All Faiths, All Backgrounds
JEWISH LIGHTS Publishing
Woodstock, Vermont

Torah of the Earth: Exploring 4,000 Years of Ecology in Jewish Thought
Vol. 2: Zionism & Eco-Judaism

Except where otherwise stated, copyright for the individual essays published in this volume remains with the authors, and the contributions are included here by permission. We gratefully acknowledge permission from the following:

"The Environment: A Shared Interest" by Smith and Abu Diab; "Pollution and Peace," an Interview with Yossi Sarid; and "Our Shared Environment" by Robin Twite reprinted from *The Palestine-Israel Journal of Politics, Economics and Culture,* vol. V, no. 1, 1998, by permission of *PIJ*.

Excerpts from "Guarding the Garden" reprinted by permission of Margot L. Stein, David Schechter, and Evi Seidman.

"Metaphors of God" from *Standing Again at Sinai* by Judith Plaskow (HarperCollins Publishers, 1990) reprinted by permission of author and publisher.

"Nadie la Tiene: Land, Ecology, and Nationalism" by Aurora Levins Morales originally appeared in *Bridges: A Journal for Jewish Feminists & Our Friends,* and also appears in the author's collection, *Medicine Stories: History, Culture, and the Politic of Integrity* (South End, 1998). Reprinted by permission of the author.

"Technical Civilization and Shabbat," excerpts from "Architecture of Time" and "Beyond Civilization" in *The Sabbath* by Abraham Joshua Heschel. Copyright © 1951 by Abraham Joshua Heschel. Copyright renewed © 1979 by Sylvia Heschel. Reprinted by permission of Farrar, Straus, and Giroux, LLC.

"To Work It and Guard It" by Rabbi Arthur Green, from *Seek My Face, Speak My Name* © 1992, Jason Aronson Inc. Reprinted by permission of the author.

"The Way of the Sabbath" from *You Shall Be As Gods,* by Erich Fromm, © 1966 by Erich Fromm. Reprinted by permission of Henry Holt and Company, LLC

For information regarding permission to reprint material from this book, please mail or fax your request in writing to Jewish Lights Publishing, Permissions Department, at the address/fax number listed below.

Library of Congress Cataloging-in-Publication Data

Torah of the earth : exploring 4,000 years of ecology in Jewish thought / edited by Arthur Waskow.
p.   cm.
Includes bibliographical references.
ISBN 1-58023-086-5 (v. 1) — ISBN 1-58023-087-3 (v. 2)
1. Human ecology—Religious aspects—Judaism. 2. Nature—Religious aspects—Judaism. 3. Human ecology—Israel. I. Waskow, Arthur Ocean, 1933–
BM538.H85T67 2000
296.3'8—dc21

00-008696

First Edition

10 9 8 7 6 5 4 3 2 1

Manufactured in the United States of America
Printed on recycled paper.

Cover design: Casey Nuttall
Text design: Sans Serif Inc.

Published by Jewish Lights Publishing,
A Division of LongHill Partners, Inc.
Sunset Farm Offices, Route 4
P.O. Box 237, Woodstock, VT 05091
Tel: (802) 457-4000   Fax: (802)457-4004
www.jewishlights.com

For our children
Shoshana and Michael, David and Ketura, Morissa, Joshua;
For their children
and the children of their children;
For all children:

May you live to see your world fulfilled, your planet healed.

May you be our link to future worlds, and may your hope encompass all
the generations of all life yet to be.

May your heart conceive with understanding, may your mouth speak
wisdom, and your tongue be stirred with songs of joy.

May your gaze be straight and sure, your eyes be lit with Torah's lamp, your
face aglow with heaven's radiance, your lips speak words of knowledge.

May your innards rejoice in foods whose seeds are righteousness.

And may you always rush with eagerness to hear the truths
of the Unity who is more ancient than all time
and ever present in all beings.

Talmud Bavli: B'rachot 17a
(adapted from translation by Joel Rosenberg in the
Reconstructionist prayerbook, *Kol Haneshamah*)

Contents

INTRODUCTION

EARTH AND EARTHLING, *ADAM* AND *ADAMAH*

Perhaps the most profound Jewish statement about the relationship between human beings and the earth is bound up in two words of Hebrew—two words that do not even need a sentence to connect them: *Adam. Adamah.*

The first means "human being"; the second, "earth." The two words are connected to teach us that human beings and the earth are intertwined. In English, this connection would be obvious only if the everyday word for "human being" were "earthling," or perhaps if the ordinary word for "earth" were "humus." With either of these configurations, no one could say the name of earth or of human without hearing an echo of the other. Intertwined. Not identical, but intertwined.

What differences make us not identical? Genesis 2:5–7 explains:

There was no *adam* to serve/work the *adamah*, but a flow would well up upon the ground and water all the face of the *adamah*. And YHWH [by some understood as "Breath of the

World," from the sound of the letters "pronounced" with no vowels, producing only an outbreath] shaped the *adam* out of dust from the *adamah,* and blew into its nostrils the breath of life, and the *adam* became a living being, a breathing being.

The human being lost the breathing "-ah" sound at the end of *adamah.*

At the level of individual life-history, the human being loses the unconscious placental breathing that connects the enwombed human with the all-enfolding earth—and gains a new, more conscious, more deliberate breath.

At the level of the evolutionary history of humankind, *adam* lost the unconscious breathing that connected the earliest human beings with the earth from which they had just emerged—little different, to begin with, from the other primates round about them. And that "-ah" was replaced with a new kind of breath—a conscious breath from the Breath of the World. In separating from the earth, in being born, the *adam* becomes more conscious.

The earth-human relationship takes on a complex, ironic tone. Small wonder that humans eat what the earth grows in a way that bespeaks their alienation and brings upon them and the earth a still deeper alienation: "Damned be *adamah* on your account; with painful labor shall you eat from it."

If this is a myth of births and beginnings, it is also a myth of every new beginning. Not once only has the human race separated itself from the earth, but over and over.

On each occasion, as our sacred stories and our secular histories teach us, we have had to learn a new depth of connection and community with the earth from which we have separated. When we did not, we shattered the localities and regions of our earth and birth—and were shattered in return. For none can eat unscathed from the food into which they have poured out poison.

Today we are living in a crisis of this spiral. Epoch after epoch, the more and more knowledgeable human race has alienated itself more deeply, then realized more deeply its need for connection and built some new sense of community with the earth. Once this meant learning to raise fewer goats in fragile local ecosystems. Now it means learning not to destroy the global ozone layer. The upward turning of the spiral of human power to Make and to Do has faced every community and tradition on the planet with the task of learning better how to Be and how to Love.

In some ways it is in our own generation that we have most vehemently gobbled up that fruit of plenty that grew from the Tree of Knowing, and in our own generation that we face most sharply the danger that the earth will war against us.

So during this past generation Jews have been looking back, with much more urgency, into our own teachings about *adam* and *adamah*. We who were once a down-to-earth people, an indigenous people—what can we learn and teach to heal ourselves and our neighbors and the neighborhood itself—*adam* and *adamah*?

This Jewish conversation has only begun. Much of it has been carried out in a muttered undertone, mostly among a few people who were especially knowledgeable and concerned. This book brings together some of the most important explorations, to make the conversation more public and to make it more possible for the Jewish people as a whole to assess its own part in addressing a planetary crisis.

There have been four basic life-stances from which the Jewish people has addressed these questions: Biblical Israel, Rabbinic Judaism, Zionism, and most recently, Eco-Judaism. These four stances are not merely chronological periods (indeed, the last two of them overlap in time); they embody four different ways of connecting with the earth. For that reason, they have seemed to offer an organic pattern for organizing this book.

CONNECTIONS OF LAND AND PEOPLE

Four millennia ago, among Western Semitic nomads in the land of Canaan, there were stirrings of response and resistance to the new imperial agriculture of Babylonia. At some point in the next five hundred years, one of the communities that emerged from this simmering stew began to tell stories of a clan that became the seedbed of the people that came to call itself the Children of Israel—the Godwrestlers—and *Ivrim,* "Hebrews" in rough transliteration but, more important, in translation "boundary-crossers."

For they wrestled with the deepest questions of the universe, and they crossed the boundaries not only of territorial fiefdoms but of cultures and proprieties and social structures.

As they crossed over and wrestled, wrestled and crossed over, they drew from their hearing of the universe words they told and retold and wove into new patterns and turned into stories, poetry, drama, law, daily life-practice, philosophical musings.

These words became what we call the Bible, and one of its great themes was how to make a sacred relationship with the earth. In the Biblical Era that ensued, these Israelites/Hebrews/Jews not only lived intimately with a particular piece of earth but lived in a way that made them—collectively, as a people—responsible for how human beings acted toward the earth and how the earth responded.

This Biblical Era finally was shattered. There followed almost two thousand years in which one of the defining characteristics of

Jewish life was that the people Israel no longer had a direct physical connection with the land of Israel. During these centuries of what we call Rabbinic Judaism, Jews shaped the *adam/adamah* relationship much more as scattered households or communities than as a united people.

The Rabbinic community developed some loose guidelines for a sacred relationship to the earth. Since the lands of the Diaspora were so distant and so different from each other as ecosystems, and since interhuman relationships seemed of higher priority during this period, Rabbinic thought sketched a broad concern for protecting the earth, but with few definitive specifics. The Rabbis were often less concerned with protecting the earth than with explaining how to use its resources to meet the urgent needs of their scattered, often impoverished, people.

In the nineteenth century, the Zionist movement focused on renewing the Jewish connection with the land in a way that would allow and require the making of a Jewish policy toward the piece of earth called Eretz Yisrael. As the State of Israel emerged, so did a set of policies. Over the years, the numbers, the technology, the religious and philosophical perspectives, and the political arrangements of Israelis—in short, the Land, the People, and the State—have all changed in relationship to one another. So, therefore, have policies toward the land.

Meanwhile, the Jewish community in the United States in the second half of the twentieth century found itself politically empowered in unprecedented ways at just the same moment that Jews, Americans, and human beings in general were realizing that the troubled relationship between *adam* and *adamah* had reached the point of planetary crisis. This confluence seemed to a growing number of American Jews to invite—even demand—a collective Jewish response to this planetary crisis.

From many seeds and roots—the Bible reexamined, the Rabbis renewed, secular Jewish poetry and other nature-focused literature, feminist theologies of relationship, Kabbalah and Hasidism—came a gathering of thought that might be called Eco-Judaism, a Judaism that had close to its very center a concern for the healing of the earth.

Although this book treats Eco-Judaism as one of four different expressions of the Jewish relationship with the earth, the book itself, of course, is also an outgrowth of that collective energy. Indeed, it is very likely that almost none of the essays gathered in this book— not even those that examine Biblical, Rabbinic, and Zionist thought, Jewish worldviews that emerged long before a sense of planetary crisis—would have been written had that sense of crisis not emerged in the last generation.

For Jews of this past generation, facing a growing sense of worldwide ecological transformation, have returned to older Jewish writings to understand what Jewish wisdom might have to say. What guidance could it give, what mistakes could it warn against? Guidance and warning not only for our own behavior but for the approaches of other spiritual communities, of the broader societies of which we are a part, of the human race as a whole.

What makes us think that looking back at ancient teachings might be of any help, as we try to dance in the midst of a planetary earthquake?

The Jewish people has faced such earthquakes before, when both political and technological/ecological transformations shook the seemingly solid ground on which we were walking. Indeed, the emergence of the people Israel and the Hebrew Bible in the form in which we know about them may have been themselves the result of such an upheaval, as imperial agriculture made its way from Babylonia into the region of the Western Semites. And the emergence of

Rabbinic Judaism, with the Talmud and all its codes and commentaries, was clearly the result of such an upheaval—the triumph of Roman-Hellenistic civilization in the Mediterranean basin.

ANCIENT TEXTS, FUTURE LIFE-PATHS

In all these situations, Jews have valued the wisdom of the past, without letting it straitjacket them. The practice of midrash, in which an old text was turned in a new direction to afford new meaning, was not just a verbal trick but a deep assertion that the wisdom of previous generations was still important, even when changes needed to be made.

Why did Jewish culture and spirituality feel so strongly this need to affirm, and transcend, the past? The past represented an achieved sense of community and identity, which was being jarred by new technologies, new economics, new politics. Riding the wave of the new might be necessary, but to lose the past entirely was to lose communal—and ecological—health. The *adam* who is born again and again and again from the *adamah* dares not lose touch with it.

That need continues in our present crisis, as it has before. So we encounter in this book materials from, and about, the most ancient of Jewish sources as well as the most recent.

Indeed, not only from ancient Israel to now, but also within each era and worldview, we affirm this pattern of reconnecting with a text while taking it in new directions. So each section of this book begins with texts that spring from the worldview of that era and then continues with writings that analyze, study, respond to, and elaborate upon those texts.

What about the sources that we do not find? Yemenite Jewish women cooks, Ethiopian Jewish farmers, Polish dairymen, all dealt with the earth. As the need and desire grows for a revitalized and earth-conscious Judaism to draw on these myriad experiences of Jews around the earth, let us hope that scholars will begin to unearth these materials as many have struggled to unearth the silenced voices of Jewish women.

Meanwhile, for what we already have we sing *Dayenu!*—It is enough for us!—even as we know that after this chorus, this pause to celebrate what we have learned so far, we will sing another verse of further learning.

We can all hope that now the scattered comments of the many who in this past generation have tuned their minds to eco-Jewish teaching can become a fuller conversation, within and beyond the Jewish people.

May the One Who sends the Rainbow to renew the covenant with all of life remind us of our share in giving life to all the many-colored cultures and species of this planet.

Arthur Ocean Waskow
On the 27th Yohrzeit of Rabbenu
Abraham Joshua Heschel
18 Tevet 5760
December 27, 1999

Zionism: One Land, Two Peoples

Beginning in the late nineteenth century, some Jews (in Eastern Europe especially) began to work toward settling large numbers of Jews in the Land of Israel, with the intention to shape and govern their own lives. The Zionist movement flowered in 1948 with the creation of the State of Israel.

From early on, this movement raised some important questions about the nature of the relationship between the Jewish people and the land—the earthy soil itself. Indeed, these questions became central to the Zionist vision in a way they had never been for Jews since the end of the Biblical Era.

Four basic currents of thought lay beneath the Zionist relationship with the Land of Israel, which for most Zionists or Israeli Jews entered the mix of Jewish policy toward the Land:

- At the heart of the original Zionist vision, the passionate hope of reconnecting the Jewish people with the soil of its ancient homeland, through agricultural labor on the land and nature-focused recreation.
- Emerging as Zionism grew, an intense desire to bring (and to birth) as many Jews as possible to live in the Yishuv—the organized and semi-autonomous Jewish community in Palestine—and then in the State of Israel.
- An intense desire to "settle" the land—as much land as possible—with people, trees, and crops, to mark out national Jewish turf that could be distinguished from Arab-held land.
- A drive for modernity, economic development, and industrialism that could support a large and prosperous Jewish population and a strong military force.

But this program faced two problems.

First, this program bore internal contradictions, so that the first of these four values sometimes was at odds with the others. The hope of empathy with the land was often overwhelmed by the desire for economic development of the land.

Second, the whole Zionist program faced the presence of another community living in the same land. That Palestinian Arab community had for many years shaped its own relationship with the land. From the beginning of the influx of large numbers of Jews in the twentieth century, most of the Jews and most of the Arabs saw themselves as culturally and economically distinct from each other, and they had different visions for the biological/geological future of the land itself, as well as for its politics.

As the struggle between the two communities intensified, the

Palestinian national identity became clearer and clearer, more and more connected to national political institutions of its own. Its public and its leadership felt a strong need to shape its own future policy toward the soil, the air, and the water.

It may be that similar differences were at the heart of ancient distinctions and conflicts between the Israelites and the Hittites, Jebusites, and other peoples of Canaan. As we live with the realities of the national-ecological struggles of today, we may find ourselves looking with new eyes at the biblical history examined in Volume 1 of this anthology.

We may find ourselves asking, What may have been the ecological content of the ancient struggles that the Bible described as battles against idolatry? We read biblical stories of struggles over wells of water. What else was at stake? Did those other peoples of Canaan observe the seventh year as one of rest for the land? Did they deal the same way with tithes of grain and fruit? Were differences in sacrificial practices crystallizations of different worldviews about the relationship between human beings, the earth, and the Divine? We do not know; these possible ancient disagreements over "environmental policy" are now hazy for us.

We do know that in the century of Jewish resettlement and self-government in the Land, collisions between the two peoples have had deep environmental effects, and environmental issues have exacerbated the national conflicts. From the Jewish standpoint, the drive toward population increase, expansion of Jewish turf, and economic modernization have usually overridden concerns about the health of the various species, ecosystems, and habitats of the Land of Israel.

Only in the 1990s did support grow for a holistic reassessment of the relationships between human numbers, human technology, political/national configurations, and the climate, water, soil, air, plants, and animals of the Land. And only then did efforts begin to join the two peoples in discussions of protecting their common piece of earth, and of shaping their economies and polities toward that protection.

These discussions have rarely made a conscious or explicit connection between ecological planning and the Biblical or Rabbinic outlooks on the relationship between humanity and earth. Expressions of spiritual connectedness with the earth today have rarely invoked the religious symbols or practices of the past. Human communities, in the very process of wrestling with their ongoing lives, do generate thoughts, feelings, and practices that look toward larger wholes and unities, which are "religious" and "spiritual." As ecological consciousness emerges in Israel over the next generations, we can expect both some new religious languages and some efforts to unfold the old Jewish languages to express contemporary realities.

This part begins with two texts. The first, aggadic (that is, philosophical and spiritual) in tone, is a classic statement of the early Zionist hope for a rapprochement between the Jewish people and the earth—a text by A. D. Gordon from the early twentieth century. The second was spoken (in an interview) almost a century later by Yossi Sarid, then the leader of an opposition party in the Knesset who had been Minister of the Environment in a previous Israeli government. His words have a quasi-halakhic tone, outlining specifically what needs to be done in order for the two peoples living in one land to heal the wounds they each and together inflicted on its earth, air, and water.

Using the labels *aggadah* and *halakhah* for these texts is metaphoric, since neither is grounded directly in the Rabbinic tradition in which these terms emerged. But the analogy in tone is unmistakable.

Then we move on to an article by Fred Dobb on the

environmental approaches of four Jewish thinkers of the twentieth century: the same A. D. Gordon whose text begins this part, and Martin Buber, Avraham Yitzhak Kook, and Samson Raphael Hirsch. The first three were Zionists who spent large parts of their lives living in the Land of Israel. All of them held a strong vision of rapprochement with the earth as one of the goals of Zionism. Hirsch was included in Dobb's paper because he, like the others, was responding to dark sides of Modernity. But his life and thought were focused on Torah-connected Jews in the Diaspora, and he represents an effort to bring the Rabbinic tradition (see Volume 1) into a more fully self-aware sense of resistance to Modernity.

The next two articles—by Alon Tal and David Brooks—show that in the crucible of history, the vision of an eco-Zionism was overwhelmed by the goals of increasing Jewish population, marking national territory, and succeeding as an industrial power. They also describe the tentative beginnings of frail movements to apply the early eco-Zionist vision to the realities of Israeli life.

Tal's article, written earlier, was also written with a darker, more pessimistic pen than Brooks'. Tal voices deep concern that basic policies of the State, rooted in profound Zionist assumptions about population increase and economic development, may endanger the Land in ways that will be hard to reverse. Over the several years between the writing of his article and the one by Brooks, public environmental awareness in Israel rose. Whether that will be enough to change the direction of public policy and social behavior to heal the Land, or whether Tal's earlier concerns prove prophetic, is yet to be seen.

From focusing on the issues within Israeli society, we turn to the relationships of two peoples striving to live in the same land. The difficulties and possibilities are set forth in two articles that appeared together in 1998 in *Palestine-Israel Journal,* a quarterly not only jointly named but jointly sponsored and edited by Palestinians and Israelis. Indeed, one of the articles is co-authored by a Palestinian and an Israeli. Both articles address the question of how two peoples, evolving toward two nation-states, can cooperate on environmental questions so as to heal the land both peoples love.

The earth-and-human history of Israel and Palestine during the twentieth century maps in microcosm the earth-and-human history of most nations and peoples on the planet in the same century. For Jews of the next century, wherever they may live, the schoolhouse of Zionism demands we consider the following questions for life in a larger sphere:

- On a planet where ecosystems cross national and cultural boundaries, can different peoples cooperate to heal wounds in the earth, or are different peoples obligated to act on their own to master and control as much of the earth as possible, to whatever degree is necessary, to make their own nations more safe, more prosperous, more successful?

- Do we need to reexamine and redirect the urge to increase population, whether rooted in ancient teachings or in contemporary national competitions, so as to be in tune with the rhythms of the earth? Or can new approaches to earth-human relationships absorb indefinitely larger numbers of the human race without damaging the earth?

- Must ancient stories, metaphors, and symbols of the sacred be plowed under as irrelevant—either to an industrial era or to the creation of an eco-sensitive future? Or can new flowers blossom from those old trees, so

that older cultures can take part in renewing the sacredness of earth under new conditions?

And, of course, Israel itself and the neighboring peoples still
face the same questions.

Through facing the physical degeneration of the earth, air, and
water of the Land, suggest Alon Tal and David Brooks, there may yet
come—with enough compassion, alertness, and commitment—a
new ecological approach to Zionism. Through facing these same
questions, suggest Smith, Abu Diab, and Twite, there may yet emerge
a new depth of understanding and cooperation between Israelis and
Palestinians.

If so, they make clear, each people must be more attuned to the
reality that Modernity bears dangers as well as benefits, and to the
necessity of sharing efforts with the other people that lives in the
same land, breathes the same air, and drinks the same water.

A. *AGGADAH:* VARIATIONS ON THE THEME OF THE FUTURE

A. D. Gordon, translated by Jeremy Schwartz

And it shall come to pass,
O child of Adam,
when you return to Nature,
on that day you shall open your eyes,
and you shall peer directly
into Nature's eyes
and there you shall see
your own image.
You shall know that you have returned to yourself,
for in hiding from Nature,
you hid from yourself.

Rabbi Jeremy Schwartz is a teacher, translator, and author who lives in the greater Boston area. He is a graduate of the Reconstructionist Rabbinical College and served as the first assistant director at Kolel: The Adult Centre for Liberal Jewish Learning, located in Toronto.

And furthermore, you shall see,
that from upon you,
from upon your hands and feet,
from upon your body and soul,
fragments are peeling and falling,
crumbling and falling.
Heavy fragments,
> *hard,*
>> *oppressive;*
you straighten yourself,
> *you stand up tall,*
>> *you grow.*
And you will know that these are the shards of your shell, your kelippah,
in which you had constricted yourself
in your bewilderment,
and out of which you have finally grown.
And you will recognize on that day:
nothing had been according to your measure,
you must renew everything:

your food   and   your drink,
your dress   and   your home,
the character of your work   and   the way that you learn
—everything. . . .

And on that day, with all the power of your heart, you will sense the pressure with which the walls of the houses in the city—and even in the village—press upon your soul, and you will sense the slightest barrier which stands between your Self and the Boundless Space of the World, between your Self and the Boundless Life of the World. And so, when you build a house, you will not set your heart on the multiplication of its rooms and closets but you will set your entire heart on this: that there be nothing in it that separates from Boundless Space, from Boundless Life, for when you sit in your house, when you lie down and when you rise up, at every moment and every hour, your entire being will be in the midst of that Space, in the midst of that Life. And thus also will you build houses of Torah and wisdom, also houses of labor and work, setting a space between one house and another—a large space, so that no house will rob or conceal from another its place in this world. You will learn Torah from the mouth of Nature, the Torah of building and fashioning, and you will learn to do as it does in all that you build and in all that you fashion.

On that day you will know and take to heart, O child of Adam, that you had been wandering aimlessly until you returned to this point. For you didn't know life. Even after you stopped eating from the pre-made, you still didn't recognize the Nature of life; you didn't stop living from the pre-made, whether made by you or by others. A different life, a life not from the pre-made, a life in the midst of the making of life, in the midst of the fashioning of life: this you didn't know. And so your life was torn into two tatters: one very small tatter of life and one very large tatter of non-life—of labor, of trouble, and of bother. "Shabbat"—and "pre-Shabbat." And you didn't think, it didn't occur to you, that there is no life in living from the pre-made, if there is not life in the act of making. Doesn't Nature also live in the midst of creating life, in the midst of fashioning life? And so, all your days, you were a seeker of life, a pursuer of life—and not alive. Your life was dangling before you: either in the past or in the future; present you didn't know. When you saw that your own life was small and poor, you craved to annex to yourself the lives of others. So you would rob, plunder, and extort as much as possible from whomever and whatever you thought to have life. You sucked, you drank, you drained your comrades' blood, if they didn't succeed in sucking your blood. To you, the life of a parasite became the sign of greatness, strength and splendor; wealth the sign of happiness, the rule of one human over another the sign of strength and glory. You didn't sense, you didn't perceive, that the pre-made life which you swallowed became a rot in your bones. And even your prophets, who arose to repair your world and renew your life, prophesied falsehood and emptiness. They added nothing at all to the teaching, "Those who took the trouble to prepare before Shabbat will enter the Shabbat and eat." They only taught you to put a bit in your mouth and in the mouth of those eating with you from the communal plate, a bit with which to prevent yourself and the others from eating more than your share, more than you prepared "before Shabbat." But you, child of Adam, do you not desire life also "before Shabbat," and at every time and every hour, at every single instant? What good is the bit in your mouth to you?

And it shall come to pass on that day, O child of Adam, that you shall receive a new spirit, you shall feel a new feeling, a new hunger— not a hunger for bread, nor a thirst for money, but for labor. You will find delight in every labor and in every deed that you do, like the delight you find in eating and drinking. On that day, you will take care to make your labor pleasurable and appealing, like you now take care to make your food appealing, and like you now take care to increase the fruit of your labor—money. You will know to work your fill every day, no more and no less. Most of all, though, you will take care to do all your labor and all your deeds in the midst of Nature, in the midst of the Boundless Space of the World. That is how you will do your work in the field and that is how you will do your work in the house, for that is how you will build your house.

And it shall come to pass when you work at your labor, that the spacious expanse of the universe will seem to be your work-place, and you and Nature the workers. The two of you will be of one heart and of one spirit. You will say on that day: Nature is beautiful on its surface, but it is seven times more beautiful in the spirit of its life, in its labor. And when you stop for a moment to straighten your back, and to take a breath, you will breathe in not only air, but you will feel that you are breathing in something more, something subtle which you can't identify, but which will make your emotions and your thoughts bear fruit, which will add life and light to your spirit. Indeed, you will have moments as if your entire being were melting into the Infinite. Then you will stand in speechless silence. Not only speech, but even song, even thought, will seem to you a desecration of that which is holy. You will grasp the hidden truth of silence and its holiness. You will experience something which cannot be expressed except by labor. So you will labor powerfully, with strength and joy. And you will hear a divine voice issuing forth from your labor and saying, "Work, children of Adam, all of you, work!" Then you will know and internalize, that in labor there is a reservoir of spirit, such that you can see only its outer edge, but its entirety can only be seen with many eyes, that look at it from all sides. . . . And following the divine voice, Nature answers, "Amen! Work, children of Adam! Let your labor not be belittled in your eyes. You shall complete that which I have left lacking in order that I, myself, should complete that which you lack. . . . "

On that day, the fruit of your labor, child of Adam, will be: life. For there will be life within your labor. Not a single moment of your life will be wasted. Even on a day of calamity, when afflictions come upon you, your afflictions will be significant, deep, holy. Or on a day of darkness, when you stumble a moment and sin, you will have within you enough strength, enough grandeur, to bear the sin, and enough hell-fire with which to be refined. You will know the pain that pours out a supreme, holy spirit upon you, and supreme love for all that live and suffer, and you will know nothing of the profane, you will know nothing of the petty, you will know nothing of vacuous living.

On that day, child of Adam, you shall lift your eyes round about, you shall lift your eyes upward, and you will see the earth and all that exists therein, and you will see the heavens with all their legions, with all the incomprehensible, endless numbers of worlds that are there, and lo, all of them, all of them are near to your Self, all of them bring You blessing. Then you will grasp the eternity that inhabits the moment. Then you will know how great is your wealth, how great the blessing, that life carries to you. Then you will know, and say in your heart: How poor, how wretched is life appropriated from others, rule over others, light gotten from others! On that day you will love all that exists, you will love the children of Adam, you will even love yourself—for your heart will be filled with love. You will believe in yourself, you will believe in humankind, you will believe in all that one has to believe—for you will be entirely filled with life.

Your emotions and thoughts, your spirit, will be like the swelling stream—ever new, ever your own. You will also feel your entire self, and behold, you are ever new, ever your own. Thus will you seem to yourself and thus will you seem to your comrades—for your source will be blessed.

On that day, human will no longer be a burden to human, which the bearer bears for an hour—and becomes weary. For there will be sufficient space for every person, and sufficient distance between one person and another, that one will not fall to another, but will ever and always draw the other near.

On that day, child of Adam, you will know Nature, for your eyes and all your senses will be sufficiently clear, your heart sufficiently open, your mind sufficiently deep. On that day, the light of your wisdom and your science will no longer be a cold and terrible light, but it will be a living light, flowing abundantly from all of the worlds.

On that day, child of Adam, you will know how to live with Nature, for *it will be your will* to know. . . .

B. *HALAKHAH:*
POLLUTION AND PEACE:
AN INTERVIEW WITH YOSSI SARID

In 1998, Member of Knesset Yossi Sarid, former Minister of the Environment, was interviewed by the Palestine-Israel Journal.

*T*he *Palestine-Israel Journal:* According to the Hebrew daily *Ha'aretz* (May 10, 1998), a Palestinian spokesperson repeated the Palestinian stand that they would not cooperate with Jewish settlements on environmental problems. Do you think this policy towards the settlements, which stems from the Palestinians' refusal to

---

Yossi Sarid was Minister of the Environment in the Israeli government during the prime ministerships of Yitzhak Rabin and Shimon Peres, from 1992 to 1996. He is a leader of the Meretz party and in 1999 reentered the government coalition led by Ehud Barak.

give them legitimacy, is justified? Is this primarily an environmental or political problem, in your view? Do you see a way out?

Yossi Sarid: Like all such questions, this is a particularly difficult one. I will state my mind on it openly as I did when I served as the Minister of the Environment. Environmental problems have nothing to do with politics. You know my attitude toward the Jewish settlements in the occupied territories. I am one of the very few people on the Israeli political scene who opposed the very founding of all the settlements in the occupied territories, with no exception whatsoever. In this respect, my record with regard to the Jewish settlements is absolutely clear.

However, environmental problems are of a different nature, and without cooperation between all those involved, there is not the slightest chance to even try to begin solving the problems. There is a political debate which will decide the future fate of the Jewish settlements. As far as I am concerned, most of them will either be uprooted or will fall under Palestinian sovereignty. But whatever the political solution, they will be there and the environmental problems will be there, and they are not going to change. So, when I was Minister of the Environment, we all came to the conclusion—the Palestinians as well as the Israelis—that without cooperation there will be nothing. And I believe that this was not only a theoretical conclusion. It was a practical one. I still remember very vividly that some European governments said that they are ready to help with regard to environmental difficulties and very severe problems everywhere, but in the occupied territories in particular, and they were ready to sponsor joint projects. As far as I could judge, the Europeans were very enthusiastic about assisting in this respect because, first, they like to support joint ventures; second, because it was a very concrete project; third, because the Europeans think—surprisingly enough—

that sewage, for example, is very dangerous, even a threat, to everybody. The German government, for example, asked the Palestinian Authority and the Israeli government to sign a joint letter in order to facilitate or to enable the beginning of new, very promising projects. As far as I remember, I signed the letter on behalf of the Israeli government and Mr. Nabil Sha'ath signed on behalf of the Palestinian Authority.

Then came May 29, 1996, and the Netanyahu government. Everything was stopped, like all joint projects with the Palestinians. This is to say, the Palestinian Authority was ready to cooperate in this respect, regardless of the future and the final status of the occupied territories and of the Jewish settlements. The settlements are not going to be wiped out. They will be there either under one sovereignty or another.

Even though we have to draw a distinction between environmental problems and political problems, this is very difficult in practice because life is much more complicated than theories. On the ground today there is, in general, no Israeli-Palestinian cooperation and there is no cooperation in the environmental field. It is very unfortunate and we are running out of time, but what can we do about it? Without political progress there is no progress on the environmental aspect.

So what are the prospects?

We are polluting the Palestinians and the Palestinians are polluting us, and if the Palestinians take care of their own environmental business and we take care of ours, nothing will come out of it. The occupied territories, environmentally speaking, were very neglected by us, by the Israelis, during the last 30 years. The Palestinian Authority is not at this stage in a financial position to facilitate and to sponsor major environmental projects. They cannot afford it. Cooperation is necessary, but I believe that the Palestinian Authority is not very enthusiastic now about cooperation, and I do not feel that the Israeli government is very enthusiastic about it, as far as I know.

There was a special budget of the Ministry of the Environment dedicated to those joint projects, and as far as I understand, such a budget no longer exists. The budget totally disappeared. That is to say that the intention of the Israeli government is not towards cooperation. I believe that this is also the attitude at the present moment of the Palestinian Authority, and that's it. It is to be regretted. After we have neglected the environment in the occupied territories in the West Bank for 30 years, this situation at the present moment indicates that it is likely to continue to be ignored, and we are approaching total catastrophe from an environmental point of view. We are not talking politics now.

I will give you a scoop, which may surprise you. When I served as Minister of the Environment, I, more than previous ministers, supported the agencies dealing with environmental issues in the Jewish settlements. My friends asked me, Why do you do that? Why do you support them? I said, Because whatever the future of these settlements will be, they will be there. They are polluting very severely and very dangerously, and that problem must be solved. I believe that this is the right thing to do.

They are polluting into Palestinian areas.

Into Palestinian areas, into Israeli areas, everywhere. You know, sewage has a very strange nature. It knows no boundaries and it flows from east to west. Whatever flows from the east comes westward into Israel. When it comes to environmental problems, it is a reality that there are no boundaries. I looked very carefully into ensuring that those budgets would be dedicated exclusively to the environment and not to any other projects. And I am quite sure that I did the right thing.

This is the irony of history. One day, when we hope that there will be peace and coexistence between us and the Palestinians, the solution will be found. I can assure you that without solving the environmental problems, we will give the Palestinians hell and the Palestinians will give us hell, and it will pollute the peace. The peace will be very polluted, and we will hate the Palestinians for what they are doing to us and the Palestinians will hate us for what we are doing to them.

We can often define environmental problems as existential problems. People don't understand it, but it is true because they relate to the quality of the water we drink, the quality of the air we breathe and the quality of the ground we live on. So we are talking about deadly and very serious problems.

Can you end by saying a few words about how you see the very strong criticism on Israeli environmental policy at home, as recently published by the Greenpeace people?

We talked before about the fact that Israel neglected environmental problems in the West Bank and in the Gaza Strip, but the same is true with regard to Israel as such. Environmental issues are, unfortunately, not at the top of our national agenda. I'm not too objective, of course, but at least I believe that I had some success in placing the environmental issue higher on our national agenda when I served as minister.

Now the issue has disappeared, vanished. I do not think that the present Minister of the Environment is very interested in the environment, and I do not think that the Ministry is as active and as determined as it was when I was minister. So I understand why the Green community, all those involved with environmental issues, are highly frustrated about the present situation.

Greenpeace representatives came to see me recently and it is a fact that I was the only Minister of the Environment in the region to maintain very close relations with the Green community, and the Green community, including their more militant wing, saw me as their representative. They are not easy people, by the way, but I greatly appreciate the role they are playing. Now, under the present government, there is a different situation and nobody is really very interested in environmental issues.

How can that be? How can people be so short-sighted? It sounds irrational.

This question is very relevant not only to this area of life. Here, it is because the Palestinians, as well as the Israelis, are very deeply involved in what they see as existential problems. So they mislead themselves into believing that they can ignore environmental problems for the time being. But this is a mistake, a very grave mistake, and we are going to pay a very heavy price for this illusion, all of us.

FOUR MODERN TEACHERS: HIRSCH, KOOK, GORDON, AND BUBER

Fred Dobb

T he advent of modernity is well-known for its effects on West-ern Jewry. New religious notions were needed to keep pace with emancipation, technology, and new intellectual and political currents. The pace of change, especially in the tumultuous modern century between 1848's European revolutions and 1948's birth of Israel, was staggering. Yet some of the agents of change within the Jewish community were also concerned with conservation. I speak not of religious or social conservatism, but of ecological awareness.

Rabbi Fred Dobb was ordained in 1997 by Philadelphia's Reconstructionist Rab-binical College. Ever since an environmental education walk across the United States ten years ago, he has been writing, teaching, and organizing around ecology and Ju-daism. He serves on the board of trustees of COEJL and the Teva Learning Center and as rabbi of Adat Shalom Reconstructionist Congregation in Bethesda, Maryland.

The proto-environmentalism of modern Jewry is best seen in four thinkers: Samson Raphael Hirsch, Avraham Yitzhak Kook, Aaron David Gordon, and Martin Buber. This study centers on gleanings from the words of these men. (No women, alas, seem to have been in a position to explore these issues and be heard.)

Attitudes toward nature in the modern era are multivalent and rarely clear. Even these leading thinkers speak only in the context of the "larger" issues of their day, such as building up the land, revitalizing the people, expounding the mystical secrets of the Torah, and drawing Jews back to Orthodoxy. Not until our own contemporary era, when social and scientific awareness of the environment constitutes a category unto itself, can we speak of ecological Judaism per se. Nevertheless, their thoughts can help us construct a Jewish-environmental ethic for our day. A look at the modern period offers numerous and valuable "sparks" to be lifted up toward the great *tikkun* ("repair") of our day.

I. SAMSON RAPHAEL HIRSCH

Neo-Orthodoxy, *austritt* (secession from the dominant Jewish community), *Torah im derekh eretz* (Torah with the ways of the world)— all of these critical concepts and trends in modern Jewish history owe their existence to the heterodox orthodox Rabbi Samson Raphael Hirsch (1808–1888). Hirsch maintained most of the Central European orthodoxy of his upbringing even as he studied Kant and modern science. From his pulpit in the growing community of Frankfurt he became among the most influential leaders of his time. Liberal in his view of non-Jews (*Ben Uziel* 81) and even Darwin's new theory of evolution (*Judaism Eternal* 11), yet quite traditional regarding the role of women in Judaism (52), this enigmatic thinker has left a rich environmental legacy.

> Not thine is the earth, but thou belongest to the earth, to re-spect it as Divine soil and to deem every one of its creatures a creature of God, thy fellow-being. (*Ben Uziel* 33)

A key Jewish ecological concept concerns the ownership of creation, as in Psalm 24:1—"the Earth is God's, and the fullness thereof." Both earth and people, as part of the "fullness," belong to God. But above, Hirsch takes it one step further—we belong to the earth as well as to God! Unique to this day, Hirsch's notion deserves a central place within our contemporary construction of a Jewish ecological ethic.

> Yea, "Do not destroy anything!" is the first and most general call of God which comes to you . . . when you realize yourself as master of the earth. . . .
> " . . . the things around you. I lent them to you for wise use only; never forget that I lent them to you. As soon as you use them unwisely, be it the greatest or the smallest, you commit treachery against My world, you commit murder and robbery against My property, you sin against Me!" This is what God calls unto you . . . (*Horeb* 56)

Hirsch makes "God as ultimate owner" the Jewish rallying cry, which in turn illuminates the latent environmental sensitivity in many traditional teachings. Here he highlights the "eco-law" of *bal tashhit,* the prohibition of wanton waste derived from the dictum of Deuteronomy 20:19 against cutting down an enemy's trees in wartime. To my mind, Hirsch is more passionate about *bal tashhit* than any other thinker in the whole of Jewish history.

In his *Chumash,* Hirsch expounds on Deuteronomy 20:20: "The 'do not destroy' of our text becomes the most comprehensive warning to human beings not to misuse the position which God has given them as masters of the world and its matter." He warns against "capricious, passionate, or merely thoughtless wasteful destruction of anything on earth." And linking *bal tashhit* with the "dominion" of Gen. 1:28, he adds, "Only for wise use has God laid the world at our feet when He said to Man [*sic*] 'subdue the world and have dominion.'"

> Sabbath in our time! To cease for a whole day from all business, from all work, in the frenzied hurry-scurry of our time! To close the exchanges, the workshops and factories, to stop all railway services—great heavens! How would it be possible? The pulse of life would stop beating and the world perish!
>
> The world perish? On the contrary, it would be saved.
> ("The Jewish Sabbath," in *Judaism Eternal* 30)

As with *bal tashhit,* Hirsch's innovative approach brings new ecological meaning to the observance of the Sabbath, which Hirsch says was given to man [*sic*] "in order that he should not grow overweening in his dominion" of God's creation—again, a reference to and limitation of Genesis 1:28 (*Ben Uziel* 125). *Shabbat,* ownership, and Divine ownership come together in his system: a person "should refrain on this day from exercising his human sway over the things of earth, should not place his hand upon any object for the purpose of human dominion, that is, to employ it for any human end; he must, as it were, return the borrowed world to its Divine Owner in order to realize that it is but lent to him."

Commenting on Exodus 20:10, Hirsch poetically adds: "On Sabbath you strip yourself of your glorious mastery over the matter of the world, and lay yourself and your world acknowledgingly at the feet of the Eternal your God." In all of this he seems to presage Abraham Joshua Heschel and his famous "to set apart one day a week for freedom" passage (*The Sabbath* 28) nearly a century later. From thoughts like these, many liberal Jewish environmentalists now reclaim the traditional *Shabbat* as a central institution.

> One glorious chain of love, of giving and receiving, unites all creatures; none is by or for itself, but all things exist in continual reciprocal activity—the one for the All; the All for the One. (*Ben Uziel* 29)

Perhaps Hirsch's greatest contribution to a Jewish ecological ethic lies not in his understanding of ownership but in the "mutual interdependence" of God's wise creation. Above is his most famous utterance in this vein.

Offering yet another fresh approach to the human dominance of Genesis 1:28, Hirsch expands on his "reciprocal activity"—in *Ben Uziel*, the human stance is "neither as god nor as slave . . . in the midst of the creatures of the earth-world; but as brother, as co-working brother" (*Ben Uziel* 44). Though man [*sic*] occupies "the rank of first-born among his brother beings, because of the peculiar nature and extent of his service," nowhere in this system are we allowed to cheat or injure our "brothers," much less cause their extinction. Rather we are to administer the "whole Divine estate . . . [and] provide and care for all therein according to the will of God."

This theme of cosmic interdependence will resurface in each of the following thinkers. As Mordecai Kaplan echoed it in the introduction to his 1945 Reconstructionist Prayer Book: "Each of us should learn to think of himself [*sic*] as though he were a cell in some living organism—which, in a sense, he actually is—in his relation to the universe or cosmos." Almost word for word, this expresses the yet unnamed Gaia hypothesis, wherein each creature is like a cell of the self-regulating organism known as Earth. Kaplan adds that the world "is more than nature; it is nature with a soul. That soul is God." Hirsch took the first steps toward reaching such a Jewish understanding of Gaia; Rav Kook picked up the baton from him.

II. RAV ABRAHAM ISAAC KOOK

Like Hirsch before him, Rav Kook (1865–1935) was a remarkably open-minded Orthodox rabbi who lived in tumultuous times. Just as Hirsch turned down "better" job offers to take the Frankfurt pulpit, the Latvian-born Kook also risked much in accepting a job in Jaffa in 1904. After being stranded in Europe during World War I, Kook returned to Jerusalem in 1919 to become the Chief Ashkenazic Rabbi of Palestine. His breadth of Jewish and secular knowledge, creative synthesis of Zionism with Hasidic mysticism, early support of women's suffrage and civic equality, and ability to reach out to people far outside of his community all lead contemporary Kook scholar Ben Zion Bokser to call him "one of the most remarkable figures in the spiritual history of [hu]mankind" (*Essential Writings* 1).

> The doctrine of evolution that is presently gaining acceptance in the world has a greater affinity with the secret teachings of the Cabbalah than all other philosophies. Evolution, which proceeds on a course of improvement, offers us the basis of optimism in the world. How can we despair when we realize that everything evolves and improves? . . .
>
> Evolution sheds light on all the ways of God. All existence evolves and ascends, as this may be discerned in some of its

parts. . . . This is its general ascent: No particularity will remain outside, not a spark will be lost from the ensemble. All will share in the climactic culmination. (*Lights of Holiness,* in *E. W.* 220–221)

Kook's warm embrace of evolution, in the same decade as the Scopes "Monkey Trial" in Tennessee, is radical enough. Even more important for our ongoing construction of a Jewish ecological ethic, however, is a powerful message about biodiversity. The gradual evolution of distant cousins apart from one another, or *speciation,* has made the earth so biologically rich. If "not a spark will be lost from the ensemble" in (God's) evolutionary plan, then humanity's destructive actions are an affront to the Divine. Moreover, Kook's "basis of optimism in the world" is shattered when we realize that "a fifth or more of the species of plants and animals could vanish or be doomed to early extinction by the year 2020 unless better efforts are made to save them" (*Wilson* 346). Were Kook alive in our ecocidal era, I believe that he would have taken action on this urgent issue.

> Genuine science teaches us the unity of the world, of body and soul, of imagination and reason, of the lowly and the exalted. . . . We cannot make any absolute distinction between various levels of being; their difference is merely one of degree.
>
> Everything is full of riches and greatness, everything aspires to ascend, to be purified and to be elevated. Everything recites a song, offers praise, magnifies, exalts; everything builds, serves, perfects, elevates, aspires to unite and to be integrated. (*Orot HaKodesh* I:405; II:386)

Kook takes up Hirsch's theme of cosmic unity with vigor. Indeed, at the heart of Kook's system lies the interdependence and animated quality of all creation: "The nature of all existence and every particular creature . . . must be seen from one comprehensive perspective, as one essence constituent of many particularities" (*Lights of Penitence,* in *E. W.* 50).

Kook anticipates Kaplan and the Gaia hypothesizers: The further we go in perfecting the world, he says, "the more its constituent elements are seen as embraced in a comprehensive unity, and its nature as one organism becomes more clearly discernible" (*Arpele Tohar,* in *E.W.* 10). More remarkable still is Kook's teaching that "we cannot make any absolute distinction between various levels of being." This seems to imply the sharing of essential rights among all creatures, thus opening the door for today's deep ecology movement.

> When we contemplate the physical creation as a whole, we realize that it is all as one organism, that the parts are linked in varying gradations to each other. We see this in every plant, in every living being. . . .
>
> The realization dawns on us that were it not for the lower beings, the uncouth and the unseemly, the higher beings could not have emerged in their splendor, their esteem and their luminous quality. We continually become more conscious of the integration and unity of existence. (*Orot HaKodesh* II:431, in *E. W.* 167–168)

Along with powerfully reiterating his support for this proto-Gaian vision, Kook implies here that we gain a great deal from the very existence of "the lower beings," even the "uncouth and the unseemly." This notion may be part of what guided Kook to at least partial vegetarianism (varied accounts have him eating a small amount of meat, only on *Shabbat* and *Yom Tov,* only on *Yom Tov,* or not at all). Here, and given the effect of the meat industry on habitat loss and other environmental issues, Kook remains an inspiration for Jewish vegetarians of our day. In Kook's famous poem, "A Fourfold Song"

(*Lights of Holiness,* in *E.W.* 228–229), the ultimate level of existence is attained by "one who rises toward wider horizons, until he links himself with all existence, with all God's creatures, with all worlds, and he sings his song with all of them." Much of Kook's thought still revolves around the three "lower" levels of self, nation, and humanity; moreover, the ideal is to sing the song of all four worlds at once. Nevertheless, the highest level in Kook's system is the one which embraces the entire created order—rocks and trees and cows and people alike.

III. A. D. Gordon

Aaron David Gordon (1856–1922), a critical thinker and essayist in early Zionist history, practiced the very Labor Zionism that he preached. Most of his essays were written by candlelight after a hard day's labor in the land of Israel, to which he moved from Lithuania at age forty-eight. Beset by illness and tragedy all his life, Gordon nevertheless kept faith with his deepest-held beliefs. Still revered at his beloved [kibbutz] Degania and throughout the kibbutz movement, Gordon stands as a modern prophet of labor, of Zionism, and of nature.

> It is obvious that even in the lands of the diaspora, Jews must look to labor, to nature; they must strive to recreate their own lives. We should engage in all forms of labor, especially in the tilling of the soil; we should avoid the exploitation of the labor of others; we should inject the spirit of the family into our economic life—these are the things we must start to do. (Gordon, 79)

Gordon's system is encapsulated in the phrase "to labor, to nature." The two go hand in hand. A return to labor means a return to nature, an end to the estrangement of two millennia, and an honest reassessment of our comparatively humble place within the natural world. Along with his socialist concern for economic justice, Gordon was an early "dove" on Arab-Jewish relations whose stance against "exploitation of the labor of others" bespeaks his relevance to today's concerns of environmental justice. Though, importantly, he speaks about nature in the diaspora, Gordon placed a special emphasis on the sacred soil of Israel. Consider his powerful analogy of the Jewish people to a tree:

> We come to our Homeland in order to be planted in our natural soil from which we have been uprooted, to strike our roots deep into its life-giving substances, and to stretch out our branches in the sustaining and creating air and sunlight of the Homeland.... We, who have been torn away from nature, who have lost the savor of natural living—if we desire life, we must establish a new relationship with nature. (Hertzberg 381)
>
> What has man [sic] done within nature that it should be for him an unfailing source of wealth? The grain, the garden which men do not work but own, the forest, considered the property of men because business is tied up with it, and so on—what does all this imply? Is there any spiritual affinity to the plant as a plant, to the whole field, to the garden, *per se*? Do not people, for example, cut down entire groves and even virginal forests that are not only an ornament of nature but also beneficial to the health of both man and plant? Do not people cut them down merely for the sake of money? Or a waterfall which has been utilized for water power—what does this imply? Countless are the questions along this line.... (Hertzberg 242)
>
> Such, too, is the attitude toward living creatures. What is the

beast, the animal, the fowl, and so on, to man? Either beneficial or harmful. . . . Are not men ready to annihilate whole species of beasts merely for the sake of material gains derived from them? Does not man kill the elephant, for example, the most intelligent, the most sensitive of beasts, for the sake of its ivory tusks which net him a considerable price? And one can go on enumerating these examples. . . . (Hertzberg 244)

Gordon's relevance in our time is nowhere clearer than this, on protecting the glory and diversity of God's creation. Here he might be naming 1990's issues of clear-cutting old growth forests or damming rivers in the Pacific Northwest. He is prophetic not only about habitat loss, but about species extinction in general. This similarity between contemporary environmental issues and those faced by our forebears should only reinforce our own current efforts to end such evils as bad forestry ("entire groves and even virginal forests"), choking rivers ("a waterfall which has been utilized for water power"), and trade in endangered species ("its ivory tusks which net him a considerable price").

The categoric imperative of the spirit of man, therefore, does not lie in the glib phrase of the culture today: "Know nature and love it!" Rather it is to be found in the wordless notes, inaudible in our culture, of the voice that coos like a dove in the searching soul, that beats like the wings of a bird in its narrow cage: "Live Nature!" (Hertzberg 181)

And when, O Man, you will return to Nature—on that day your eyes will open, you will gaze straight into the eyes of Nature, and in its mirror you will see your own image. . . . On that day you will know that your former life did not befit you, that you must renew all things: your food and your drink, your dress and your home, your manner of work and your mode of study—everything! On that day, O Man, deep in your heart you will know that you had been wandering until you returned to Nature. (Hertzberg 371)

Gordon's assertion that "everything" changes with a return to nature rings truer than ever. But more than simply an environmental thinker and leader, Gordon is a philosopher of Gaia. "Gordon's world view is rooted in the conviction that the cosmos has unity, that nature and man are one, and that all men are but organic parts of the cosmos" (Bergman 103). If nature's mirror reveals ourselves, the distinction between human and non-human nature is blurred. This emphasis on interconnectedness within the biosphere is again reminiscent of Hirsch, Kook, and the Gaia hypothesis—witness his prescription for "spiritual preparation, a deep awareness of the unity in cosmic life" (Hertzberg 247).

Concluding once again with reference to Genesis 1:28, Gordon holds that "man (*sic*) should return to his source, to nature, on condition that he be neither a slave nor a master of nature, but a trustworthy companion to nature in life and a trustworthy partner in creation" (Hertzberg 241). As with Kook's image of all creatures as brothers, this egalitarian approach to nature is among Gordon's contributions to our emerging Jewish ecological ethic. Though less textually oriented than Hirsch or Kook, by commenting on our place in God's creation, Gordon joins the ongoing conversation with the Jewish tradition.

IV. MARTIN BUBER

The modern Jewish philosopher par excellence, whose renown outside the Jewish community even exceeds his standing within it,

Martin Buber was born in Vienna in 1878. He spent his early professional years in Germany, some as director of the famous Freie Jüdisches Lehrhaus in Frankfurt, and lived in Israel from 1938 until his death in 1965. Buber's relational worldview is set forth in his 1923 classic *I and Thou,* "one of the few generally recognized masterpieces of twentieth-century philosophy" (Gillman 173), and later applied to Judaism in a number of important works. His legacy is not only as a philosopher but also a mystic, a scholar, a peace activist, a translator, a socialist, a Zionist.

In addition to all of these memorable contributions, some also see in Buber a touch of naturalist, even "environmentalist." With the caveat that his environmental ideas generally arise in the context of other issues, nature does seem to be of great concern for him. To illustrate this, we start with his overall scheme of relationship.

Buber's system starts with two primary words, I–Thou and I–It. One is always spoken with the whole being, the other never; one is a thing, while the other is nothing. I–Thou is a framework, a stance, of relationship (*I and Thou* 3–4). The world of Thou is preferable, but it is impossible to sustain permanently: "without It man [*sic*] cannot live. But he who lives with It alone is not a man" (34).

Amidst our meager I's and Thou's is God, the Eternal Thou, the ultimate Spoken With The Whole Being, Unbounded Nothing. God is where the "extended lines of relations meet" (75). The Eternal Thou represents everything: "Of course God is the 'wholly Other'; but He [*sic*] is also the wholly Same, the wholly Present. Of course He is the Mysterium Tremendum that appears and overthrows; but He is also the mystery of the self-evident, nearer to me than my I" (79).

Within this system "I–Thou moments," which make life worth living, occasionally and unpredictably occur. These are also the moments which renew our relationship with God, since "Every particular Thou is a glimpse through to the eternal Thou" (75). Moreover, this notion of I and Thou is "organic"—the life-force of relationship pulses through it. But to pursue this thought further, let us consider a tree.

Buber's first analysis of an I–Thou relationship begins with that simple, famous line, "I consider a tree" (7). He explains all the things he could do with the tree—view it as a static picture, perceive it as active movement, classify and study it, subdue it (cut it down), or treat it as a number. But among all these options, "the tree remains my object, occupies space and time, and has its nature and constitution. It can, however, also come about, if I have both will and grace, that in considering the tree I become bound up in relation to it. The tree is now no longer It. . . . " By entering into mutual relation, Buber shares an I–Thou moment with the tree.

The very possibility of such a relationship implies an obvious question, which Buber is unable to answer: "The tree will have a consciousness, then, similar to our own? Of that I have no experience . . . I encounter no soul . . . of the tree, but the tree itself" (8). Buber neither anthropomorphizes nor anthropocentrizes. Yet he holds that in the ultimate spiritual realm, one can indeed have the same relationship with human and tree alike.

The tree seems central to Buber; he returns to it often, as in one of the most striking images of *I and Thou:* "The central reality of the everyday hour on earth, with a streak of sun on a maple twig and the glimpse of the eternal Thou, is greater for us than all enigmatic webs on the brink of being" (88). Elsewhere it is a rich metaphor capping a discussion of Jewish identity: "What is the condition of the roots themselves? Are they still healthy enough to send fresh sap into the remaining stump and to produce a fresh shoot from it? . . . Let us recognize ourselves: we are the keepers of the roots" (*On Judaism* 201). He even explains that Eve's initial relationship with the initial Edenic tree was of the I–Thou variety (*On the Bible* 15). It is no coincidence then that naturalist Annie Dillard quotes Buber repeatedly (31, 202); her recollections of such an I–Thou moment include "the tree with the lights in it . . . grass that was wholly fire." Later in the book, Buber speaks with equal eloquence about a similar moment with a cat (*On the Bible* 97–98). But the tree remains central enough to deserve revisitation in his 1957 postscript (126):

> It is part of our concept of a plant that it cannot react to our action towards it: it cannot "respond." Yet this does not mean that here we are given simply no reciprocity at all. . . . That living wholeness and unity of the tree, which denies itself to the sharpest glance of the mere investigator and discloses itself to the glance of one who says Thou, is there when he, the sayer of Thou, is there: it is he who vouchsafes to the tree that it manifest this unity and wholeness; and now the tree which is in being manifests them.

Here the relationship with the tree seems still more vivid, and more mutual, than it did in 1923. Interestingly, Buber has three examples of I–Thou relationships with beings in the natural world: a tree, a stone, and a cat. This list is "significant by exclusion, for he does not refer to manufactured objects. Manufactured articles are evidently not beings with which one can potentially have an *I-Thou* relationship but are experienced, used" (*Harris* 106). Buber demonstrates not only a tremendous respect for the created order, but also an apparent devaluation of humanity's labors in comparison with God's works. This is itself an ecologically relevant notion, since like Heschel, Buber holds that materialists "adore the god 'Success'" (*Israel and the World* 117); today, and perhaps in Buber's day as well, such idolatrous overconsumption is a key ecological concern. "The more a people rejects love of the spirit, preferring success, the more void will it be in the face of eternity" (*On Judaism* 136). Better for that people to "extricate itself from the whirling frenzy" (136), as Hirsch advocated regarding the Sabbath, and to grow in spiritual rather than material directions.

We now turn to our second area of Buberian thought, in which it is easy to confuse him with another bearded, mystical Zionist. Like Rav Kook, Buber dwells on the theme of unity; there is no room for dualism in his system. In *I and Thou* (107), he attacks those who divide life "between a real relation with God and an unreal relation . . . with the world —you cannot both truly pray to God and profit by the world. He who knows the world as something by which he is to profit knows God also in the same way." What a profound anti-materialistic and environmental statement! In *On Judaism* (18), he echoes it (and Gordon) when decrying Jewish "intellectuality—out of touch with life, out of balance, inorganic, as it were—[which] fed on the fact that, for millennia, we did not know a healthy, rooted life, determined by the rhythm of nature."

Like those before him, Buber spares no eloquence regarding the unity of the cosmos. Like Kook he sees in all of creation a "striving for unity: for unity within individual man; for unity between divisions of the nation, and between nations; for unity between mankind and every living thing; and for unity between God and the world" (*On Judaism* 27). And in yet another reference to the opening chapters of Genesis, Buber asserts that the wordplay of *Adam* (person/man) and *Adamah* (Earth/ground) is no coincidence, and neither is "the Roman derivation of *homo* from *humus* because man is declared to have been 'born out of the earth'." Buber, like Gordon, focuses on the interdependence of people and soil in one of his strongest "environmental" statements:

> Man [*sic*] and the earth are united one with the other from the beginning and to the very end of time . . . [there is] an existential *communion* of the two, a communion which develops into a special kind of *solidarity*. . . . They are bound up with one another for better and for worse, but in such a way that it is man who determines the fate of the earth by his conduct, the fate which in turn becomes his own. (*On Zion* 11–12)

This last line is among the clearest statements of ecological responsibility in all of Jewish literature. But Buber does not end there; beyond the interdependence of creation lies cosmic unity. He sees the created order as one element of the Divine, one which daily offers its almost pantheistic testimony: "Nature, as a whole and in all its elements, enunciates something that may be regarded as a self-communication of God to all those ready to receive it. This is what the psalm means that has heaven and earth 'declare,' wordlessly, the glory of God" (*On Judaism* 221). Finally, this idea is taken to its extreme as Buber exhorts us to eco-theological consciousness:

> . . . real relationship to God cannot be achieved on earth if real relationships to the world and to mankind are lacking. Both love of the Creator and love of that which [God] has created are finally one and the same.
>
> In order to achieve this unity, man must indeed accept creation from God's hands, not in order to possess it but lovingly to take part in the still uncompleted work of creation. . . . (*On Judaism* 209)

As with Hirsch, we "accept creation from God's hands" by acknowledging that God is the true Owner of all that is. Commenting on the Sabbatical laws of Leviticus 25, Buber writes that "This idea of God as the sole owner of all land [Ps. 24:1] . . . is the cornerstone of the Jewish social concept" (*On Judaism* 116). Allying himself with today's environmental justice movement, Buber goes on to spell out the human dimension of this social and ecological concept: "The Landlord makes a harmonious balance of property ownership, lest inequality arise, grow, and break the bond between the members of the community. Holiness penetrates nature without violating it" (*Israel and the World* 92). The Sabbatical and Jubilee years sacralize agriculture, says Buber; the seventh year is a "ritually conceived fallowness" (*On Zion* 15). And Buber radically offers that the Sabbatical exists for the sake of the land itself, that our presence upon it not become too wearisome: "It can be said in fact that the idea is that the earth is for a time to be free, so as not to be subjected to the will of man, but left to its own nature, to be like no-man's-land" (*On Zion* 154).

Our study concludes with Buber's rootedness in the soil. The interdependence of humans with land is clearest in his essay "The Holy Way," written near the close of World War I:

> The establishment of a true community cannot come about unless the agrarian life, a life that draws its strength from the soil, is elevated to a service of God and spreads to the other social classes, binding them, as it were, to God and to the soil. The laws of the spirit are the laws of the soil, correctly understood; they carry out the dictates of a nature that has become humanized and God-directed.
>
> Our revolution, the revolutionary settlement, signifies the elective fulfillment of a task with which our tradition has charged us. We must choose in this tradition the elements that constitute closeness to the soil, hallowed worldliness, and absorption of the Divine in nature; and reject in this tradition the elements that constitute remoteness from the soil, detached

rationality, and nature's banishment from the presence of God. (*On Judaism* 144–145)

Buber's use of ecological criteria for selectively appropriating the tradition is useful for those of us now trying to reconstruct an authentic, holistic, and ecologically sound Judaism. Also in this passage Buber echoes both Gordon and Kook, the same two intellectual kinsmen with whom he culminates his treatise *On Zion*. Buber favorably quotes Kook's messianic and naturalistic vision (153): "The holiness in Nature breaks through its barriers, it goes out in power to join the Holy that is above Nature. . . . Elijah has come to proclaim peace. . . . We are all coming near to Nature and Nature is coming near to us." Truly Buber and Kook, despite their tremendous differences regarding religion and Jewish law, often manifest between them the very unity of which they both speak.

Lastly and even more powerfully, Buber concludes *On Zion* with a profile of the man he considers to be "without peer in the Jewry of our day" (153), A. D. Gordon. Buber first likens Gordon to, and then raises him above, the famous American naturalists Walt Whitman and Henry David Thoreau—for while these merely romanticize pioneering, "Gordon *is* the pioneer" (156–157). Buber remembers the worker-philosopher's words: "It is our land that speaks to the people . . . the land is waiting for you" (161). Clearly, Buber has heard the voice of the land, as well as that of its spokesperson, Gordon.

With palpable admiration, Buber eulogizes the one who achieved true unity with the object of their mutual affection: "He has really merged into one with the land, it has indeed empowered him to speak for it . . . just as a man's heart empowers his mouth, so he has become the mouth of the land" (161). That Buber should shower such accolades on Gordon is no surprise, since to this day,

the two stand side by side among the modern prophets of both
Zion and Nature.

V. CONCLUSION

The resources these moderns offer us as we construct/reconstruct a
Jewish environmental philosophy, theology, and praxis are remarkable.

From Hirsch we learn to emphasize that God owns creation,
and that we belong to the earth. We reconsider waste *(bal tashhit)*
and rest *(Shabbat)* in their legal, moral, and spiritual dimensions. And
we contemplate the "one glorious chain of love" that unites all
being.

From Kook we learn God's intention that nothing be lost from
God's ensemble, redoubling our own commitment to protecting endangered habitat and species. We sense the interdependence within
the cosmos even to the point of deep ecology. And we question our
individual and societal consumption of animal flesh.

From Gordon we learn the value of labor, land, and nature. We
are reminded that sweat and soil must have a place in our evolving
system. We bolster our commitment to a host of contemporary issues, from logging practices to water management, by learning of
them in another time and place. And we again emphasize the ever-
present themes of species protection and cosmic unity.

Finally, Buber revisits and reframes such all-important concerns as soil, species, interdependence, Divine ownership, and cosmic unity. He also makes our heads spin with new ideas: trees and
cats and relationality; a critique of consumerism; environmental
justice; the common fate of *Adam* and *Adamah,* of people and
planet; eco-theology.

Bibliography

Bergman, Samuel Hugo. *Faith and Reason: Modern Jewish Thought* (tr. Alfred Jospe). NY: Schocken, 1961.

Buber, Martin. *I and Thou* (tr. Ronald Gregor Smith). NY: Scribners, 1923/1958.

———. *Israel and the World.* NY: Schocken, 1948/1963.

———. *On Judaism* (ed. Nahum Glatzer). NY: Schocken, 1967.

———. *On the Bible* (ed. Nahum Glatzer). NY: Schocken, 1968.

———. *On Zion* (tr. Stanley Godman). NY: Schocken, 1944/1973.

Dillard, Annie. *Pilgrim at Tinker Creek.* NY: Bantam, 1974.

Gillman, Neil. *Sacred Fragments.* Phila: JPS, 1990.

Gordon, Aaron David. *Selected Essays* (tr. Frances Burnce). NY: League for Labor Palestine.

Harris, Monford. "Ecology: A Covenantal Approach." In *CCAR Journal* 23(1976):101–8.

Helfand, Jonathan. "The Earth is the Lord's: Judaism and Environmental Ethics." In *Religion and Environmental Crisis* (ed. Eugene C. Hargrove). Athens: Univ. of Georgia, 1986, pp. 38–52.

Hertzberg, Arthur. *The Zionist Idea.* NY: Harper and Row, 1959.

Heschel, Abraham Joshua. *The Sabbath.* NY: Farrar, Straus & Young, 1951.

Hirsch, Samson Raphael. *Horeb* (tr. Isidor Grunfeld). London: Soncino, 1962.

———. *Judaism Eternal, Vol. II* (ed. Isidor Grunfeld). London: Soncino, 1956.

———. *The Nineteen Letters of Ben Uziel* (tr. Bernard Drachman). NY: Funk and Wagnalls, 1899.

Kaplan, Mordecai M. *Siddur.* NY: Reconstructionist Press, 1945.

Kook, Rav Abraham Isaac. *The Essential Writings of Abraham Isaac Kook* (ed. Ben Zion Bokser). Amity, NY: Amity House, 1988.

———. *Abraham Isaac Kook* (ed. Ben Zion Bokser). NY: Paulist Press, 1978.

Wilson, Edward O. *The Diversity of Life.* Cambridge, MA: Harvard Univ., 1992.

AN IMPERILED PROMISED LAND

Alon Tal

INTRODUCTION: ISRAEL'S ENVIRONMENTAL CRISES

The miraculous redemption of a "barren" land has always been touted as one of Israel's most impressive achievements. Ecological criteria and environmental data, nevertheless, present a far less complimentary picture of stewardship during the third Jewish Commonwealth. Since Israel's establishment in 1948, there have indeed been notable achievements in such diverse areas as water conservation, forestry, solar energy, and anti-desertification (IME, *Environmental Quality in Israel,* 1992). Yet, when viewed in a broader

Dr. Alon Tal is the director of the Environmental Policy Research Center at the Arava Institute for Environmental Studies. He also teaches environmental law and environmental politics as an adjunct lecturer at Tel Aviv and Hebrew University. Dr. Tal serves as chairman of Life and Environment, the umbrella organization for Israel's environmental groups. He lives on Kibbutz Ketura with his wife and three daughters.

environmental context, the first century of Zionist settlement can primarily be characterized as a nonsustainable gallop toward ecological disaster.

Although a small country with a total land area of 20,000 square kilometers, Israel is blessed with a geographic and biological diversity that more than matches its spiritual and historical dimensions. The southern half of the country—a desert region with rainfall limited to 20 to 250 mm of water annually—is a landscape completely different from the tropical and alpine environments in the north. The "Rift Valley" that dominates the eastern side of the country for 400 kilometers encompasses the world's lowest point at the Dead Sea and offers a dramatic contrast to the limestone mountains of the Galilee in the north and the central Judean Hills. The rich landscape supports a remarkable biodiversity including 2,500 plant types (150 of which are indigenous to Israel), 350 bird species, 70 mammals, and 88 reptiles/amphibians (IME, *The Environment in Israel,* 1995).

Because of Israel's diminutive size, it did not take long for the full force of environmental degradation to be felt. Beginning in the 1970s, emissions of most conventional air pollutants doubled every ten years, largely due to the burgeoning fleet of automobiles. The number of "exceedances" from national ambient standards has increased accordingly. During the years 1994–1996, an average of 300 violations of air quality standards occurred in the Tel Aviv area alone (ICBS, 1995).

By 1993, Hebrew University Professor Menahem Luria, a leading expert in air quality monitoring, estimated that air pollution in Jerusalem would exceed present levels in Mexico City by the year 2010 (Luria, 1994). According to estimates of Professor Noam Gavrielli of the Technion University Medical School in Haifa, particulate emissions, only one of many problematic Israeli air pollutants, are associated with 1,000 deaths each year (Gavrielli, 1995).

The water flowing in most of the country's streams and rivers is predominantly poorly treated, putrid municipal sewage. Groundwater has become so contaminated that vast parts of the nation's largest aquifer have been disqualified, even for agricultural usage. In 1992, 30–40 percent of the wells exhibited microbial contamination (IME, *Environmental Quality in Israel,* 1992). While eutrophication in Lake Kinneret (the Sea of Galilee), the country's only fresh water lake, appears to have been stemmed during the past two decades as a result of intensive government management activities (Berman, 1996), expanded tourism around the banks threatens the precarious equilibrium.

Green open spaces and undeveloped natural areas are being paved over to accommodate an increasingly consumerist society's appetite for automobiles, backyards, and villas. The urban sprawl, once associated with the greater Tel Aviv region, stretches throughout the Central region, creating the so-called N'Ashdod (Netanya to Ashdod) coastal megalopolis. As the suburban development moves eastward to the Judean Hills in Jerusalem, it devours much of Israel's natural beauty in its wake (Sagai, 1996).

There are other disturbing trends as well. Toxic and municipal solid waste is generated in growing amounts with no comprehensive policy for source reduction or treatment. Pesticides are used almost indiscriminately with one of the highest per-hectare usage rates in the world (Richter, 1994). Some 10 percent of produce contains pesticide residues in excess of national standards. Factories lying in the residential areas often store considerable quantities of hazardous chemicals with no meaningful emergency response plans in place.

Leading Israeli journalist and author Amos Kenan declared

recently that "Jews have caused more damage to the Holy Land during the last fifty years than that cumulatively produced by a litany of conquerors during the past two thousand." As this essay will document, such a critical view is not without empirical support.

How did the Zionist adventure, springing from an ideology that adored the land of Israel, produce such degradation? The first part of this essay offers a cursory environmental history of Israel from the time of its independence, tracing the origins of specific environmental problems to rapid industrialization, massive population growth, and government policies. Next, it is argued that a new era of environmentalism began to emerge at the end of the 1980s with the creation of an environmental ministry and enhanced public awareness. In the final section, a discussion of the requisite policy and environmental paradigm shifts focuses on the primary ideological and practical challenges facing Israeli decision makers and society. Fundamental changes are imperative if the Jewish state is to embark on a more sustainable route and return a modicum of harmony between the inhabitants and the very land Zionists came to redeem.

THE ORIGINS OF
ISRAEL'S ENVIRONMENTAL CRISES

Development and the Zionist Imperative

While Zionist visionaries in Europe dreamed about what a Jewish state might be and argued about philosophical dogma, it was a practical, energetic generation that forged Israel's physical reality (Elon,

1971). The Zionist pioneers, largely a self-selected population, preferred tangible achievements to time-consuming, thorough planning. It can be argued that a pragmatic myopia emerged as the dominant approach to national development during the period prior to Israel independence, when "creating facts on the ground" constituted a political imperative. The so-called "stockade and tower" settlements, created overnight to circumvent British mandatory building restrictions, remain a symbol of the efficacy and orientation of the Zionist enterprise (Ben Gurion, 1955).

These pioneers frequently perceived the natural world as a challenging, hostile wilderness to be tamed through diligent Jewish settlement. Songs extolling production, the beauty of concrete, and the importance of construction became part of a nationalistic liturgy. While Israeli Zionists were certainly not unaware of the splendor of the land of Israel, the task of nation building dominated their senses (Odenheimer, 1991).

The pre-state Zionist community was also home to many figures who deviated from the dominant anthropocentric ideology, which deemed economic and political development to be paramount. The preaching of Second Aliya philosopher A. D. Gordon, as expressed in his seminal work, *Man and Nature,* offered a romantic and inspirational alternative (Gordon, 1951). Gordon waxed reflective about an organic rapport between the Jews and their land that would replace the Diaspora dissonance and alienation from the natural world, and he wrote of the edifying benefits of manual, agricultural labor. A complementary, ecological voice can be found in the rich images penned by "Rachel," the lyrical, melancholy poet, who wrote on the banks of the Kinneret Lake during the early third of this century (Blubstein, 1978). Yet their ideals, while widely admired, were never integrated into macro-decision making on physical planning and policy issues.

The almost exclusive focus of the *Yishuv* (the Jewish settlement in British Palestine) and later Israeli planners and politicians on economic and security exigencies ensured that even the most successful enterprises would give rise to severe environmental problems. Over-pumping in Tel Aviv during the 1930s and 1940s led to closure of wells due to massive salt-water infiltration. The draining of the Hulah Swamp in the northern of tip of Israel during the 1950s, once hailed as a visionary act of Zionist competence, today is largely considered ecological folly (Merom, 1960). Recently, a small area of the reclaimed but largely unproductive farmland was returned to wetlands.

A more recent example, the construction of Tel Aviv's Reading Dalid Power Plant in the 1960s (through a statutory circumvention of Israel's own planning law), reflects the prevailing development paradigm. The country's immediate energy needs were met with little thought to the sulfur and nitrogen dioxide levels in the surrounding metropolitan area (Laster, 1973). The prevailing, short-sighted impatience was exacerbated by a pervasive lack of national environmental consciousness. Basic concepts such as impact statements, emissions controls, and endangered species were not part of the Hebrew scientific or conservational nomenclature for the first two-thirds of the twentieth century. In this sense, Israel was little different from many other Western nations. But as a very small country, with minimal resources, its margin for error was, and remains, perilously small.

Indeed, as long as Israel remained a sparsely populated, relatively indigent country, with an apparent surplus of basic resources, the effects of the aggressive development policy were not conspicuous. Yet, as the population grew almost tenfold between 1940 and 1996, so did the ecological damage (IMI, 1992). The same aggressive Zionist ideology that, despite unrelenting security threats, galvanized a nation to transform swamps and deserts into a modern prosperous state, left deep scars on the land of Israel.

Antiquated Paradigms in the Face of Limited Resources

Perhaps the single greatest cause of Israel's present environmental crises is the concomitant increase in population and rapid economic development (Brachya, 1996). Together, these place enormous pressures on Israel's limited and fragile resources. The symptoms emerged so rapidly that it has been difficult for decision makers to meet the challenges. When government decision makers faced the constraints of limited national resources, hard, frequently politically unpopular decisions were required but rarely made.

It would be wrong to suggest that physical planning had no place during the initial years of statehood. A National Master Plan designed in 1950 by a team of planners headed by Ariel Sharon (no relation to the general/politician of the same name) established the physical blueprint for the Israel of today. This twenty-year plan created such landmarks as the port of Ashdod, the National Water Carrier, and most development towns. Yet, the strategies for national development had no mechanism for integrating environmental considerations. Moreover, the underlying orientation and consequent objectives created environmental impacts that eventually became intolerable (Mazor, 1995).

Beyond rapid economic growth to absorb immigration population, demographic dispersal to guarantee Jewish sovereignty was one of the Sharon Plan's paramount objectives. Professor Adam Mazor, one of Israel's most distinguished experts in physical planning, has diagnosed the prevailing orientation of early planners as "agoraphobia," or a fear of open spaces. According to this view, the major objective of planners was to fill up the country's seemingly vast empty stretches. This manifested itself in strategies that sprayed dozens of new development towns and agricultural settlements across Israel's landscape and encouraged new immigrants (with only modest success) to settle on Israel's periphery. Even within Israeli cities, high-rise buildings were relatively rare.

Within the span of a few decades, Israel was transformed from a relatively unpopulated land to one of the industrialized world's most crowded countries. While in 1948 the legitimacy of scattered and dispersed construction may have been self-evident, Mazor argues that by the 1960s, several waves of immigration made this strategy inappropriate, given Israel's diminutive size (Mazor, 1995).

The resulting sprawl today is bemoaned by environmentalists as "the Los Angelization" of Israel. The phenomenon has been exacerbated by an explosion of hasty development and construction during the early 1990s, exploiting an Emergency Planning Law (enacted to meet the mass immigration from the former Soviet Union) that circumvented normal approval procedures (Gouldman, 1996). The results have been profound. Mazor's recent contrast of aerial photographs between 1948 and 1993 suggests that the amount of land transformed from undeveloped or natural sites to urbanized construction increased from 3 to 17 percent.

Agriculture is another area where national policy was unable to envision the environmental ramifications of "success." The return of the "Jewish farmer" and the greening of the desert, a central tenet of modern Zionism and modern Israeli policies, ultimately had grave ecological impacts. Heavy use of fertilizers, pesticides, and waste water irrigation led to alarming deterioration in ground water quality.

While Israel's Water Commissioner is granted almost unrestricted authority to regulate and reduce pollution of water resources, historically commissioners have done very little to reverse the on-going contamination. Selected by the Minister of Agriculture, the political orientation of those holding the position has always been clear. Water prices, controlled by a powerful farm lobby (supported by historically high representation in Israel's Knesset), reflect massive agricultural subsidies. Agriculture's share of the national water budget typically reached 60 percent (Schwartz, 1994).

As is frequently the case with subsidized commodities, water was often squandered, particularly by the farming sector. This often led to cases of over-pumping of underground aquifers and a subsequent increase in salinity levels. Until the State Comptroller issued a scathing report in 1990 castigating the irresponsible policies of the Water Commissioner (ISC, 1990), however, no serious national debate about the wisdom of agriculture's water allocation occurred. Here again, deeply rooted national ideological commitments failed to accommodate the dramatic rise in population/pollution and a corresponding drop in available resources.

Present commitments to encourage access to automobiles as the primary form of transportation is yet another example of policymakers' inability to bring old dogma in line with new ecological reality (Garb, 1996). Proactive measures to temper the impacts of the geometric expansion of the domestic fleet from 70,000 vehicles in 1960 to roughly 1.5 million today were never seriously considered. Hence, the level of mass transit services deteriorated during this period, and the quality of gasoline often made the catalytic converters, which were only installed in cars during the early 1990s, largely ineffective (Tal, 1992). The associated congestion on Israeli roads, particularly during rush hours, and the pernicious air pollution levels have not yet registered with decision makers, who continue to reduce investment and subsidies for public transportation while dramatically expanding Israel's road network.

Of course the most fundamental conventional Israeli paradigm that requires rethinking in light of new ecological realities is a blind commitment to unfettered economic growth. Increasing GNP and productivity has been the raison d'être of Israel's economic policy since the country's establishment, regardless of the ruling political party. National policy assumes that the general welfare and happiness of citizens automatically improves as the economy expands. While strategies vary under Finance Ministers—from the early heavy industry emphasis of Sapir to the more recent, high-tech models of Shochat and Meridor—the pursuit of speedy, high-return projects with little or no regard to long-term impacts on the environment is consistent. By the end of the 1980s, however, the damage wrought by expanded production and consumption on the quality of Israel's air, land, and water could no longer be disregarded by decision makers with impunity.

Historically, within Israeli economic circles there has been little interest in alternative paradigms. The country's many influential artists and intellectuals, so vociferous on a range of societal issues, never seriously raised questions about the limited time horizons of economic planners or industrial and agricultural producers' propensity for destroying the very resources upon which they rely. Paradoxically, while the "polluter pays" ethic, prohibiting the taking of public resources for private economic gain, increasingly found expression in Israeli environmental statutes, implementation of such principles lagged drastically (Tal, 1994).

Hence, while international awareness following the 1972 Stockholm convention caused a ripple in Israeli society, and were followed by the promulgation of the first ambient air quality standards (Abatement of Nuisances Regulations, 1972) and tough new environmental amendments to the Water Law 29 (Adam Teva V'din, 1992) environmental controls, in practice, were rarely demanded from industries, particularly if they threatened short-term profits. Similarly, municipalities were not required to meet their legislative responsibility to treat sewage and dispose of garbage in a sanitary manner.

THE PARADOX OF ISRAEL'S ENVIRONMENTAL MOVEMENT

Despite the bleak picture just described, a strong environmental movement emerged in Israel during the country's first four decades (Sofer, 1991). Its efforts focused almost exclusively on nature preservation and conservation. In retrospect, it is not clear whether this narrow agenda was the result of superficial consciousness or tactical considerations (likelihood for success) given the political problems associated with tackling the powerful, vested economic interests that created the acute pollution problems. With very little environmental monitoring during this period, it may well have simply been due to a lack of understanding regarding the extent of deterioration.

Notwithstanding the inadequate attention directed toward pollution prevention, preservation efforts undertaken by the Israeli government agencies during this period are unquestionably impressive. A 1963 law established the Nature Reserves and National Park system, and it was promptly followed by an aggressive conservation plan, largely associated with the charismatic Avram Yoffe, who headed the Nature Reserves Authority. A former general, Yoffe shepherded National Master Plan Number 8 for establishing nature reserves and parks through the bureaucracy of the Ministry of Interior. Commissioned in 1970 and submitted and approved in 1979 and 1981, respectively, the plan includes 278 sites (143 reserves and

78 parks) covering more than a million acres of land or a full quarter of the real estate lying inside pre-1967 Israel.

Numerous caveats must be mentioned when presenting Israel's Nature Reserves system (IME, *The Environment in Israel,* 1995). Many of the reserves have yet to be formally declared and appear only as potential sites on the Master Plan drawing board. Other reserves are located inside firing zones and training grounds of the Israeli army, which is not duty bound by law to respect the Nature Reserves Authority. On a deeper level, it is often argued that because of centuries of human interaction with the environment and the diminutive size of the country and parks, it is practically impossible in Israel to set aside critical masses of land where nature is not only preserved but can continue to evolve without anthropogenic disturbance.

Yet, the system of nature reserves and the attendant protection of hundreds of plant and animal species under the Nature Reserve Law's "Natural Assets Regulations" remains a very bright spot in the midst of the period's overall development fervor. The relatively few extinctions recorded this century (involving seven mammal species, including the bear and the cheetah; fourteen birds, including the ostrich and field owl; and two reptiles, including the crocodile) almost all pre-date the establishment of Israel.

Other quasi-government groups enjoyed comparable success in the area of nature conservation campaigns. The Jewish National Fund's tree-planting initiatives have led to the planting of 200 million trees over hundreds of thousands of acres. These activities received a significant boost with the recent passage of Master Plan Number 21, which will enable the JNF to double the forested lands in Israel in the future. The magnitude of the forestry activities is unprecedented internationally and a justifiable source of national pride. Furthermore, the Society for Protection of Nature in Israel (SPNI), established in 1954, leveraged a national passion for hiking and outings to grow into the nation's largest nongovernment organization with thousands of members. Their highly successful educational campaign to eliminate the picking of wildflowers and expansive network of field schools is indicative of both their influence and limited focus during this period.

Ultimately, however, the national pollution problem was not addressed by either the government or the nongovernment sector. In the absence of an independent Environmental Ministry, limited regulatory efforts were centered at the Environmental Protection Service, established in 1973 and located for the most part in the Interior Ministry. Yet, lack of enforcement authorities and marginal influence within the Ministry placed formidable limitations on the activities of the Service's small but highly energetic professional staff.

Regulatory initiatives that did succeed (e.g., marine pollution prevention catalyzed by international efforts to protect the Mediterranean Sea) were never in response to demands by a nongovernmental "green" sector that remained largely indifferent to the pollution levels spiraling out of control. The environmental movement's orientation during the 1970s and 1980s led a noted Israeli environmentalist to characterize the country's environmental movement as "standing in a toxic waste dump and watching the birds."

The paradox of Israeli environmentalism through the 1980s continues to puzzle many local commentators. On the one hand, an extensive network of nature reserves, parks, and field schools nurtured a remarkable culture of hiking and retreats. On the other hand, unsustainable development and an industrial sector that was rarely required to internalize pollution control costs produced unhealthy ambient pollution levels in the cities and a parallel massive deterioration of natural resources. Ironically, the watershed event that began the changes in Israel's environmental activities had little to do with the severity of the problem.

THE NEW ERA OF ISRAELI ENVIRONMENTALISM

Israel's attitude toward the environment underwent a drastic change during the 1990s. While this "greening" has not yet translated into broad-based environmental gains, the political climate is finally ripe for comprehensive environmental regulations and fundamental changes in Israeli society's attitude towards responsible ecological living. While it is difficult to single out a particular event that has led to the transition, three phenomena that served to reinforce each other are identifiable:

- Creation of the Environmental Ministry
- Expansion of environmental activism within the non-governmental sector
- Dramatic expansion of environmental education and media coverage

The 1988 elections resulted in a stalemate requiring a national unity government containing both the Labor and Likud parties. Under the coalition agreement, the two adversaries were to have an equal number of cabinet ministers. Faced with an odd number of existing portfolios, a Ministry of Environment was created to provide a cabinet entrée for the talented young Likud politician (and later Mayor of Tel Aviv) Ronni Milo. Environmentalists were ecstatic at the promise of a single, cabinet-level entity holding the requisite authority to confront the full range of pollution problems. (They were also relieved to discover that rumors about the creation of an alternative "Sports Ministry" were unfounded.)

Once established, however, the Ministry got off to a shaky start. As a "low-prestige" Ministry, the office itself proved to be a turnstile for ambitious politicians. During its first seven years, the Ministry has seen five different administrators at its helm from five different political parties, leading to striking inconsistencies in policy. For instance, Minister of the Environment Ora Namir (1992–1993) implicitly set solid waste as her top priority and was a fervent advocate of incineration. Her successor, Yossi Sarid, became resigned to the inevitability of trash burial and to a lesser degree supported recycling, green labeling, and reduced packaging. Raful Eitan, the present Minister, appears to be channeling resources to litter control and has also voiced support for incineration proposals.

Other disappointments involve budget and statutory authorities. For its first three years, the Environmental Ministry's budget was a paltry ten million dollars (ICBS, 1996). Even when this level of appropriations increased fourfold as a result of Minister Sarid's extensive efforts, it was still inadequate to cover the costs of highly skilled personnel, monitoring equipment, media campaigns, significant policy research, and assessment. Even more problematic is the lack of substantive authorities. Many key environmental areas remain largely in the hands of other government ministries. Control of mobile-source air pollution sources remains within the purview of the Ministry of Transportation, and public transport is even more fragmented. Sewage treatment is funded by the Ministry of Interior and monitored by the Health Ministry. Radiation is largely regulated by the Prime Minister's office. Enforcement of water quality laws is still primarily in the hands of a Ministry of Agriculture appointee, the Water Commissioner (Tal, 1993).

Nonetheless, the creation of the Environmental Ministry provided a cabinet-level advocate for environmental interests. Minister Ronni Milo's immediate battle to impose stiff emission standards on the Haifa Oil Refineries and Electric Company, despite competing litigation by both industry and environmentalists and subsequent compromise, was ultimately responsible for a drastic reduction in sulfur dioxide concentrations in the Haifa area (ICBS, 1995).

The Ministry has also begun the first criminal prosecutions of municipal authorities who do not meet environmental standards. While used only sparingly, high-profile prosecutions, such as the trial of Eilat Mayor Raffi Hochman for illegal sewage discharges into the Red Sea, signaled that the Ministry means business (Warburg, 1993).

At the same time, the environmental movement in Israel at both the national and local levels began to stir. The public, suffering from what is increasingly perceived to be unreasonable exposures, wanted activities beyond nature appreciation. The creation and subsequent aggressive activities of Adam Teva V'din, the Israel Union for Environmental Defense, a national public interest law and science group, is indicative of the growing public militancy and professional demand for better compliance with environmental laws (Silver, 1994).

The burgeoning number of effective local groups is also impressive. According to a recent survey, over 80 environmental organizations have been active over the past decade; from Kiryat Shmoneh to Eilat, citizens across the gamut of Israeli life organized to improve the quality of their immediate environment (Bar-David and Tal, 1996). Farmers in the Jezreel valley successfully stopped a sanitary landfill in a neighboring forest; residents of the Maccabim settlement in 1994 received a Supreme Court order enjoining construction of part of the planned Modi'in city to protect sensitive archaeological areas; in 1990, Haifa's "Citizens Against Air Pollution" coalition prevented the expansion of the local power plant in the country's most polluted city. Even ultra-Orthodox communities such as B'nei Brak, not traditionally associated with environmental activism, have undertaken campaigns to abate pollution from small businesses, culminating in a Supreme Court petition.

Environmental education in Israel has also entered the modern age. It has been pointed out that the nature awareness approach characterizing pedagogical efforts failed to produce a broad cadre of committed environmental lawyers, economists, scientists, and activists. The new environmental curriculum is more promising. By the 1990s, numerous high schools began to offer special environmental tracks with a strong science emphasis, including the opportunity for testing in high school matriculation examinations. New advanced degree programs in environmental studies were established at the Technion, Tel Aviv, Ben Gurion, Haifa, and Hebrew Universities, and most recently a special Middle East regional environmental program opened at the Arava Institute for Environmental Studies. These interdisciplinary programs, relatively anomalous within Israeli academia, are appropriate given the variegated nature of the subject matter.

Formal and informal environmental education also reached new levels during the 1993–1994 "Year of the Environment." Public schools introduced a mandatory environmental component into the curriculum of each grade. A series of public campaigns including battery collection, introduction of a government-sponsored "green seal" for environmentally friendly products, national beach cleanup, and many independent initiatives by youth movements and communities complemented school-room theory (IME, *Environmental Quality in Israel,* 1995).

Moreover, national environmental awareness grew as a result of expanded media coverage. In 1989 only two national newspapers,

HaAretz and the *Jerusalem Post,* had a reporter working a part-time beat to cover environmental issues. By 1994 the environment had become a major media issue, with all dailies and periodicals ear-marking staff to ensure scoops and provide ongoing coverage. Environmental topics and environmentalists began to make the television talk-show circuit and received extensive attention on the new local cable stations. Clearly, Israel's savvy press had come to believe that the public was interested in the environmental story.

Despite the concern and enthusiasm generated by educational activities, little change has been registered in environmental indicators. Notwithstanding the high rainfalls during the past years and major reductions in agricultural allocation of water that returned much of the aquifers' water deficit, salinity levels in the coastal aquifer continue to rise precipitously. The number of air pollution episodes and exceedance of national standards also grew, at an even faster pace. Hazardous waste remains largely unaccounted for, and environmental regulation of pesticides is still rare. Environmentalists' future challenge involves harnessing the enhanced Israeli ecological consciousness to prompt policy changes and better enforcement on the one hand, while galvanizing a heightened commitment to environmentally responsible individual conduct on the other.

THE DEMANDS FOR A SUSTAINABLE FUTURE

Sustainability has emerged internationally as a key ecological concept that, while vague, generally encourages development that does not degrade basic environmental resources. This requires a move from a linear approach to production and natural resources to a cyclical one. Given the country's population growth and economic boom, such an approach is long overdue in Israel. Already, much damage is irreversible.

Flora and fauna supplanted by proliferation of urban sprawl and agricultural development probably will never return. In a recent lecture, director of Water Quality in Israel's Ministry of Environment, Yeshayahu Bar Or, declared the coastal aquifer (a reservoir that holds a full third of Israel's fresh water supply) to be "moribund." In his pessimistic view, because of the pollutants already present in the soil that have percolated toward the groundwater and because of the high pace of the salinization process, it is only a matter of time until the entire aquifer becomes unfit for human consumption as well as agricultural use.

Much remains that can be saved. The Nature Reserves Authority's Hai Bar program, which is returning many of the 20 animal species that have become extinct locally to their natural habitats, should serve as an inspiration. If Israel is going to have an inhabitable environment for future generations, ecology must adopt an aggressive preemptive and restorative approach—preventing pollution and repairing the land. The recent establishment of a Rivers Administration to reclaim Israel's polluted streams constitutes just this kind of initiative. In the final analysis, business as usual is no longer sustainable, and basic values, behavior, and conventions must be altered dramatically. The following are some of the essential challenges that must be on Israel's environmental agenda.

Institutional Expansion

The Ministry of Environment, as mentioned, is not succeeding in concentrating key powers in its hands. Water pollution, arguably

Israel's number one environmental priority, is an example of where the Ministry of Environment is relegated to a secondary supporting role. The Water Commissioner's authority must be transferred from the Ministry of Agriculture to an alternative, more independent environmental Ministry.

During the tenure of Minister Rafael Eitan, who coincidentally holds both the environment and agriculture portfolios, such a institutional transition should be remarkably easy. Similar measures are needed in other problematic areas such as pesticide registration and application. Progress cannot be expected without clear authority, wielded by a committed agency to regulate mobile-source emissions, radiation, mining and even the composition of petroleum products.

Environmental Planning

Israel must realize that as land becomes more scarce, it must be preserved with fanatical stinginess. In practice, this means a return from the hasty habits spawned by the Emergency Legislation of the 1990s to the cautious and thoughtful planning process that Israel's Planning and Building Law mandates. The use of environmental impact statements needs to be expanded and should become an integral part of every major construction initiative, thus guaranteeing the public's right to know the full implications of a development project. Most important, particularly in undeveloped areas, Planning Committees must be willing to say no, even if this results in reduced tax revenues to local authorities or short-term forgone business opportunities.

Greater resources must go to expedite preservation of undeveloped lands, both for use by future generations as well as a critical mass of territory for sustaining ecological viable food webs. A National Master Plan for preservation of open spaces should be quickly prepared to ensure that the most aesthetically and ecological valuable lands remain unspoiled. Recommendations of Adam Mazor's long-range 2020 Program should be implemented with regard to greater efficiency in land use. This includes policies that discourage and limit development of single-story structures in the center and north of the country with corresponding incentives for construction and purchase of well-designed, attractive high-rise structures.

While new settlements have always been part of the Zionist package, it is time to freeze the map in its present state and meet population growth through expansion of existing towns. New settlements, particularly one- and two-story suburban communities, serve to pave over development options for future generations. Finally, the Negev desert, a region where there is ample room for growth, should be the focus of environmentally sensitive development efforts, with Beersheva expanded to constitute the country's third and ultimately largest metropolis.

Public Transportation

In a country as small as Israel, there is insufficient space for a highway system that can accommodate the three million private vehicles that will serve the eight million people expected to live in Israel after the new millennium begins. Convenient, high-speed public transportation is the only serious hope from both an ecological and traffic management/safety point of view. The pragmatic Israeli public will ultimately come to realize that only first-class trains and buses can break the gridlock in congested urban areas. They also offer the attendant benefits of curbing air pollution and preserving open spaces.

Existing incentives for private automobile ownership, including import tax benefits for immigrants and salary perks for public servants and other employees, should be replaced with public transportation subsidies. An emergency plan to implement "designated public transport lanes" should make traveling by bus faster than driving private cars. Parking freezes, additional fuel taxes, expanded pedestrian walkways, carpool incentives, and bicycle lanes are solutions that must be considered, with regulation of automobile usage a last resort that may very likely become unavoidable.

The remarkable success of the recently opened Rehovoth/Tel Aviv line, which without any advertising is flooded by pragmatic Israeli commuters, confounds the pessimistic conventional wisdom that Israelis are too addicted to their cars to travel by rail (Shlisberg, 1996).

Enforcement

In most areas, Israel has environmental standards that are compatible with international criteria for protection of public health and welfare. For instance, the 1992 ambient air quality standards control more pollutants and are generally more stringent than the national air quality criteria of the United States (Adam, Teva V'din, 1993). It is the widespread violations of these standards that serve as the primary challenge to policymakers.

Efficient and professional enforcement activities have proven successful in cleaning air and water around the world. Israel's marine pollution prevention efforts, as part of the national commitment to comply with the Barcelona Convention for protection of the Mediterranean, is the one area where an ongoing inspection and monitoring program has existed since the 1980s. It is therefore not coincidental that marine pollution is also the one environmental medium where pollution levels actually retreated during the 1980s. For example, tar along Israel's beaches has dropped by over 1,000 percent in the period following 1975 (Whitman, 1988).

In order for enforcement efforts to be credible, however, the Attorney General and the District Attorney's offices must make prosecutions a priority. The Ministry of Environment has received authorization to prosecute violators of several environmental laws and has hired a few private law offices on a "retainer" basis to file cases on its behalf. Yet, the number of prosecutions is marginal relative to the pervasiveness of the violations (IME, 1996).

A strong inspection program requires uncompromising political backing, as it inevitably leads to conflict with powerful business interests. Enforcement personnel at all levels must be ready to implement a societal decision to prefer quality of life and protection of natural resources over short-term economic profits. Israel's many environmental laws express a general legislative intent to deal rigorously with polluters, but this is not reflected in the priorities of the State or District Attorney's office.

In public policy realms, from health care to rescue missions, Israel makes ostensibly economically "inefficient" decisions because human and Jewish values are deemed more important. Politicians recognize that such policies are highly popular and receive favorable media attention. There must be similar support by the public for bold environmental actions, if the political equation regarding pollution is to change and environmental objectives attained.

In theory, it can be argued that Israeli environmental policies should begin to integrate economic incentives for nonpolluting behavior—adding the proverbial carrot to the regulatory stick. Yet, for this theory to be compelling, certain conditions must be met. First and foremost, precise data must be available. Without accurate information about what is coming out of smoke stacks and the chemical makeup of effluents discharged by a factory into a sewage system, it is impossible to know whether a trade or tax incentive has actually helped the environment.

Experience from around the world has led to a consensus that economic incentive programs require no less oversight and enforcement than conventional "command and control" policies. In Israel, basic information and enforcement capabilities in the field are still woefully lacking. A freedom of information law still languishes in the Knesset, leaving the public without access to many key environmental data sets. Hence, enforcing existing Israeli standards should be seen as a prerequisite before attempting innovative pollution reduction strategies.

Population Policy

Meeting the environmental challenge honestly may call some of the fundamental beliefs of Israeli society into question. Israel's commitment to expanding its Jewish population is a so-called "sacred cow" and constitutes a non-negotiable public policy. There are many reasons for this dynamic, including residual trauma from anti-Semitic persecution and a sense of isolation and vulnerability when faced with the hostility of the entire Arab world. Yet, when seen in a European context, the picture is very different. Today the population of Israel approaches that of Switzerland and more people speak Hebrew than Norwegian.

After fifty years of population growth at roughly one million people per decade, Israel needs to reconsider its demographic policies. While the ingathering of the Jewish exiles will remain the raison d'être of the country, with an open emigration policy a central tenet of mainstream ideology, it is not certain that ongoing subsidies to large families make sense. While the birthrate is dropping, it remains among the highest in the Western world, despite Israel's diminutive geographic size. In the long run, continued demographic expansion spells ecological and probably economic disaster. Sooner or later, the issue will have to be confronted—better sooner than later.

Education and Environmental Values

As the State of Israel enters the second half of its first century, its pollution profile has changed. No longer can the industrial corporate world be vilified as the primary environmental enemy that must be unconditionally vanquished for total ecological victory. In fact, contamination is increasingly caused by hundreds of small polluters and the seemingly banal activities of an anonymous, dispersed population. Agriculture, automobiles, sewage treatment, dry cleaners, and private home developers are at the heart of Israel's environmental crisis. If Israelis seek an environmental enemy on whom to pin their ecological distress, increasingly "it is us." In such a context, an effective strategy for Israel's environmental movement must go beyond symptoms to the cause of the maladies.

When so many actors are responsible for environmental problems, "command and control" regulation may not offer the most efficacious strategy unless it enjoys broad-based voluntary support from the public. The current educational focus on ecological awareness must be expanded to demand individual participation—from energy conservation to consumption patterns and environmentally friendly shopping. Modern Israel has increasingly come to adopt Western values. Many values, such as respect for human rights and free access to information, are ecologically neutral or even positive.

Yet, the growing materialism and emergence of a consumer society has created a glut of solid waste, short-term economic plans, and irresponsible polluting behavior.

Polluters are ultimately tolerated because society identifies with their singular pursuit of profits at the expense of public values and quality of life. Even though they may be responsible for criminally high levels of pollution, they are not treated as criminals. To enter a sustainable era, Israel must rethink its commitment to conventional, quantitative economic measurements of success.

While no Israeli citizen should be denied a minimal level of comfort, prosperity should not be confused with greed. In an age where emigration from Israel is an option available to many Israelis, the decision to live in the Jewish state is largely a matter of choice. For most citizens, a higher quality of life offers a sufficiently compelling reason to remain and build a country, despite a modest sacrifice in monetary standard of living.

Environmental education must therefore continue to emphasize the connection between quality of life and a clean environment, with access to a healthy natural world. While a credible case can be made in economic terms for such policies (particularly given the importance of tourism to the national economy), it is wrong to define happiness and national well-being strictly along economic lines. Expanded GNP often does not reflect expanded total utility and invariably ignores substantial unaccounted losses of the earth's natural resources.

CONCLUSION

Israel has proven during its brief history that it is capable of making remarkable achievements in environmentally related fields It leads the world in areas such as waste water reuse and solar heating of water. It may be the only country in the world where the desert is clearly in retreat and arid land reclamation has succeeded on a macrolevel (IME, *The Environment in Israel,* 1992). Yet, for a variety of reasons, for too long most pollution problems have "sat on the back burner" and today have reached a critical stage where irreversible damage is beginning to emerge. Environmental indicators across virtually all media are negative: the air, water, and land are degrading rapidly and the unique landscape of the Holy Land is spoiled by sprawl and unimaginative development.

With the advent of peace, the environmental challenges will only grow. A recent independent catalogue of proposed regional development projects likely to impact Israel's environment reached a full 53 pages (Ecopeace, 1995). Greater societal resources must focus on reducing pollution and more must be asked in revising the ecologically unfriendly lifestyles of Israeli citizens who are living in the Western world's most crowded country.

As a country founded on an ideology of land reclamation, it is imperative that the State of Israel integrate modern principles of sustainability across the board in its government policies. Linear development and production patterns have left a land suffocating in the residuals. A cyclical approach to production and waste management that perceives the land, air, and water as fragile and very limited resources is in fact consonant with traditional Jewish values. Israeli society meticulously preserves and nurtures the holy sites which it holds in trust for four of the world's major faiths as well as the generations ahead. A commitment of similar magnitude along with true ingenuity will be required to keep the Holy Land whole.

References

Bar-David, S., and Alon Tal. *Harnessing Activism to Protect Israel's Environment: A Survey of Public Interest Activity and Potential.* Adam Teva V'din, Tel Aviv, 1996.

Ben Gurion, David. *Israel, Years of Challenge.* Massadah, Tel Aviv, 1955.

Berman, T. "Lake Kinneret: Fluctuations in Ecosystem Parameters from 1970 to 1994." In *Proceedings of the Sixth International Conference of the Israeli Society for Ecology and Environmental Quality Sciences,* (1996), p. 881.

Blubstein, Rachel. *Shirat Rachel.* Davar, Tel Aviv, 1978.

Brachya, Valerie. "Towards Sustainable Development in Israel." In *Proceedings of the Sixth International Conference of the Israeli Society for Ecology and Environmental Quality Sciences,* (1996), p. 350.

EcoPeace: Middle East Environmental NGO Forum, *An Inventory of New Development Projects.* EcoPeace, Tel Aviv, 1995.

Elon, Amos. *The Israelis Founders and Sons.* Holt, New York, 1971.

Fletcher, Elaine. "Israeli Transportation and the Environment: Learning from the European Experience." In *Our Shared Environment,* ed. T. Twite and J. Isaac. Israel/Palestine Center for Research and Information, Jerusalem, 1994, p. 215.

Garb, Yaakov. "Fighting the Cross Israel Highway." *Sustainable Transport* (Summer 1996).

Gavrielli Noam. "New Findings on Additional Mortality as a Result of Particulate Air Pollutants." In *Particulate Air Pollution.* Technion, Haifa, 1995.

Gordon, A. D. *Man and Nature.* Zionist Library, Jerusalem, 1951. (In Hebrew)

Gouldman, M. Dennis. "Agricultural Land and the Prevention of Urban Sprawl." In *Proceedings of the Sixth International Conference of the Israeli Society for Ecology and Environmental Quality Sciences* (1996), p. 332.

Hadar, Almog. "Is There an Improvement in Air Quality?" *Proceedings of the 25th Annual Conference of the Israeli Society for Ecology and Environmental Quality Sciences* (1994), p. 23.

ICBS (Israel Central Bureau of Statistics). *Expenditures of Public Services for Environmental Protection.* No. 46. Jerusalem, 1996.

———. *Statistical Abstracts of Israel.* No. 46. Jerusalem, 1995.

IME (Israel Ministry of Environment). "Enforcement Update-February 29, 1992". (Internal document on file with author. 1996.

———. *The Environment in Israel,* ed. Shoshana Gabbay. National Report to the United Nations on Environment and Development. Jerusalem, 1992; 1995.

———. *Environmental Quality in Israel.* Annual Report. Israel Government Printing Office, 1992. (In Hebrew)

——. *Environmental Quality in Israel.* Annual Report. Israel Government Printing Office, 1995. (In Hebrew)

IMI (Israel Ministry of Interior). *National Master Plan for Immigrant Absorption.* Jerusalem, 1992.

ISC (Israel State Comptroller). *Israel Water System.* Special Report. Jerusalem, 1990.

Laster, Richard. "Planning and Building or Building and Then Planning?" *Israel Law Review* 481 (1973):8.

Luria, Menahem, et al. "Forecast of Photochemical Pollution for the Year 2010." In *Proceedings of the 25th Annual Conference of the Israeli Society for Ecology and Environmental Quality Sciences* (1994), p. 26.

Mazor, Adam, et al. *Israel in 2020.* Technion Press, 1995.

Merom, Peter. *Song of a Dying Lake Yefet.* Tel Aviv, 1960.

Odenheimer, M. "Retrieving the Garden of Eden." *The Melton Journal* 24(1991):1.

Postel, Sandra. *Last Oasis, Facing Water Scarcity.* World Watch, New York, 1992.

Pruginin, A., and Y. Glass. *The Environment in Israel in the Year 2000.* Ministry of Environment, Jerusalem, 1990.

Richter, Eliyahu. "Sustainable Agriculture and Pesticides: Problems, Perspectives, and Programs." In *Our Shared Environment,* ed. R. Twite and J. Isaac. Israel/Palestine Center for Research and Information, Jerusalem, 1994, p. 182.

Sagai, Yoav. "Open Landscape Preservation in Areas Exposed to Massive Development Pressure—the Israeli Example." In *Proceedings of the Sixth International Conference of the Israeli Society for Ecology and Environmental Quality Sciences,* (1996), p. 335.

Schwartz, Joshua. "Management of Israel's Water Resources." In *Water and Peace in the Middle East,* ed. Isaac Shuval. Elsevier, Amsterdam, 1994.

Shlisberg, Rebecca. "Why Tel Aviv Needs High-Capacity Rail Transit." In *Proceedings of the Sixth International Conference of the Israeli Society for Ecology and Environmental Quality Sciences* (1996), p. 298.

Silver, Eric. "The New Pioneers." *The Jerusalem Report.* (April 1994):12.

Sofer, Barbara. "A Movement Sweeps Israel." *Hadassah Magazine* (May 1991):18.

Tal, Alon. "Law of the Environment." In *Israel Law and Business Guide.* Kelluwer Law and Taxation publishers, Deventer, Netherlands, 1994, p. 341.

——. "Reform in Air Pollution Prevention from Mobile Sources, Towards the Era of the Catalytic Converter." *The Biosphere* 22(1992):4 (In Hebrew).

——. "Six Reasons Behind Israel's Environmental Crises." *Politics* 47/48 (1993). (In Hebrew)

Warburg, Philip. *Implementation, Enforcement and Oversight of a Gulf of Aqaba Report: Protecting the Gulf of Aqaba: A Regional Environmental Challenge.* Environmental Law Institute, Washington, 1993, p. 375.

Whitman, Joyce. *The Environment in Israel.* State of Israel: Jerusalem, 1988.

Worchaizer, Susan, ed. *Israel's Environmental Legislation.* Adam Teva V'din, Jerusalem, 1993.

THE STRUGGLE
FOR ISRAEL'S ENVIRONMENT:
TOUGHER THAN EVER

David B. Brooks

This article on the State of Israel and its ecology—and more
particularly the continuing struggle to protect the two together—is written in four parts. The first part is a very brief
overview of the ecology and of its neglect in the early years of Israel. The next three parts reflect both the recent history of that
struggle and the stages in which this article was written. The original versions were published at the start of the 1990s: first in *Reconstructionist,*[1] later, in a modest revision prepared with the assistance
of Joseph Shadur (at the time with the Society for the Protection of

Dr. David B. Brooks works in a part of Canada's international aid program that
supports research on natural resources and environmental management in developing
countries. His most recent book is *Watershed: The Role of Fresh Water in the Israeli-
Palestinian Conflict.*

Nature in Israel), in a special environmental issue of *Conservative Judaism*.[2] Towards the middle of the decade, it seemed that the article might be reprinted, and, with the advent of a new Likud-led government in Israel, an annex was added both to update key events in the struggle and to suggest something about the changes that a more business-oriented government might bring. This version was never published, but the mid-decade annex now forms the next part of this article. Now, at the end of the decade, the original article (again somewhat revised) will indeed be reprinted, and ironically again just after a change of government back to a Labor-led coalition. A further update and additional suggestions are called for, and they form the final part of the article.

Thus, taken in series, the last three parts of the article offer snapshots not so much of the environment in Israel as of the struggle to protect that environment at three points over a ten-year period, each with a different government in power. The only constants over the decade are (a) the diversity and beauty of ecology in the tiny nation of Israel; and (b) the lack of much evident will on the part of any Israeli government to do much to protect that diversity and beauty.

ECOLOGY AND BUILDING A NATION

We have long seen Israel, located at the junction of three continents, as lying athwart trade routes and political interests. In a similar way it straddles ecosystems—close to the southern limit for northern habitats and the northern limit for southern ones. This means that her 20,000 square kilometers, well over half of them arid or semi-arid, constitute an amazingly varied and highly sensitive environment with a wealth of landscape and species diversity. Some 2,600 species of plant life (150 of which are indigenous to Israel), 454 bird species, 128 mammals, 8 amphibians, and 90 species of reptiles were native to Israel, though some have not been found recently and can be assumed to have been extirpated.[3]

In view of the decided ambiguity in the traditional Jewish approach to nature,[4] and widespread lack of understanding of the role of the environment among many if not most of Israel's planners and builders, ecological problems were almost totally ignored by the early generations of nation builders. Under the imperative to find housing and jobs for hundreds of thousands of displaced Jews and to encourage immigration, plus the necessity of securing the defenses and establishing an infrastructure for the new nation, they unwittingly—perhaps in some cases, regretfully—destroyed dozens of unique natural values. More recently, the development of Israel as a modern nation, with the twin forces of aspirations for Northern standards of living and high rates of population growth, has placed even greater pressure upon the nation's delicately balanced, vulnerable ecosystems—but without the excuses that could reasonably have been offered by those working in the first decades of the nation's history.

Spurred by the alarming damage to hallowed and beautiful landscapes, the loss of habitat, and the evident disappearance of flora and fauna, a non-governmental environmental movement arose and was punctuated in 1953 with the creation of the Society for the Protection of Nature in Israel (SPNI). In the years that followed, other environmental non-governmental groups (ENGOs) sprung up, though none has yet matched the size or international standing of SPNI. From hesitant beginnings, the ENGO movement has become a major force in Israel with emphasis initially on education and nature conservation, but increasingly on activism as well. For example, SPNI initiated and campaigned for, in the 1960s and 1970s, legislation to set aside protected nature reserves throughout the country and to establish the Nature Reserves Authority as an effective statutory enforcement agency. However important, this campaign reflected the environmental movement's traditional stance with emphasis on preservation rather than conservation, and on natural ecology to the neglect of human ecology. Gradually, the movement came to understand that not only the health of Israel's citizens but the health of its economy depends on careful protection (and, in too many cases, restoration) of the total environment. The lesson was brought to much of the public, and even to some politicians.

SNAPSHOT ONE: ENTERING THE LAST DECADE OF THE CENTURY

The 40th year of the State of Israel, 1988, looked promising with respect to her natural environment. For the first time, a Ministry of the Environment was established by the government. The origins of the new ministry were anything but glorious. A new Labor government was being formed, and the political shuffling required an additional cabinet seat to balance the coalition. The choice fell to environment, and the Ministry of the Environment came into being. This is not the kind of history from which legends are made, and it was late in coming, but it was nevertheless welcome. A step long advocated by the nation's fledgling environmental movement and by many biologists, ecologists, and even a few economists had finally come about.

The New Ministry

In order to create the Ministry of the Environment, the previously existing Environmental Protection Service (EPS), an agency of rather circumscribed powers within the Ministry of the Interior, became the core of the new Ministry, and Dr. Uri Marinov, the competent head of EPS, became its Director-General. The EPS had been created in 1973 following the first United Nations Conference on the Environment and Development in 1972, and Marinov had headed the office for its entire life. Despite a chronically inadequate budget, the EPS had developed a good professional staff and had made a significant start at tackling the gamut of environmental problems in Israel.[5]

What was needed above all in Israel was to place environmental affairs on an authoritative footing within the Government so as to give them higher priority in decisions involving natural resources. The Ministry of the Environment was given primary authority in the fields of air and marine water quality, noise pollution, solid and hazardous wastes. It shared responsibility for environmental planning and for Israel's protected nature and historic areas—national parks and nature reserves. However, further jurisdictional progress was slow. Other ministries, becoming aware of the growing political power in environmental affairs, clung tenaciously to their "turf." For example, the Ministry of Agriculture controlled pesticides and water policies, and the powerful Nature Reserves Authority remained under it. The Ministry of Health had authority to enforce water quality standards. Thus, as shown many times before, the simple establishment of a new ministry was not sufficient to assure effective implementation of its purported mandate. In effect, the new ministry was given responsibility for newer fields of activity, such as air quality, but the older fields with established power structures remained beyond its mandate.

The Environmental Movement

Given the combination of political uncertainty and administrative vacillation, the prime moving force on behalf of Israel's environment came to be the concerned public. The role and initiatives of ENGOs as self-appointed watchdogs were then (and still remain) crucial. This is not to say that there are no people in government or in politics who understand or sympathize with environmental causes. Over the decade, some two to three dozen Knesset members, from all parties, could be counted on to pursue environmental issues consistently and often to table relevant legislation. But their initiatives are typically restrained by political considerations and by the overbearing influence of politically influential if private interests.

Over the years since formal organizations were created, the environmental movement has learned the necessity of adopting broader (and more expensive) tactics. In particular, with the need to take a more activist stance, the movement has had to develop its own research capacity. SPNI was among the first environmental groups in the world to establish its own research capability, an approach that was later followed by other ENGOs, even to the extent of funding their own chemical and biological laboratories. Much of SPNI's research is carried out in the organization's field stations, and in some cases the results have proven critical to its political and social goals. For example, it was SPNI research that demonstrated the potential in detailed knowledge of bird migration to avoid collisions with aircraft and resulting losses of life and equipment (see Box 1). In addition, the existence of in-house research capacity has led to closer cooperation in planning between experts working for (or with) ENGOs and some of the key governmental construction agencies, such as the Public Works Department of the Ministry of Housing.

Education and Awareness

Over the years, both the Ministry of the Environment and the ENGO movement have been active in developing an extensive nature awareness and environmental education program that has made Israel a model for both advanced and developing countries. Some parts of this program involved unique information and enforcement mechanisms. For example, in support of its anti-litter campaign, the Ministry of the Environment, with the full cooperation of the ENGO movement, has enlisted volunteer inspectors and trustees from the general public to report violations of the Cleanliness and Anti-Litter Law. Among the first of many achievements has been the near-reflex reaction inculcated in every Israeli child—and most adults—to desist from picking wildflowers. As a direct result, many threatened species, such as the beautiful black iris, have recovered, and magnificent carpets of wildflowers have returned to embellish the countryside.

The public at large has been kept abreast of and involved in environmental issues by intensive ENGO-initiated media exposure—though, until recently, the media itself lagged in developing its own environmentally aware cadre of journalists. Close cooperation also exists with the Youth Division of the Ministry of Education for programs involving school hikes and outings that incorporate components for environmental education. These activities have had a significant side benefit for ENGOs and particularly for SPNI. Because they were delivering environmental awareness and educational programs to school groups, the army, and tourists, the Ministry of the Environment could rationalize the provision of sizable financial contributions from government coffers, something that was particularly important in the early days of the movement.

Prior to about 1990, the education and awareness programs of

ENGOs concentrated almost entirely on delivering positive messages and on providing information to the public. In this decade, however, Israeli ENGOs have adopted the practices of their colleagues abroad and initiated politically oriented programs. Perhaps the first really significant effort of this kind centered on opposition to the construction of a mammoth Voice of America transmitter station in the Aravah Valley in the Negev desert. As indicated in Box 2, the tower would present many potential hazards to ecosystems, landscapes, and historical sites and—not least—to the inhabitants of the central Aravah valley. It will be interesting to see whether government subsidies continue in the face of this new-found activist stance.

Major Problems Remain

With emphasis upon urgent nature and landscape conservation measures, less attention was paid (particularly by the environmental movement) to increasingly severe but less evident problems of a more dispersed kind. Disappearing wildflowers, poisoned birds of prey, hunted gazelles, and littered beauty spots are much more visible and emotionally stirring than the gradual onslaught of emphysema from air pollution, toxic effluents seeping into ground water, or proper disposal of human and industrial wastes. There was no shortage of such issues at the start of the 1990s. Among them:[6]

- Air pollution in Israel, particularly from automobiles, was soaring. In just eight years, from 1980 to 1988, carbon monoxide, lead, and hydrocarbon emissions all went up by around 50 percent, and nitrogen oxides (one of the sources of acid rain), by nearly 79 percent.

- The need for a suitable toxic waste treatment facility had been long evident. The existing site at Ramat Hovav in the Negev had been improperly maintained, with toxic leachates endangering water supplies. Budget cuts had regularly deferred new construction, and illegal dumping was common.

- The Jordan, with all its hallowed associations and its unique landscape of flowing water in a dry land, was over-exploited and threatened with near disappearance by further water diversion projects. The once-beautiful Yarqon river, flowing through Tel Aviv, was little more than an industrial sewer.

- Per hectare use of pesticides in Israel rated (and still rates) among the highest in the world, and regulations to protect domestic consumers from pesticide residues in food are quite lax, where they exist at all. (Ironically, strict regulations are enforced on pesticide residues for export crops.)

- While Israel has about 18 percent of her land in national parks and nature reserves (more than most other countries), the protected areas are inevitably quite small. Almost every one is subject to encroachment, to adverse impacts on flora and fauna from developments in surrounding areas, and even to excessive public use (including tourism). Large areas of nature reserve and open-space landscape, especially in the Judean and Negev deserts, are used for military training, which causes irreversible damage to their natural ecosystems.

And the list is longer still.

State of the Environment Reporting

These and other problems were summarized in the 1988 edition of *The Environment in Israel,* Israel's official state of the environment report. This was Israel's fourth state of the environment report, though the first to be issued since 1979. Despite the ten-year lag, publication of the report was still worthy of note when one recalls that the United States has never managed to produce a full state of the environment report, and Canada published its first one only in 1986.[7]

The report includes chapters on Land Use Planning, Energy, Resource Management, and Pollution Control (divided into Water, Marine Water, and Air), Solid Waste, Toxic Substances, and Noise. Most of these chapters follow a common pattern. The major sources of the problem are first identified, and then the efforts, by no means always successful, to deal with the problems are described. Subsequent sections cover research, legal framework, and special considerations. Most chapters conclude with a section entitled "Future Trends."

As an official statement, *The Environment in Israel* is remarkably frank. The report refers, for example, to "flagrant violations" of pollution control orders by specific companies. Military aircraft are the "worst offenders" in producing noise in excess of permissible levels. The process of setting standards for pesticide residues "has moved at a snail's pace." In a few cases the frankness falters, as when the term "flexible implementation plan" makes a delay in building the second phase of a toxic waste treatment facility seem less of a problem than it was. (The chapter on toxic substances is one of the few which fails to include a section on future trends!)

Nevertheless, the tone of the 1988 state of the environment report was generally upbeat. The marine chapter highlighted one of the key accomplishments of recent years: a law prohibiting marine pollution from land-based sources. This law complemented an existing one prohibiting pollution from ships and thus gave Israel a comprehensive base for protection of the marine environment. As one result, the amount of tar washing up on beaches decreased by a factor of 150 during the 1980s. This gain reflected the ability (and the courage) of the fledgling Ministry, and of the EPS before it, in moving forcefully into areas that had not been captured by vested interests in other ministries.

There is a special angle to the success story in the marine environment. Recognizing their common interests in protecting the sea from pollution, 16 nations had come together in 1976 to form the Mediterranean Action Plan. Supported by the United Nations Environment Program, the Plan became a model of regional cooperation—and one largely free of the acrimony that has poisoned other efforts at cooperation between Israel and her Arab neighbors.

The chapter on fresh water describes how Israel became a world leader in recycling sewage for agricultural use. In 1970, there was only one sewage treatment plant in all Israel; most human waste just flowed into rivers or the sea. By 1988, despite a more than doubling of the volume of sewage, 90 percent of municipal sewage was collected in sewers, 80 percent was treated and 60 percent re-used.

Fresh water quality, in contrast, was continuing (and still continues) to deteriorate, in significant part because of agricultural and industrial practices in place before environmental quality was an issue. The result: growing pollution loads in rivers and increased incursions of brackish water into critical aquifers as fresh water is pumped out. Israel was close to the point where the availability of potable water would actually decline. With the influx of hundreds of thousands of new immigrants, the issue required immediate solutions. The powerful post of State Comptroller had taken note of the imbalance in water use between agriculture and other sectors,[8] and

Israeli economists were challenging the huge gap between prices paid for water and costs incurred in supplying water.[9] The options are few; conservation of water could clearly help, but by the start of the 1990s it was clear that, despite the traditional place of agriculture in the history of Zionism, its current role in Israel's economy and export had declined to the point where large volumes of water would have to be reallocated from irrigating crops to industrial and household uses.[10]

The record shows that early efforts to bring environmental issues to bear on economic accounting pay off. For example, efforts to control air quality around the large Maor David power plant at Hadera were successful because they were initiated at the planning stage, whereas those to reduce air pollution caused by Nesher Cement's aging plant in Haifa were less successful. A similar contrast is found between the watershed planning efforts of the Kinneret Limnological Lab and the Lake Kinneret Authority, established respectively in 1968 and 1971, and the continuing struggle to rehabilitate the Yarqon River against the opposition of industrial interests.

The Future

What did Israel's environmental future look like in 1990? Would its environmental quality in the year 2000 be better or worse than in 1990? On the one hand, there had been significant achievements, especially in the growing awareness by national and private planning agencies of the need for sustainable development; on the other hand, events of the past few years had exacerbated the problems and threatened to undo many environmentally progressive measures. The tremendous influx of immigration from the USSR had caught Israel's government largely unprepared. In order to meet the unquestioned need for housing and jobs, there were almost overwhelming pressures to abrogate environmentally appropriate planning processes and to discard meticulously worked out land-use determinations. Hasty *ad hoc* solutions to these problems could cause irreversible damage to precious open space landscape, water sources, and air quality. They would also seriously prejudice vital long-term needs of Israel's expanding population for outdoor recreation.

In summary, as Israel entered the 1990s, strong pressures existed to allow pollution, to relax planning procedures, and to reduce ecological reserves, and in many cases the pressure was coming from people with political clout. Then as now, it was all too easy to accept exaggerated "requirements" for electrical power put out by Israel Electric Corporation, to accede to the "need" to use more pesticides so as to increase output, to ignore the release of some pollutant as "accidental." Then as now, it was all too easy to relegate issues of environmental quality to secondary or tertiary importance. However, environmentalists in all sectors and throughout the nation were beginning to challenge this position, and were arguing that environmental protection is no less vital to the well-being—and indeed to the survival—of the Jewish state than defense, economic viability, and absorption of immigrants.

SNAPSHOT TWO: MID-DECADE AND A NEW GOVERNMENT

The first half of the 1990s had been eventful years for environmental issues in Israel, as in most other nations. The battle over the Voice of America transmitter, highlighted in Box 2, was won by the environmental movement; the tower was not erected. However, new and even worse threats arose, as with the Trans-Israel Highway.[11] Yossi

Sarid, who took office in 1993, was the first Minister of the Environment to take his post seriously, and he fought successfully for increased staff, budget, and influence. Among other things, the Ministry of the Environment took over full responsibility for national parks and nature reserves. Unhappily, the rather more important attempt to gain greater authority over water quality failed. Moreover, a new Likud-centered government coalition was poised to take power and seemed unlikely to give the environment the same priority as had its predecessor. If the struggle for Israel's environment was sharp at the start of the 1990s, it had become even sharper by mid-decade.

New Policies and Programs

Notable environmental gains were won in Israel over the first half of the 1990s:

- Creation of several new national parks, and the reintroduction into Israeli nature reserves of animals that had been extirpated.
- Construction of sewage treatment systems for Jerusalem and for Eilat, cities that formerly discharged thousands of cubic meters of raw sewage daily into wadis or the sea.
- Rehabilitation of parts of the Hula valley and of some coastal rivers, all of which once supported flourishing wildlife and provided natural water storage and purification processes.[12]

Environmental processes were also improved:

- Hebrew year 5754 was declared the Year of the Environment, and virtually the entire population of Israel was exposed to (and many participated in) environmental programs.
- State of the Environment Reports were issued in 1992 and 1994, and followed their predecessors in frankness and detail.
- Israel extended its environmental impact assessment process until it became without doubt the best in the Middle East;[13] in parallel state-of-the-art monitoring systems to track pollution were put into place.

Despite these gains, none of the really critical problems identified at the start of the decade were resolved:

- Except for lower sulfur emissions from electrical generation, air quality continued to decline, with automobiles replacing industry as the main problem.[14]
- Water quality also continued to decline in many areas, and, as feared in 1990, resulted in an actual loss of useful water.
- Barely 2 percent of Israel's solid waste was recycled in 1991, and five years later the target was still just 10 percent.
- Toxic waste disposal, notably at Ramat Hovav, continued to be "a tale of high expectations and dashed hopes."[15]

Environment in the Peace Process

When the Middle East Peace Process was initiated in 1992, the United States and the Soviet Union were understandably concerned that the bilateral political discussions between Israel and each of her neighbors would break down. They therefore created a parallel set of multilateral "technical" discussions to focus on five subjects, among them Water Resources and Environment. These meetings are attended not only by parties to the Israeli–Palestinian conflict but also by other Arab nations, most OECD countries, and international agencies such as the World Bank.[16]

Although nothing in the Middle East (or in environment) is exclusively technical, the Multilateral Working Groups on Water Resources and on Environment met regularly over the ensuing four years, and registered significant progress. For example, agreement was reached to create a regional water data base, a regional environmental training center, and a regional code of environmental conduct. A few projects were put on the ground, including a Canadian test of rooftop rainwater catchment systems for Gaza and emergency oil spill teams on both coasts.

Environmental Organizations

In the 1980s SPNI and a few other organizations represented the spectrum of ENGOs in Israel. By the mid-1990s there were at least a half dozen strong national ENGOs and perhaps 20 regional or sectoral ones. (The Autumn 1992 issue of *Israel Environment Bulletin* provides a directory.) Notable among them was the Israel Union for Environmental Defense (UED), which was formed in 1991 to use law to tackle the nation's environmental problems. Armed with results from its own labs, UED used the courts to ensure that government agencies enforce their own rules. For example, only after UED took the Water Commissioner to court did his office take action against kibbutzim and communities that were violating the wastewater disposal rules that had been set when they received water rights.

Some ENGOs are making connections between environment and peace. The Israel/Palestine Centre for Research and Information (I/PCRI), formed in 1989, was perhaps the first group to recognize the importance of this link. Among other activities, I/PCRI used its roundtable process to organize conferences and edit books on environmental problems.[17] EcoPeace was formed in 1995 as the first group to focus explicitly on peace and environment as a multinational regional issue. With Israeli and Palestinian headquarters in East Jerusalem but regional offices in Amman and Cairo, EcoPeace is taking on economic issues generally ignored by other groups, such as the impact of free trade on environment.

Challenges Enough for the Future

Given her size, political situation, and ecological position, Israel faces environmental challenges unique among developed countries. Certainly no other developed nation expects a doubling of population and a tripling of built space over the next 30 to 35 years.[18] In the 1948–1951 period, a comprehensive plan for development in Israel was prepared and largely followed for the next two decades. The 2020 Master Plan was an attempt to replicate that process. Although not due to report until 1997, it was already clear by 1995 that the focus would be on concentration of population and on efficiency of land and resource use. What was less clear was whether the 2020 Master Plan would adopt concepts contained within the general rubric of sustainable development (which are applied to Israel in the Spring

1996 issue of *Israel Environment Bulletin*). However, given the reluctance of much of the Israeli bureaucracy to take environmental issues seriously, it would be foolish not to anticipate controversy. Perhaps the key issue in urban areas will be limiting the role of the automobile, something the Ministry of Transport is unlikely to accept easily. The key issue in rural areas north of the Negev will be shifting toward ecological agriculture, something that will be even harder for Israel's chemically oriented Ministry of Agriculture to accept. From any perspective—environment, development, peace—fresh water continues to be the single most critical issue. Although options for resolution are available,[19] prospects are not hopeful for fundamental reform of the highly politicized water sector. Farming still takes the largest share of the nation's water, and, even though Israeli drip irrigation is highly efficient in getting water to the roots of crops, it is expensive and capital-intensive. Many farmers require government subsidies in the form of low prices for water in order to make a profit. Except in irrigation, Israel has long since lost its role as a leader in water-use efficiency, yet, ironically, it is the irrigation sector that must reduce use the most to allow for improvements in environmental quality, to improve macroeconomic prospects, and to permit a peace settlement.

Finally, any survey of environmental challenges in Israel in the middle of the 1990s had to take account of the Likud victory in the 1996 elections. In one of its first actions, the new government relegated the Ministry of the Environment to second-class status by forcing it to share ministers. The fact that the new Minister was Rafael Eitan and that his main responsibility (and interest) was as Minister of Agriculture sent up danger signals, as did the appointment of Ariel Sharon, Eitan's closest ally in Cabinet, to a newly created post as Minister for Infrastructure with responsibilities that included highways, new housing (on both sides of the Green Line), and water. Clearly, the challenges were the same, but prospects for dealing with them in the last half of the 1990s were decidedly less positive than in the first half of the decade.

Snapshot Three: The End of the Decade, and Again a New Government

The preceding part of this article was originally drafted just after the Netanyahu government had taken office. Given the business-oriented character of that government, my statement that "the new Likud government seemed unlikely to give environment the same priority [as the previous Labor coalition]" was hardly prescient. In fact, it turned out to be an understatement. As noted, when Environment was simply added to the Agriculture portfolio, Rafael Eitan became Minister of the Environment and Agriculture, which created an impossible conflict of interest in respect of both ministerial time and sectoral stakeholders. The not-surprising result was that environment fell to the bottom of the Government's priorities.

Some environmental gains were registered in the second half of the 1990s. Programs got underway to restore the heavily polluted coastal rivers, recycling of at least some solid waste was initiated, and Israel's best-known eyesore, the huge dump just outside Ben Gurion airport, was finally closed. As well, a new state-of-the-art plant for disposal of hazardous wastes opened at Ramat Hovav. Another hopeful sign, and one for which one we thank the neo-classical economic policies of Likud, was the increase in the price of water, particularly to urban consumers, which finally began to reflect its true value. (In the case of farmers, prices for irrigation water did go up but by no means enough to cover the full costs of delivery, much less the value, of the water.[20])

However, these gains were more than offset by the adverse effects of new highways, inadequate control of toxic waste shipments, near-total absence of land planning, loss of shoreline and wetlands, and industrial effluents (commonly from plants built just across the Green Line to avoid Israeli regulation). The new plant at Ramat Hovav can keep up with the generation of hazardous wastes, but will do little to reduce the backlog, which remains as dangerous as ever. The availability of high-quality water continues to decline, and even irrigation water is threatened by increasing levels of chemicals from continued re-circulation of reclaimed sewage now laden with fertilizer and pesticide residues. Both problems are of course made immeasurably worse by the current drought, which is as severe as any in recent history. Had it not been for the continued efforts of the dedicated staff of the Israeli Ministry of the Environment, and for increased activism by the environmental movement, the results would have been still worse. Indeed, judging by the information published periodically by the Ministry, it would appear that the number of ENGOs has continued to grow during this period. Perhaps the biggest successes have come from the efforts of the Israel Union for Environmental Defense, which has extended its activities in the courts to win a number of path-breaking decisions in areas beyond pollution, as with the protection of open space and access to shorelines. Another notable step came when Ecopeace was accepted into the international network of Friends of the Earth to represent the Middle East.

Palestinian Contributions

For its part, the Palestinian Authority took early action to create an environmental protection agency, but for the first few years of its existence those efforts hung up among conflicting objectives, ill-defined powers, and a surplus of chiefs. Only in the last three years has the Palestinian Environmental Authority been really operational. However, just as in Israel, the organization is staffed with capable and committed people, and it is showing signs that it intends to act with greater vigor in the future. The task it faces is formidable as almost all indicators show that environmental and human health conditions are less favorable on the Palestinian side of the border, and of course financial resources are more limited. The Authority faces all of the normal problems of environmental management plus a legacy of 50 years of environmental neglect.[21] Moreover, development plans, as with the deep-water port in Gaza, call for intensive environmental assessment, and it is by no means certain that time and money will be devoted to the task.

Some key insults to the environment on the West Bank and in Gaza are beyond the reach of Palestinian officials. Notably, sewage and other effluents from Jewish settlements, which are typically located on hilltops, continue to flow untreated onto nearby farmland. In direct violation of the Oslo agreement, Israel refuses to accept toxic wastes from Palestinian sources.[22] (The latter is not without reason; authorities fear that bombs might be concealed in the waste.) Even if Ramat Hovav were opened to hazardous wastes from Palestine, no system exists to control the movement of those wastes, and most authorities agree that risks are highest when wastes are in transportation. Fortunately, the extent of industrial operations generating hazardous wastes in Palestine is small—limited mainly to some chemical operations, tanneries, and electroplating, and pharmaceutical plants.

Efforts within the Palestinian Authority to protect the

environment are enhanced by the role of local ENGOs. Indeed, throughout the period of occupation and the Civil Administration, non-governmental organizations were responsible for delivering many if not most of the services in Palestine.[23] Those services were not limited to health and welfare, where they might have been expected to play a role, but extended to natural resources management. For example, the Palestinian Hydrology Group may be an ENGO with no formal authority, but it has the scientific capabilities of hydrological survey organizations in most nations. The Palestinian Agricultural Relief Committees is the match for agricultural extension services in developing countries around the world. And the Applied Research Institute of Jerusalem has analytical capabilities for environment and natural resources management comparable to those of many governments.

Just as with their Israeli counterparts, Palestinian ENGOs focusing strictly on the environment have tended to restrict their initial activities to education and awareness campaigns. Even so, they have played an important role in stimulating greater efforts at environmental protection, and, as more land comes under the control of the Palestinian Authority, one can expect to see a greater degree of environmental activism from these same groups. At the same time, difficulties must be expected as, in the process of state building for Palestine, some activities formerly undertaken by ENGOs come to be taken over by formal government processes or incorporated into government agencies.

Peace Process

In the wake of the Netanyahu government's continued construction of settlements around Jerusalem, formal sessions of the Multilateral Track of the Peace Process ceased in 1997. Plenaries were no longer held but some "inter-sessional" activities and projects continued to operate. For reasons not entirely the fault of the Israeli government, the Environment Working Group of the Multilateral Track of the peace process was largely dormant, except for a few relatively "safe" areas, such as environmental education. Only recently are there signs that the Environment Working Group is reviving. In contrast, under the more forceful gavel of the United States,[24] the Water Resources Working Group did manage to remain active, and to produce some impressive results in developing common data bases and scenarios on future water use. (The scenarios show that there are many political and economic futures under which adequate fresh water would be available for both Israelis and Palestinians for the next couple of decades, but almost no scenario in which Jordanians will not continue to suffer severe shortages.) There is every reason to expect both working groups to operate with considerable success in the coming years, and, if progress is made in the Bilateral Track, for Syria and Lebanon, which have boycotted the Multilateral Track from its inception, to join at least these two working groups where their interests are so close to those of Israelis and Palestinians.

International Activities

Israel continued to participate actively in most of the important international conventions on environment, with particular emphasis on those involving protection of the shared seas and measures to counter desertification. The Palestinian Authority does not generally act as a party to international conventions (because it is not formally a state), but it is gradually playing a greater role in those conventions of direct concern. In contrast, the Palestinian Authority is a full partner in the peace negotiations. Despite the nominal freeze on plenaries in the Multilateral Track, it has participated actively in the inter-sessional activities and project meetings, even when, as in the development of joint data bases and school programs, this implied a form of "normalization." Palestinians have also participated actively in a number of joint research programs with Israeli counterparts. For example, among those financed by Canada's International Development Research Centre[25] are studies of sustainable development for the Dead Sea region, joint management of the Mountain Aquifer, and public health conditions.[26] On a much larger scale, the Agency for International Development in the United States funds the Middle East Regional Cooperation program, which involves actual construction and implementation of sewage treatment and other necessary elements of infrastructure to protect the environment.

New State of the Environment Report

Finally, despite its lack of influence in decision-making, the Ministry of the Environment did manage to bring out a new edition of *The Environment in Israel*.[27] (The previous one came out in 1994.) This state of the environment report maintains the tradition of earlier volumes in combining good analysis with something almost unique in such reports: good writing. The report is considerably longer, but perhaps somewhat less critical of Israeli policies, than past editions. This tendency is evident less in what the report says than in what it does not say. For example, an otherwise excellent article on sustainable transportation says nothing about the inducement to automobile and truck traffic implied by the Trans-Israel Highway, and the ambitious discussion of the Israel 2020 Master Plan in the previous report is replaced here by an equally ambitious but policy-poor discussion of sustainable development.

The Future: Déja Vu All Over Again[28]

Ironically, just as with the first annex, this annex is being written as a new government takes office in Israel. However, this time it is much more difficult to predict what will be the stance of the coalition led by Ehud Barak toward environmental issues. Past Labor governments have not been notably progressive on the environment, but this coalition is distinctly more broadly based than any past one has been. The new minister is Dalia Itzik from Labor; she is relatively young but has served in the Knesset since 1992. None of her previous roles on, among other things, the Finance Committee, the Education and Culture Committee, and the Committee on Women (as Chair) are directly linked to environment; on the other hand, each is certainly relevant in its own way.

Perhaps the greatest threat to the environment in Israel comes not from any proposed highway or development plan but from the absence of a concerted broadly based public lobby for the environment. True, there are more ENGOs than ever before, and they are rather more sophisticated than they have been in the past, but public interest organizations are only part of civil society, and very much less than a true public lobby. Even on those occasions when the government has been forced to back down, as with the Voice of America transmitter, one suspects that external rather than internal pressure deserves the bulk of the credit. Today's need is probably for a more militant environmental movement even at the risk of alienating some sectors of government. Indeed, the fact that government subsidies to some of the larger ENGOs have been sharply cut back could be a blessing in disguise. It could free both sides for a more mature and, over the long term, more productive relationship. Together with people in all parts of the media, including particularly those few who are well informed about environmental issues, civil society in Israel would be well on its way toward creating a lobby that could be mobilized not just against specific proposals but in favor of a major role for environment in all decision making.

In summary, as stated in the Introduction to the 1998 edition of *The Environment in Israel,* important as environmental protection may be throughout the world, "It is especially critical in a small, densely populated and arid country such as Israel." Whether the new government will recognize what is termed "our moral obligation to place the environment high on the list of national priorities" remains to be seen.

Box 1:

Saving Migratory Birds—and Air Force Pilots

Because of its location at the junction of continents, Israel is a funnel for the major south to north (spring) and north to south (fall) migrations of tens of millions of birds, including raptors, storks, pelicans, and smaller species. Damages from collisions with aircraft (mainly military jets, which fly horizontally at low altitudes, just as do birds, but of course at much higher speeds) were causing not merely a loss of birdlife but of planes and pilots. In collaboration with the military, SPNI initiated a three-dimensional mapping of migration routes and climatic factors that, together with radar and volunteer ground spotters, is now so accurate that the timing and location of bird flocks can be predicted within close time and distance parameters. At critical times and locations, military flights are diverted to higher altitudes or grounded altogether. The benefits are evident: collisions between birds and planes have been reduced to nil, yet the times of restricted flying are minimal. Total cost of the project was only about $500,000. And, as a bonus, the SPNI research was the first full-scale demonstration of the potential for gliders to study migration patterns and to map migration routes.

BOX 2:

Fighting the Voice of America Transmitter

Israel's arid regions in the Negev and Judean desert, including the Aravah in the Great Rift Valley, are the only part of Israel where pristine wilderness can still be experienced. They offer the last refuge in the world for certain species of wildlife, such as the Negev Lappet-Faced Vulture. Claiming imperative security needs, over 80 percent of the Negev is today closed by the military for training areas. As a result, portions of the fragile desert have been damaged beyond repair.

A new threat arose to the small remaining parts of the Negev still open to unrestricted public use. The Government of Israel signed an agreement with the United States permitting construction of a Voice of America transmitting station in the Aravah. It was to be among the largest and most powerful in the world. Indeed, so large and powerful would it be that the Israel Air Force found it would endanger its training runs and demanded access into one of the last open and protected parts of the region.

Under the lead of Israeli environmentalists, European, African and American environmental groups fought the proposed transmitter. More than half the members of the Knesset signed a petition to Prime Minister Shamir urging him to deny approval. A coalition of important United States environmental groups raised the issue in the Congress and pointed out that the project may violate the U.S. environmental impact assessment regulations. Important parts of the environmental studies required by the Israel government were left incomplete, and the effect on the million of migratory birds that pass over the Aravah is unknown.

Pressure to build the Voice of America transmitter was great. The Israeli National Council for Planning and Construction at first blocked construction and then set aside its own decision. Alleging that undue political pressures were exerted on Council members, the SPNI and the settlers of the Aravah Regional Council appealed to the Israel High Court of Justice, which issued a temporary restraining order.

A one-year delay proved critical. In one of the few cases in which an environmental lobby could be said to have mobilized in Israel, plans for the transmitter were permanently shelved.

The Environment:
A Shared Interest for
Palestinians and Israelis

Paul Pesach Smith and Thaer Abu Diab

Palestinians and Israelis are inextricably linked in many ways, but especially so through their environment. The two communities share a small area, containing common ecological systems. Within this geographical unit, there are shared surface and subsurface water basins, shared seas and bodies of water, and the same flora and fauna and natural resources. The same aquifers feed our wells, the same rains water our fields, the same limestone quarries supply our builders, and the same soils sustain our crops.

Together, all the elements of our environment compose one

Paul Pesach Smith is co-director of the Palestinian-Israeli Environmental Secretariat.

Thaer Abu Diab is co-director of the Palestinian-Israeli Environmental Secretariat.

delicately balanced organic whole, each part existing only in relation to the others. The consequences of sharing these natural resources are clear. Any harm to the environment almost inevitably affects the other side, both in terms of direct environmental damage to the natural resources in the region and to the people living in the area. No aquifer turns brackish without the ripple effects reaching not only all living Palestinians and Israelis, but all their generations yet to come. In short, there is no Palestinian environmental problem without bearing on Israelis, and no Israeli problem without consequences for Palestinians.

The close proximity of the two communities and the need to address regional environmental issues necessitate cooperation. As difficult as this may be, no alternative exists if the one environment both peoples share is to be sustained and cherished now and in the future. While this article will not discuss in detail the severe environmental challenges facing the region, the broad picture is well known. The region faces chronic water shortages, making responsible management of water resources essential. Water supplies themselves are often dangerously contaminated.

Other serious problems include inadequate and environmentally destructive solid waste disposal practices, unsustainable methods of farming and livestock breeding, tree destruction, soil erosion, and air pollution. It is becoming increasingly clear that the development of sustainable systems of mass transport is essential in order to minimize the environmental hazards that result as the number of cars increases dramatically each year, and more roads are built in an attempt to accommodate increased traffic. As the available open space in the region decreases steadily, the physical development of Israel and the Palestinian Authority becomes an environmental issue of great concern. While national and political considerations may guide the responsible authorities, it is incumbent on environmentalists from both sides to ensure that the impact of short-sighted planning is considered.

MATERIALLY ADVANTAGEOUS COOPERATION

Although the two governments have started to create mechanisms for formal cooperation, particularly with the creation of the Environmental Experts Committee as specified in Oslo II, there continues to be a need to facilitate cooperation between the two non-governmental communities and other segments of society. This informal sector containing youth, students, teachers, academics, specialists, and environmental non-governmental organizations (NGOs), can contribute much to protecting our shared environment. These bodies are often, by definition, less constrained than governmental groups and are able to nimbly accommodate themselves to changing realities in the execution of projects. It was against this background that the Palestinian-Israeli Environmental Secretariat (PIES) was created, in order to forge a joint commitment to protecting the environment by encouraging different sectors to become active and involved.

With regard to many of the topics mentioned above and other environmental hazards, Palestinian-Israeli cooperation is a prerequisite for a successful and comprehensive treatment of these problems. In some other fields, such cooperation is clearly mutually advantageous. A case in point is the area of eco-tourism. Additionally, as a result of its strategic location at the junction of three continents, our region has an exceptional avian population, with extensive migration in the summer months. This region has been blessed with

abundant natural beauty and an ancient and rich social and historical heritage. Attracting nature lovers to the region, using bird-
watching, hiking trails, and village tourism as a focus, will result in
clear economic benefit and development.

For this benefit to be maximized, there is a need to open the
whole area to eco-tourists, so that overseas and local tourists can
tour the region in its entirety. Aside from its clear economic benefits, eco-tourism has a positive environmental impact, as natural sites
are maintained and developed.

Because of the historical and political reality in the area, there
exists a need to strengthen the Palestinian environmental community and infrastructure in order to create a balance between project
partners. Environmental cooperation can play a role in this regard.
Cooperation in the field of eco-tourism is a good example of a
project which can involve Palestinian and Israeli groups in generating new ideas. Projects such as this can be catalysts both for joint activities and for the development of an environmental infrastructure
in the Palestinian Authority.

"PEOPLE-TO-PEOPLE" DIALOGUE

Another aspect of environmental cooperation is the contact established between participants in the joint programs and the overcoming of long-standing barriers resulting from this. While the Oslo
peace negotiations held during the early 1990s, and subsequent ac-
cords, represent the commitment of political leaders to resolve the
Israeli-Palestinian conflict, the achievement of peace cannot be the
work of political decision makers alone. In order to cement the political process initiated, civilian and grassroots interaction must be

strengthened among all elements of the society by developing a "people-to-people" dialogue. This would create a network of inter-personal contacts, particularly among those sharing a common in-terest, in order to initiate substantive attitudinal reorientation and, in turn, to strengthen the peace process. Therefore, this shared interest in the environment and this passion for the land they live on can pave the path for joint activities, both of which are effective instru-ments for the prevention of crises and for the resolution of conflicts.

This dialogue, or, in this case, joint environmental activity, needs to be conducted on an open, mutually beneficial basis in order for it to succeed. Projects need to be built by both sides, and to meet both sides' interests if they are to be successful. These in-terests are not always identical, and different processes may be used within the same project to achieve acceptable outputs for the par-ties. Because of the existing reality in the region, this may involve developing Palestinian infrastructure in some projects before joint activity is commenced. It is our experience that cooperation must be built on a basis of equality and parity in the real, substantive sense, as opposed to a sometimes empty numerical equality of form only.

JOINT PROJECTS

In order to illustrate some of the principles outlined above, and to provide examples of joint environmental work currently being un-dertaken, it is necessary to present some projects being implemented in the area. It has been our experience that NGOs can be especially successful in the field of environmental education and public aware-ness. The fact that extensive infrastructures are not needed, involving the authorization of numerous agencies, allows NGOs to directly interact with youth or communities. Naturally, these activities are of crucial importance in educating a new generation with a shared sense of urgency to protect our most precious resources.

An interesting example of a project that managed to educate Palestinians and Israelis towards a shared commitment to protecting their environment is the Environmental Summer School held over the summer of 1997 in the Galilee and near Jericho, followed by subsequent seminars. Israeli and Palestinian teenagers gathered together to spend ten days learning about their common environment. Bonding between the youth was created, heightening the level of trust and friendship, which managed to transcend political and cultural differences and changed the way the students and counselors perceived each other.

A further project that will address an important joint need, that of controlling environmental hazards emanating from industry, is the Sustainable Environmental Management Program for Palestinian and Israeli Business Leadership. Business and industry, while obviously leading economic development in the region, also have a major environmental impact on their surroundings, stemming from the improper treatment of solid and liquid waste produced, and on air pollution. With the rapid growth in industry and physical development in Israel and the Palestinian Authority, there exists a real need for both sides to meet, share their expertise, and define joint procedures for environmental management.

A FAIR APPROACH TO
REAL CONCERNS

An additional need the project meets is to encourage regional economic development, thus creating the prosperity and stability necessary to build a sustainable and lasting peace. Sound environmental management has proved to be a significantly profitable business strategy for major European and North American companies. It is largely recognized today that there exists a business rationale for "being green," that pollution prevention and cleaner production pays, both in terms of the specific company involved and in terms of national budgetary considerations. This program, by encouraging the adoption of such principles by Israeli and Palestinian industries, will encourage sustainable regional economic development.

During the program, a group of Palestinian and Israeli business leaders will undergo a joint, specialized learning experience concerning the use of eco-efficient/friendly principles in their industries. The use of Israeli expertise and advanced technologies will be discussed, and leading industrial complexes visited, for the benefit of all sides. This program will allow for direct contact to be made between Palestinian and Israeli business leadership, with the aim of contributing to environmental protection and sustainable economic development in the area.

It is important to understand the above-mentioned projects in the light of our initial comments. Clearly, there is a need for Palestinians and Israelis to work together in joint activities for the protection of our environment. This cooperation can take place between many different sectors and concerning a variety of projects. Nonetheless, it should always be remembered that, in order for these activities to be successful, they need to address real concerns in both communities in a fair and equitable manner.

SHARED ENVIRONMENT

Robin Twite

W hen many years ago I worked as a journalist in London, my editor, who had been trained at *The Times,* warned me solemnly never to use the first person in my articles. Nobody cares, he said truly if hurtfully, what you think. However, I decided to use it on this occasion since the actual and potential deterioration of the quality of life in both Israel and Palestine is something which concerns me as an individual who is neither a doctor, or a scientist, or any kind of expert. In this article, I want to explain why it concerns me and how non-governmental agencies (NGOs) working with small budgets and limited personnel can help to prevent it.

It is my belief that only when many, many people (experts and professionals alongside ordinary citizens) do take a personal interest

Robin Twite is a former director of the British Council in Israel. He has worked on conflict resolution at Hebrew University and coordinates work on environmental issues for the Israel/Palestine Center for Research and Information.

in environmental questions that the chances of preventing the long-term deterioration of the quality of life will be reduced. In neither Israel nor Palestine are those concerned with the environment, whether as government officials, representatives of NGOs, or private citizens, strong enough to put environmental concerns in the forefront of affairs, to forestall adverse environmental decisions or insist on action. However, if concerned Israelis and Palestinians work together, they will be more effective than if they work separately. Working within the Israel/Palestine Center for Research and Information (IPCRI), a modest size NGO managed jointly by Israelis and Palestinians, I have tried to facilitate cooperative activities which will help Israelis and Palestinians work together on a wide range of environmental issues, most recently on those relating to public health.

Leave It to "Them"

In some ways, of course, public indifference to the more technical and professional aspects of the environment, such as the question of water quality or disease prevention and control, is understandable. After all, for much of the world's population, and more especially those in North America, Europe, and other economically successful countries, they have improved. The average citizen in countries such as the United States, Britain, or Israel can be forgiven for thinking that we can leave it to "them," the experts who deal in such matters. However, the facts now emerging worldwide make this a rash assumption. It seems that the authorities everywhere are slow to realize the implications of environmental degradation and reluctant to spend money to combat it.

Of course, in some areas, such as the destruction of open spaces and the threat to wildlife, environmental damage is more obvious and it has proved easier to organize effective lobbies and to fight against destructive proposals, but society at large needs also to be concerned about other, less emotive questions, some of which are scientifically complex and therefore more difficult for the layman to understand.

Even if the caring minority does exert itself, success is not assured. To take a local example, very few of those concerned with the Israeli environment believe that the proposed Road No. 6, a multilane highway linking the north and south of the country, can be anything but detrimental to the physical environment of Israel and diminish the quality of life in the country, but in spite of their best efforts, the road goes forward.

Matters are made more serious in both Israel and Palestine by the fact that both societies are looking for development as the prime national aim. In Israel, such attitudes are deeply engrained. I remember when, in the sixties, the Hula Basin was drained to provide more agricultural land, a few farsighted naturalists and others objected, but their voices were not heard. There was a consensus that such large projects were the natural fulfillment of Israel's existence and its ability to get the best out of "the land." Today, much of the Hula Basin is being gradually reflooded in belated recognition that the decision to drain it at all was an economic mistake and one that reduced the biodiversity of the region by wiping out several small species.

In Palestine too, where unemployment levels are intolerably high, it is no small wonder that the minds of both government and people are more drawn to finding employment than thinking about environmental questions. Sheer survival takes precedence over such things as the future of the environment.

THE MUTUAL BENEFITS OF COOPERATION

Only when those concerned with the environment in both Israel and Palestine work together and support one another can the worst impacts of unrestrained development be avoided and a better quality of life be secured for both peoples. The people who have given time and energy to developing Israeli-Palestinian environmental cooperation over a period of years can now be clearly identified. Some of them have been working for many years as individuals within their institutions to facilitate such cooperation.

However, when in 1994, IPCRI held its first conference under the general heading "Our Shared Environment," and published a background book on environmental issues (which, though it is a little out of date, still remains an excellent statement as to the type of problems facing the two societies), there were not many NGOs actively pushing for cooperation.

I have never lost the conviction that, by working together on environmental questions, Israelis and Palestinians can both benefit themselves and those who come after them. They can also contribute to peace by developing mutual respect for one another's capabilities and methods of decision making. Mutual cooperation can be beneficial in itself and develop traditions and methods of work which can be helpful in other areas.

While a mutual effort to maintain or improve the environmental quality of life will benefit both communities, it remains a fact that the quality of life is not an easy concept to define. For example, while there is general agreement that nature reserves are necessary and provide a much-needed amenity and that species (particularly attractive species) should be preserved, there is no agreement when it comes to deciding whether or not a particular project which threatens the habitat of a species, but which also aims to provide increased revenue to the state or for investors, should be carried out. Israelis and Palestinians need to think together about their major problems, such as the supply of water for domestic, agricultural, and industrial purposes; the sort of landscape they would like to live in; how to deal with solid waste (and especially with hazardous waste); how to reduce traffic congestion; what steps to take to deal with a rapidly increasing population, and so on.

IMMEDIATE DANGERS

Of course, there are already efforts to cooperate at a government-to-government level between the Israeli authorities and the Palestinian Authority. In areas such as water quality and distribution, or the handling of difficult specialist medical problems, there is some cooperation, in spite of the ups-and-downs of the peace process.

Other health issues too need much more work on them. Perhaps the most immediate is the deterioration in the quality of water supply, especially in Gaza, caused by the pollution of the underground aquifer. It is a much quoted fact that the majority of Palestinians in the Gaza Strip now drink water that is considered harmful to health if standards drawn up by the World Health Organization are applied. Over-pumping of the aquifer by both Israelis and Palestinians has meant that there has been severe saltwater intrusion. Pesticide and industrial residues have also helped to contaminate the aquifer. Efforts to draw attention to this deplorable state of affairs have been undertaken by NGOs, such as the Applied Research Institute, Jerusalem (ARIJ), and the Palestinian Hydrology Group.

But in many areas there is still a lack of adequate data and of conceptual thinking about threats to public health. IPCRI has now started a small two-year exploratory program with the help of the Canadian International Development Research Council which is designed to help explore the dangers to public health caused by inadequate hazardous waste disposal, the incidence of dioxins (toxic chemicals produced by certain manufacturing and other processes), the effect of lead poisoning (whether from car exhausts or other sources), and the effect of overuse of pesticides on health. All these areas, and particularly the last, are already of concern to the relevant Israeli ministries and their counterparts in the Palestinian Authority, as well as to some academic researchers in both communities, but the amount of resources they have to devote to them is insufficient. Key health authorities, scientists, and officials will work together to indicate what needs to be done in each of these areas and make recommendations to government and other organizations which will almost certainly require major investment over a term of years.

THE LONG-TERM VIEW

It is the duty of the NGO community to draw the attention of the governmental agencies to the gaps and suggest how they may be filled. NGOs cannot themselves take on the responsibility for the solution of the problems, though some of the large NGOs working in Palestine have considerable socially oriented programs. But they can make the authorities and the people aware of them. Interaction with the media and, through them, with informed public opinion, is an essential part of almost all effective NGO programs. Personally, I believe that failure to respond adequately to the public health hazards posed by overuse of water resources, overcrowded towns with heavy air pollution, the destruction of open space and the consequent over-urbanization of society, and the pressure of other comparable problems will lead to a deterioration of the physical and mental health of both communities. This may not take the striking form of new epidemics, but is certainly likely to cause a rise in the incidence of debilitating conditions, such as skin disease, to weaken the immune systems of large sections of the population and to increase the number of cases of mental disturbance.

If the public authorities, research institutions, health workers, and NGOs in Israel and Palestine can think, plan, and work together, the chances of preserving and improving the health of the people of the region will be much improved. The results of their work must then be conveyed in a readily communicable form to the people themselves so that public pressure mounts, budgets are provided, and effective action is taken. If there is no action, or if only one side takes action and not the other, if either party thinks along narrow nationalist lines, the outcome will be grave for both parties, both in the short and long term. A recent study has shown that polluted water from Jerusalem takes up to 30 years to pass through the mountains of the West Bank down to Ein Fashkha on the shore of the Dead Sea. Now the water at Ein Fashkha is of good quality. What will it be like in 30 years? Long-term deterioration of the environment cannot be limited by political boundaries; viruses do not distinguish between Arab and Jew. NGOs must take the lead in defining the difficulties and having effective action taken to overcome them.

PART 2

Eco-Judaism:
One Earth, Many Peoples

During the same generation in which the State of Israel was struggling toward stability and a sense of security, the American Jewish community was becoming something almost unprecedented: a Diaspora community with real political clout, living in a society that treated Jewish ethnicity and religion with respect, free to enrich its own Jewishness without needing to surrender its citizenship in the larger society, free to make alliances with other communities and traditions without abandoning its own unique wisdoms.

And during that same generation, there was a growing sense of unease about the relationship between *adam* and *adamah,* a relationship that now seemed more and more mediated through technologies that swarmed and multiplied in power and breadth. Technologies that seemed to endanger the web of life and of human civilization. Some in that generation called into question the relevance of religious traditions rooted in eras of less powerful technologies, and suggested some wisdom in the attitudes of those traditions toward the earth.

Less than a decade after the Holocaust and the invention and use of the atomic bomb, two major Jewish thinkers—Abraham Joshua Heschel and Erich Fromm—were putting forth to general audiences, not only to Jews, a vision of Shabbat, the Sabbath, as a challenge to technological addiction and to spoliation of the earth. Their vision of the universal importance of what had traditionally been viewed by Jews as a special sign of the Jewish covenant with God was an important new development. Behind it, almost certainly, was a sense that the emerging planetary crisis was demanding a response from all the strands of human wisdom, and that Jewish wisdom in the form of Shabbat had a unique contribution to make. So passages from Fromm and Heschel are included as texts in this part of the book.

From the work of Heschel, especially, there grew a generation of Jews who began to define the issues of *adamah* as not only one important question facing Rabbinic Judaism but perhaps a central question, a major new focus for what Judaism needed to become.

For several reasons, the emergence of this Eco-Judaism was intertwined with the emergence of Feminist Judaism. As some feminists searched for new metaphors for God that are neither masculine nor hierarchical, they found themselves drawing on metaphors from nature like breath, wind, wellspring. These metaphors pointed toward a theology rooted in the interface between earth and earthling, *adamah* and *adam*.

Some feminists also concluded that the habit of treating the earth as mere object and instrument might be related to the habit of treating women as objects and instruments. So a Judaism in which women and men are to have equal voices may also need to be one in which the earth has a voice.

These factors came together to encourage American Jews to see themselves as both empowered and obligated to bring a new Judaism to bear on public policy toward the planetary issues of dying species, polluted habitats, and global threats to atmosphere, ocean, and climate. Note especially that the response was a "new Judaism," not only a new use of Jewish communal power in a narrowly political way. Increasingly, the community saw this as a spiritual issue, with strong social and political implications. And unlike much of the Zionist thought, this Eco-Judaism explicitly rooted itself in biblical and Rabbinic sources, though often midrashically reinterpreting them in unusually free-spirited ways.

Because this work is still emerging and no "fixed canon" has yet been defined, it is harder to distinguish "text" from "essay" than in the previous sections of this book. Yet there are seven writings that seem in some sense textual more than analytical. All of them are much more aggadic than halakhic in tone—much more philosophical or spiritual than legal or prescriptive.

The first two are passages from Heschel and Fromm, who were early harbingers of an emerging Eco-Judaism that is rooted in Jewish peoplehood and tradition yet looks beyond the Land of Israel to the earth as a weave of many ecosystems, and beyond the Jewish people to humankind as a weave of many cultures.

They are followed by a brief gemlike passage on earthy metaphors for God, from Judith Plaskow's central work of Jewish feminist theology.

The others are:

- Passages from "Guarding the Garden," a musical play that is a midrash on the story of the Garden of Eden and its residents—Adam, Eve, Lilith, God on High, and the earthy-immanent Divine Presence of Shekhinah. Here the intertwining of feminism and Eco-Judaism is explicit.

- Passages from a midrashic work by Leonard Yehudah Angel called *The Book of Miriam*. By using the form of a long and intricate midrashic reinterpretation of the ancient texts on Miriam's presence in Torah, Angel sets forth an eco-feminist reinterpretation of the meaning of Judaism as a whole.

  This book's form is unusual enough to bear some explanation. It is the fictional account of the discovery by a professor named Leonard Angel of a group of women in Jerusalem who have been studying an ancient text that purports to be "the Book of Miriam," parallel to the Torah we know as the books of Moses. Angel's book includes the story of this group of women, the text of *The Book of Miriam,* and the texts of women's commentaries on it.

  Angel's book as a whole bears so many marks of the movement for Jewish renewal in late-twentieth-century America that it appears here as a document of that time rather than as a historical interpretation of biblical Judaism, though it is that, too.

- A prophetic *cri de coeur* by Naomi Mara Hyman about the danger of "The Unmaking of the World."

- The editor's prophetic outcry for healing action, in the form of a new Haftarah for the Torah passage about the Flood.

After these texts, we turn to an article by Eilon Schwartz that sets forth the spectrum of debate among recent writers on Judaism and the earth, including some presented in the section on Rabbinic Judaism (in Volume 1 of this anthology) and in this section. What weight does Judaism permit giving to concern for the earth, as distinct from concern for human society and Torah?

Even though that article draws on many of the authors in the Rabbinic Judaism section, it appears here because it closes with a challenge to the new Eco-Judaism: Show that Judaism is capable of changing enough to face the onrushing earth-disaster while remaining Jewish, or leave Judaism bereft of respect and relevance. The authors in this part are attempting to make a Judaism capable of responding.

Then we turn to eight essays that explicitly, with self-awareness, explore various paths in such an Eco-Judaism.

Everett Gendler unearths a Jewish literature of lyrical earthiness, and adds to it many non-Jewish poems and passages celebrating nature that he would weave into the Judaism of tomorrow as Maimonides wove Aristotle into the Judaism of the Rabbis.

Aurora Levins Morales draws both on well-developed theory and richly lived experience: the insights of feminism and her own double tradition—Jewish and Puertoriqeña; and her memory of two different family histories and a strong sense of working-class origins, in an approach to the earth that is political, personal, ecological, and national, all at once.

Arthur Green not only points toward the general outlines of a "Judaism appropriate to a new era of Jewish history," an era of planetary crisis, but also specifies one new practice that might characterize such a new Judaism—vegetarianism as a new version of *kashrut* ("dietary laws").

Evan Eisenberg carries into the present the brilliant analysis of biblical "eco-Judaism" embodied in his essay in Volume 1 of this anthology. He does this by imagining a way to apply the logic of Shabbat, a time withdrawn from human control and management, to one-seventh of the space around us, which we might similarly withdraw from our own control and leave in wildness.

Ellen Bernstein shows how the overarching Jewish values of open land and close-knit community can be applied to the issue of earth-destroying sprawl in a very specific place, the suburbs and exurbs of Pennsylvania.

Michael Lerner urges that any attempt to grapple with ecological danger requires addressing global issues of money, corporate power, and a culture that reinforces both greed and feelings of powerlessness. He lifts up the tradition of the sabbatical year as one that can help us deal with these basic issues—one that we should therefore apply seriously in our own day.

Irene Diamond and David Seidenberg apply a very new and subtle language—contemporary critical eco-feminist social and literary analysis—to recovering and renewing a very ancient one—the symbols and practice of Torah. They try to recover an ancient sense of undivided body-mind that is expressed in both the sensuous human body and the sensuous earth. They celebrate the sensuousness that in much of classical Judaism has been tuned out in favor of the intellect, and the fuzziness and fringiness that in much of classical Judaism has been tuned out in favor of orderly distinction making.

Finally, the editor lays out a "unified theory" that attempts to explain through the Jewish language of Kabbalah how we human beings have entered the present crisis of the earth and how Jews might draw on, renew, and transform Jewish practice so as to model human actions to heal the interface of *adam* and *adamah*. The human race, he suggests, is at a point when it needs to take a major next step in "growing up." Just as individuals who are fifty years old need to act differently from those who are three or thirteen, so may the human race as a whole now have to explore a level of Torah-path that was not appropriate before.

TEXT: TECHNICAL CIVILIZATION AND SHABBAT

Abraham Joshua Heschel

Technical civilization is man's conquest of space. It is a triumph frequently achieved by sacrificing an essential ingredient of existence, namely, time. In technical civilization, we expend time to gain space. To enhance our power in the world of space is our main objective. Yet to have more does not mean to be more. The power we attain in the world of space terminates abruptly at the borderline of time. But time is the heart of existence.[1]

To gain control of the world of space is certainly one of our tasks. The danger begins when in gaining power in the realm of

---

Rabbi Abraham Joshua Heschel (d. 1972) grew up in the family tradition of great Hasidic rebbes and became known as a major theologian and then as a committed religious activist against racism and the Vietnam war while serving as professor of ethics and mysticism at the Jewish Theological Seminary. His books include *God in Search of Man, The Sabbath, The Insecurity of Freedom,* and *Moral Grandeur and Spiritual Audacity* (ed. Susannah Heschel).

space we forfeit all aspirations in the realm of time. There is a realm of time where the goal is not to have but to be, not to own but to give, not to control but to share, not to subdue but to be in accord. Life goes wrong when the control of space, the acquisition of things of space, becomes our sole concern.

Nothing is more useful than power, nothing more frightful. We have often suffered from degradation by poverty, now we are threatened with degradation through power. There is happiness in the love of labor, there is misery in the love of gain. Many hearts and pitchers are broken at the fountain of profit. Selling himself into slavery to things, man becomes a utensil that is broken at the fountain (p. 3).

Technical civilization is the product of labor, of man's exertion of power for the sake of gain, for the sake of producing goods. It begins when man, dissatisfied with what is available in nature, becomes engaged in a struggle with the forces of nature in order to enhance his safety and to increase his comfort. To use the language of the Bible, the task of civilization is to subdue the earth, to have dominion over the beast.

How proud we often are of our victories in the war with nature, proud of the multitude of instruments we have succeeded in inventing, of the abundance of commodities we have been able to produce. Yet our victories have come to resemble defeats. In spite of our triumphs, we have fallen victims to the work of our hands; it is as if the forces we had conquered have conquered us.

Is our civilization a way to disaster, as many of us are prone to believe? Is civilization essentially evil, to be rejected and condemned? The faith of the Jew is not a way out of this world, but a way of being within and above this world; not to reject but to surpass civilization. The Sabbath is the day on which we learn the art of *surpassing* civilization.

Adam was placed in the Garden of Eden "to dress it and to keep it" (Genesis 2:15). Labor is not only the destiny of man; it is endowed with divine dignity. However, after he ate of the tree of knowledge he was condemned to toil, not only to labor. "In toil shall thou eat . . . all the days of thy life" (Genesis 3:17). Labor is a blessing, toil is the misery of man.

The Sabbath as a day of abstaining from work is not a depreciation but an affirmation of labor, a divine exaltation of its dignity. Thou shalt abstain from labor on the seventh day is a sequel to the command: *Six days shalt thou labor, and do all thy work.*[2]

"Six days shalt thou labor and do all thy work; but the seventh day is Sabbath unto the Lord thy God." Just as we are commanded to keep the Sabbath, we are commanded to labor.[3] "Love work. . . . "[4] The duty to work for six days is just as much a part of God's covenant with man as the duty to abstain from work on the seventh day.[5]

To set apart one day a week for freedom, a day on which we would not use the instruments which have been so easily turned into weapons of destruction, a day for being with ourselves, a day of detachment from the vulgar, of independence of external obligations, a day on which we stop worshipping the idols of technical civilization, a day on which we use no money, a day of armistice in the economic struggle with our fellow men and the forces of nature—is there any institution that holds out a greater hope for man's progress than the Sabbath?

The solution of mankind's most vexing problem will not be found in renouncing technical civilization, but in attaining some degree of independence of it.

In regard to external gifts, to outward possessions, there is only one proper attitude—to have them and to be able to do without them. On the Sabbath we live, as it were, *independent of technical civilization:* we abstain primarily from any activity that aims at re-making or reshaping the things of space. Man's royal privilege to conquer nature is suspended on the seventh day.

What are the kinds of labor not to be done on the Sabbath? They are, according to the ancient rabbis, all those acts which were necessary for the construction and furnishing of the Sanctuary in the desert.[6] The Sabbath itself is a sanctuary which we build, *a sanctuary in time.*

It is one thing to race or be driven by the vicissitudes that menace life, and another thing to stand still and to embrace the presence of an eternal moment.

The seventh day is the armistice in man's cruel struggle for existence, a truce in all conflicts, personal and social, peace between man and man, man and nature, peace within man; a day on which handling money is considered a desecration, on which man avows his independence of that which is the world's chief idol. The seventh day is the exodus from tension, the liberation of man from his own muddiness, the installation of man as a sovereign in the world of time.

In the tempestuous ocean of time and toil there are islands of stillness where man may enter a harbor and reclaim his dignity. The island is the seventh day, the Sabbath, a day of detachment from things, instruments, and practical affairs as well as of attachment to the spirit.

TEXT: THE WAY OF THE SABBATH

Erich Fromm

There can be no doubt of the fact that the Sabbath is a, or perhaps *the,* central institution of biblical and rabbinic religion. It is commanded in the Decalogue; it is one of few religious laws emphasized by the great reforming Prophets; it has a central place in rabbinical thought, and as long as Judaism exists in its traditional customs, it was and is the most outstanding phenomenon of Jewish religious practice. It is no exaggeration to say that the spiritual and moral survival of the Jews during two thousand years of persecution and humiliation would hardly have been possible without the one day in the week when even the poorest and most wretched Jew was

---

Erich Fromm (d. 1980) was best known for drawing on psychoanalytic theory and practice to analyze and heal societal ills, in such books as E*scape from Freedom, The Art of Loving,* and *The Forgotten Language.* He is the author of *You Shall Be As Gods,* a reinterpretation of the Hebrew Bible.

transformed into a man of dignity and pride, when the beggar was changed into a king. But in order not to think that this statement is a crude exaggeration, one must have witnessed the traditional practice of the Sabbath in its authentic form.

Whoever thinks that he knows what the Sabbath is because he has seen the candles lit has little idea of the atmosphere the traditional Sabbath creates.

The reason why the Sabbath has so central a place within Jewish law lies in the fact that the Sabbath is the expression of the central idea of Judaism: the idea of freedom; the idea of complete harmony between man and nature, man and man; the idea of the anticipation of messianic time and of man's defeat of time, sadness, and death.[1]

The modern mind does not see much of a problem in the Sabbath institution. That man should rest from his work one day a week sounds to us like a self-evident, social-hygienic measure intended give him the play and spiritual rest and relaxation he needs in order not to be swallowed up by his daily work, and to enable him to work better during the six working days. No doubt this explanation is true as far as it goes, but it does not answer some questions that arise if we pay closer attention to the Sabbath law of the Bible and particularly to the Sabbath ritual as it developed in the post-biblical tradition.

Why is this social-hygienic law so important that it was placed among the Ten Commandments, which otherwise stipulate only the fundamental religious and ethical principles? Why is it explained by equating it with God's rest on the seventh day, and what does this "rest" mean? Is God pictured in such anthropomorphic terms as to need a rest after six days of hard work? Why is the Sabbath explained in the second version of the Ten Commandments in terms of freedom rather than in terms of God's rest? What is the common denominator of the two explanations? Moreover—and this is perhaps the most important question—how can we understand the intricacies of the Sabbath ritual in the light of the social-hygienic interpretation of rest?

In the Old Testament a man who "gathers sticks" (Num. 4:32 ff.) is considered a violator of the Sabbath law and punished by death. In the later development, not only work in our modern sense is forbidden, but activities such as the following: making any kind of fire, even if it is for the sake of convenience and does not require any physical effort; pulling a single blade of grass from the soil, carrying anything, even something as light as a handkerchief, on one's person. All this is not work in the sense of physical effort; its avoidance is often more of an inconvenience and discomfort than its execution would be. Are we dealing here with extravagant and compulsive exaggerations of an originally "sensible" ritual, or is our understanding of the ritual perhaps faulty and in need of revision?

A more detailed analysis of the symbolic meaning of the Sabbath ritual will show that we are dealing not with obsessive overstrictness but with a concept of work and rest that is different from our modern concept.

To begin with, the concept of work underlying the biblical and later Talmudic concepts is not one of physical effort, but it can be defined thus: *"Work" is any interference by man, be it constructive or destructive, with the physical world. "Rest" is a state of peace between man and nature.* Man must leave nature untouched, not change it in any way, either by building or by destroying anything. Even the smallest change made by man in the natural process is a violation of rest. The Sabbath is the day of complete harmony between man and nature. "Work" is any kind of disturbance of the man-nature equilibrium. On the basis of this general definition, we can understand the Sabbath ritual.

Any heavy work, like plowing or building, is work in this, as well as in our modern, sense. But lighting a match and pulling up a blade of grass, while not requiring any effort, are symbols of human interference with the natural process, a breach of peace between man and nature. On the basis of this principle, we can understand the Talmudic prohibition of carrying anything, even of little weight, on one's person. In fact, the carrying of something, as such, is not forbidden. I can carry a heavy load within my house or my estate without violating the Sabbath law. But I must not carry even a handkerchief from one domain to another—for instance, from the private domain of the house to the public domain of the street. This law is an extension of the idea of peace from the social to the natural realm. A man must not interfere with or change the natural equilibrium and he must refrain from changing the social equilibrium. That means not only not to do business but also to avoid the most primitive form of transference of property, namely, its local transference from one domain to another.

The Sabbath symbolizes a state of union between man and nature and between man and man. By not working—that is to say, by not participating in the process of natural and social change—man is free from the chains of time, although only for one day a week.

The full significance of this idea can be understood only in the context of the biblical philosophy of the relationship between man and nature and the concept of the messianic time. The Sabbath is the anticipation of the messianic time, which is sometimes called "the time of the perpetual Sabbath"; but it is not purely the *symbolic* anticipation of the messianic time—it is its real precursor. As the Talmud puts it, "If all of Israel observed two Sabbaths [consecutively] fully only once, the messiah would be here" (*Shabbat* 118a). The Sabbath is the anticipation of the messianic time, not through a magic ritual, but through a form of practice which puts man in a real situation of harmony and peace. The different practice of life transforms man. This transformation has been expressed in the Talmud in the following way: "R. Simeon b. Lakish said: 'On the eve of the Sabbath, the Holy One Blessed Be He, gives to man an additional soul, and at the close of the Sabbath he withdraws it from him'" (*Beitza* 16a).

"Rest" in the sense of the traditional Sabbath concept is quite different from "rest" being defined as not working, or not making an effort (just as "peace"—*shalom*—in the prophetic tradition is more than merely the absence of war; it expresses harmony, wholeness).[2] On the Sabbath, man ceases completely to be an animal whose main occupation is to fight for survival and to sustain his biological life. On the Sabbath, man is fully man, with no task other than to be human. In the Jewish tradition it is not work which is a supreme value, but rest, the state that has no other purpose than that of being human.

There is one other aspect of the Sabbath ritual which is relevant to its full understanding. The Sabbath seems to have been an old Babylonian holiday, celebrated every seventh day *(Shapatu)* of a moon month. But its meaning was quite different from that of the biblical Sabbath. The Babylonian *Shapatu* was a day of mourning and self-castigation. It was a somber day, dedicated to the planet Saturn (our "Saturday" is still in its name devoted to Saturn), whose wrath one wanted to placate by self-castigation and self-punishment. But in the Bible, the holy day lost the character of self-castigation and mourning; it is no longer an "evil" day but a good one; the Sabbath becomes the very opposite of the sinister *Shapatu*. It becomes the day of joy and pleasure. Eating, drinking, sexual love, in addition to studying the Scriptures and religious writings, have characterized the Jewish celebration of the Sabbath throughout the last two thousand years. From a day of submission to the evil powers of Saturn, the Sabbath has become a day of freedom and joy.

This change in mood and meaning can be fully understood only if we consider the meaning of Saturn. Saturn (in the old astrological and metaphysical tradition) symbolizes time. He is the god of time and hence the god of death. Inasmuch as man is like God, gifted with a soul, with reason, love, and freedom, he is not subject to time or death. But inasmuch as man is an animal with a body subject to the laws of nature, he is a slave to time and death. The Babylonians sought to appease the lord of time by self-castigation. The Bible, in its Sabbath concept, makes an entirely new attempt to solve the problem: by stopping interference with nature for one day, time is eliminated; where there is no change, no work, no human interference, there is no time. Instead of a Sabbath on which man bows down to the lord of time, the biblical Sabbath symbolizes man's victory over time. Time is suspended, Saturn is dethroned on his very day, Saturn's-day. Death is suspended and life rules on the Sabbath day.[3]

TEXT: METAPHORS OF GOD

Judith Plaskow

I mages of God as fountain, source, wellspring, or ground of life and being remind us that God loves and befriends us as one who brings forth all being and sustains it in existence. . . .

Metaphors of ground and source continue the reconceptualization of God's power, shifting our sense of direction from a God in the high heavens who creates through the magical word to the very ground beneath our feet that nourishes and sustains us.

As a tree draws up sustenance from the soil, so we are rooted in the source of our being that bears and maintains us even as it enables us to respond to it freely. Images of God as rock, tree of life, light, darkness, and myriad other metaphors drawn from nature teach us the intrinsic value of this wider web of being in which we dwell.

Judith Plaskow is a long-time Jewish feminist-activist and theologian of feminist Judaism who is a professor of religious studies at Manhattan College. She is the author of *Standing Again at Sinai*.

TEXT: (EXCERPTS FROM) GUARDING THE GARDEN: A NEW MUSICAL MIDRASH

Music by Margot L. Stein

Lyrics by Margot L. Stein and David Schechter

Script by David Schechter

(Additional material by Evi Seidman, Michelle Osherow, and Alon Nashman)

(Based on an idea and originally produced by David Wechsler-Azen)

David Schechter is a playwright and director based in New York City. His plays on Jewish themes include the award-winning *Hannah Senesh,* which has toured extensively throughout the United States and Israel.

Evi Seidman is a stand-up philosopher and poet, educator, and activist for environmental sanity and social justice. She now rabble-rouses in small-town politics in the Mid-Hudson Valley and is writing memoirs of personal adventures during the women's movement of the 1970s.

Rabbi Margot L. Stein is an award-winning singer/songwriter whose musical play, *Guarding the Garden,* toured North America for four seasons and was seen by some twenty thousand people. She has produced five albums of Jewish music, both solo and in collaboration with the a cappella trio MIRAJ and the ensemble Shabbat Unplugged. Their current release, *A Night of Questions,* provides original and traditional music to accompany the new Reconstructionist Haggadah.

LIL: Let me think—I'll call it . . . uh . . . this is hard! You must really work at this.

ADAM: Wait here. I'll get help from the voice up there.

LIL: Really? *(She shouts to the sky.)* Hello! Hello! Can you help me, please? Can you even hear me?

(Tree of Life theme, SHEKHINA's voice, is heard.)

(LILITH puts her ear to the ground again.)

LIL: Hello? Hello? I hear the voice down here!

(Bell rings. A rap beat begins.)

> EVE (O.S.): *Then Lilith heard the voice she'd heard before.*
> LIL: *And it definitely comes through the ground,*
>   *What's more, it also seemed to come through the grass and trees.*
> EVE: *It was the aspect of God within what one sees.*
> LIL: *And she called it "Shekhina."*
> ADAM: *As distinct from "Lord."*
>   *That's what Adam called the voice that he looked toward,*
>   *The awesome one who made the sun, the clouds,*
>   *The stars, the moon, the sky,*
>   *And the wild imaginings of his mind's eye.*

(Adam dashes off to pursue an idea.)

> LIL: *You see, "Shekhina" is a word that means "to dwell" and*
>   *the voice seemed to live,*
> EVE: *As far as she could tell,*
> LIL: *Within plants, rocks, critters and herself as well.*
> EVE: *What they heard were two aspects of just one voice*
>   *But the way that they heard it was each one's choice.*

(Musical transition to Create Out of Nothing music)

LILITH *sings:*

> *Ancient wisdom in my veins*
> *The brain tries to erase*
> *But the cold hard logic that remains*
> *Seems strangely out of place*
> *Calling, calling, calling*
> *Voices all around*
> *Asking me to listen*
> *And to tell the world*
> *What I've found*

EVE *(as God): Creation is cycles.*

LIL: *Cycles!*

EACH, *(intertwined):*

Round they all go,	*Round and round.*
Circles of meaning	*Circles of meaning.*
Endlessly flow.	*It's endless!*
Living and dying.	*Creation is cycles.*
Round they all go,	*Round and round,*
Circles of meaning.	*Circles that grow.*

> *Watch how they grow.*

LIL: It's like a spiral! Wow! This is amazing! Adam! Come here and listen. Can you hear it?

★ ★ ★

EVE *(O. S.):* Of everything that grows in the garden you may eat and if you eat the fruit of the tree in the middle of the garden, then you shall know death. [Based on Genesis 2:17]

ADAM: Well that rules out dessert.

LIL: Adam, listen to this voice down here. Can you hear it?

ADAM (listening close to LILITH's ear): All I can hear is the wind whistling in one ear and out the other!

> ADAM: *What if the rain were falling fast*
> *How long might it last?*
> LILITH: *The river is rising. Its levels are surprisingly high.*
> ADAM: *I hate to say I'm scared. But I'm frankly unprepared to die.*
> ADAM: *We've got to guard the garden.*
> LILITH: *We'll squirrel inside this tree*
> *To stay dry, we'll nest inside.*
> *Don't you agree?*
> ADAM: *Yes, we've got to guard the garden*
> *So let's chop down this tree.*
> *With you my spouse, we'll build a house*
> *And stay dry comfortably.*
> LILITH: *What if the sun were beating hot*
> *No clouds, no rain, now what*
> *Could human beings do?*
> *Should we melt into gooey pie?*
> ADAM: *I hate to say I'm scared,*
> *But I'm frankly unprepared to die.*
> LIL: *We've got to Guard the Garden*
> *For the hippos and the swan*
> *To stay cool, we'll splash in their pool*

And float to Babylon . . .

ADAM: *Yes we've got to Guard the Garden.*

We'll line a pool with stone,

Divert the river so it'll deliver

Gallons we can call our own.

BOTH: *We've got to Guard the Garden*

Protect it from disaster

Learn to imitate the birds and bees

Learn to imitate our master.

LIL: It seems to have stopped, whatever it was.

ADAM: Yeah, but you can never be too careful. *(Tree of Life theme)*

LIL: There it goes again, Adam. That voice in the ground. Can't you hear it? Listen! *(Puts her ear to the ground.)*

ADAM: You definitely have an overactive imagination. There's no voice down there. The only voice is up . . .

★ ★ ★

LIL: Listen, I want to tell you about talking to Shekhina.

ADAM: Shekhina? Who's Shekhina?

LIL: It's the voice from the ground.

ADAM: Back up, will ye? There is *no voice* down there. The Voice is Up.

LIL: Adam, I'm telling you . . .

ADAM: And I'm telling *you,* there is nothing down there but dirt!

LIL: It's not dirt! It's *soil!*

ADAM: Well, I still say that it's dirt. It gets my feet all yukky and you were rubbing your ear in it!

LIL: Oh, for crying out loud! Honey, I'm telling you, there's a very smart voice down here, and if you'd just give it another chance. . . .

ADAM *(poking a pitchfork into the ground):* And I'm telling you, there's nothing down here but "dirt"!

LIL: Knock it off! You can't stop Shekhina's voice!

ADAM: I'll do whatever I want!

LIL: I'll do whatever Shekhina wants.

★ ★ ★

LIL: The voice says we should stop right now.

ADAM: How could the ground, or the grass, or that tree have anything to say?

LIL: How come your voice has something to say but my voice doesn't have anything to say?

ADAM: It's not *my* voice or *your* voice, it's *the* voice. And if it doesn't talk to you, I'm sorry.

LIL: Well, clearly there's more than one voice!

ADAM: There can't be more than one voice.

LIL: Why not? There's more than one leaf, we keep finding more. Why can't there be more than one voice?

ADAM: There's no end to your arrogance.

LIL: Arrogance! *Arrogance!* And just what is "arrogance," please?

ADAM: It's claiming to hear voices where they don't exist.

LIL: You're just jealous because you don't hear Shekhina, and maybe the spider and the leaves, and I can hear her.

★ ★ ★

LIL: Don't take my word for it, Eve. Taste the fruit yourself and you'll know that I say is true. Taste the fruit and you'll feel connected with this marvelous web of creation. This tree breathes your stale breath and returns to you fresh air. From the soil, the tree produces fruit for you and your family to eat. And you in turn replenish the soil. The fruit contains the seed and the seed contains the tree.

What goes around comes around, all around this fruit.

Taste it Eve, Mother of All, its juice is sweet with truth. *(LILITH brings forth two scrolls with a richly patterned green fabric rolled onto them, resembling a Torah, from the slit in the backdrop, and she hands it to EVE. They dance together.)*

LIL *(sings)*: Etz hayyim hi lamacha-zikim ba v'tomche-ha me-ooshar d'rache-ha darchey no-am, darchey no-am v'hol n'tivoteha shalom.

> *A tree of life*
> *Eat her fruit and you will grow*
> *A tree of life will make you strong*

EVE *(as LILITH sings these last lines)*: Behold today I set before you blessing and curse, life and death. Choose life that your days and the days of your children will be plentiful upon the earth.

LIL and EVE: *The breath of all support her and find happiness and she will bring you all you needed all along.*

(LILITH exits and gets back in tree just before Adam enters.)

ADAM (seeing EVE with the "fruit"): What are you doing?!

EVE: Adam! Come here! Share this with me. *(She gives him one of the Torah scrolls and they hold hands as he walks around her.)*

EVE: "Remember to listen . . . "

ADAM and EVE: " . . . to love the Divine with all your heart and all your soul, then I will favor your land with rain . . . "

ADAM: " . . . and you will have an ample harvest of grain . . . "

ADAM and EVE: " . . . and wine . . . "

ALL: " . . . and oil."

ADAM and EVE: "I will assure abundance in the fields."

ALL: "You will eat to contentment!" *(ADAM steps close to her and they kiss.)*

ADAM: I'm so happy, I could die!

EVE: Adam, somehow you look different! Read some more.

ADAM *(reads):* "By the sweat of your brow shall you get bread to eat, until you return to the ground—for from it you were taken, for dust you are, and to dust you shall return!" No!

EVE: Yes. It's OK. The fruit is good. It connects us to all that is!

ADAM: Connects us to what? Dust? My soul to this . . . this dirt?! I'm going to die? Is this a joke?

EVE: It's the way things work.

ADAM: What do you know about the way things work? Everything worked fine until you came along. I warned you to stay away from that tree! And now look what you've done! And after all I did to make you more comfortable! Now look what I get in return! When the Voice finds out, I'm history. Look what you've done to me! *(He starts shaking her.)*

EVE: Adam, stop it!

LIL: No! Leave her alone!

ADAM: Lilith! You . . . ! I should have known you were behind this! You tricked me, both of you.

EVE: Adam, don't be angry at me. *She* convinced me. *She* made me eat the fruit! *She* made me!

ADAM: You snake! Get out of my tree!

TEXT: THE BOOK OF MIRIAM

Leonard Yehudah Angel

What follows are (a) passages from Angel's fictional story of explorations in Jerusalem through which he discovers the text of the ancient Book of Miriam; (b) passages from the Miriam text; and (c) passages from commentaries on the Miriam text that have been written by women over the last millennium.

Again Miriam's talk was on The Teachings of Yehudith. Now she expounded the difference between the Hebrew way, the Israelite way, and the Jewish way. It was a nutshell summary of the history presented in the Book of Miriam.

Leonard Yehudah Angel is a poet, playwright, philosopher, World Federalist activist, and Jewish meditation pacifist. His plays include *The Unveiling* and *Eleanor Marx*. His philosophical books include *How to Build a Conscious Machine* and *Enlightenment East and West*.

"In the first way, the Hebrew way," she said, "spiritual development comes with a lifestyle: the nomadic lifestyle, boundarilessness, and no territorial identification. We aren't farmers. We are wanderers in God, and so we live as tent dwellers, as wanderers in God. And God? God is the open space, the ocean without a shore, the sky, the field, the mountain, the valley. God is the cloud floating in Mystery within our heart. And why are we not farmers? Because farmers make boundaries. Without boundaries there are no farms. And with boundaries, we divide ourselves off from each other. 'This is my land, not yours,' 'This is my source of sustenance, not yours.' We end up making wars on each other for our land, saying, 'Am I my brother's keeper?' We deny our sisterliness, our brotherliness.

"Ah, the life of the wanderer. But—but—grazing depletes the land, and when there is population growth, the land can't sustain all of us wanderers in God, and we want to farm. We want to be wanderers in God, and still to farm. How can we be tent dwellers, no fixed location, when the land is scarce? And so the Israelite way is born.

"In the Israelite way, attributed to the prophetess Yehudith, we maintain the spiritual blessings of boundariless consciousness, and still farm. How do we do this? Ritually, we identify with the open spaces. We develop a path, a halachah, a way of walking, moving through boundaries so even when we farm, we break through boundaried consciousness.

"If we make a farm, we leave the corners open—hence the creation of *peah,* open-corner laws. We soften the boundaries. If we wear a four-cornered garment, symbolizing the shape of a boundaried farm, we tie fringes to it, softening the boundaries, pouring light from the center outward. If we build a house, we smear on it the ineffable name of the God of openness and breath. YHVH is smeared on the doorposts, reminding all who pass through they are passing through openness, always passing through the openness of God, that a fixed house is, spiritually speaking, a poor substitute for a tent. And every seventh day is a day of rest from all labor, for the farm life is a life of labor, and a life with Shabbat is no longer a farm life.

"We farm, but we are not farmers. And we have a seventh year, a shemitah-sabbatical fallow year ensuring everyone lives as a free roaming shepherd every seventh year, so we live with farms, and yet we Israelites remain wanderers in God, the God of boundariless openness of mind and heart. And we are a community of families, and we live with the prophets in the valleys and the hillsides. In this way, the Israelite vision fulfills the Hebrew vision and yet allows for the planting of farms and the building of cities.

"But surrounding us are pharaohs and their vassals and their armies, and kings full of the ambitions of their empires and their territories, and we are unnumbered, uncensused, uncounted, and therefore, vulnerable, being uncounted, in the valleys, and from this vulnerability, and fear, Judaism is born.

"In Hebraicism and Israelitism we identify with no territory, no boundary, living in our hearts as wanderers in God. In Judaism, we become afraid of the outsiders, so we anoint a king, saying God wants us to anoint a king to compete with other kings, even when the prophet says God lives in the tent, wandering, but no, we don't listen to the prophet, our fear anoints a King, and sure enough there is rivalry for Kingdom, and soon the new King from Judah conquers land and a city, and makes of the city, a capital, so we identify with a boundaried territory and a capital, Jerusalem, and, ultimately, tell triumphal stories about our nation leading other nations. And in Judaism, whose very name shows the triumphal role of Judah in the line of kings, how do the teachers talk about God? God is thought of as a King, the King of kings, and God is conceived of as a distinct

Being who intervenes in history, and chooses a particular people as His people.

"Especially once the Northern Kingdom was destroyed, leaving only Judah, Judaism completely overturned the original Hebraic and Israelite visions of open, unboundaried spiritual life, spiritual community, and spiritual identity. Yes, the notion of God as the womb of the world becomes the notion of God as judging King. A community living in the openness of tents becomes a community centered on a big building, a Temple, worshipping a God who sits high on the throne of a King."

Miriam HaCohen then quoted some commentators who showed that the view of this historical devolution is not merely implicit in the Book of Miriam but lies also in the Torah, though Judaism layered the later history over the earlier stories, making the unfolding from Hebraicism through Israelitism to Judaism difficult to discern in the Torah stories.

I was intrigued by this paradigm of Hebraicism, Israelitism, and Judaism. Here was someone saying that the original Hebrew/Israelite spiritual consciousness had a universality and spaciousness to it I never thought possible, and that our task now was to revive and breathe new life into the original Israelite Way, modifying Judaism perhaps, but reinstating Israelitism. My desire to study the Book of Miriam over a period of months was reinforced.

TEXT OF "THE BOOK OF MIRIAM"

Scroll One

God's beginningless beginning
begins beginning's beginnings
Heaven light sky stars planets inert
earth water plants worms birds animals
humans, and
the earth is a garden, we
gather fruits, nuts, berries, roots
the garden is rich in glistening
stones, running water
falls, fragrant trees, fruit
bearing shrubbery for
play, eating and sleeping lean to's
and fruitfully we couple innocent how
our pleasure makes children
onyx bedellium gold! running rivers
and these animals!—shall we name
the mane ones laying long lions?
Antelope loping unknowing before them
gazelle ibex bear ape, name them
without knowing
them, or anything except bathing in
Mystery, Yah, so many jumping things!
knowing only the oneness of
manwoman cleaving one-one, innocent
our pleasure makes children
Every woman knows her growing
No one knows her growing is seeded

Dawn breaks, one childbearing woman
munches pomegranates. *Pomegranates, falling*
seed the earth. Earth womb grows
pomegranate trees,
kind after kind
Eating this pomegranate, my belly fills, but
this belly's not the earth, red-blooded
Adam seeds this belly: God, my earth
She knew!
fruitbearing trees
control of seeds
all benefit and harm that flows therefrom—
the farm
Big bellied Lifewoman, children
children in her belly
nurses them, feeds
man her knowledge of seeds
This, then, is the curse of the fruit
of the tree of knowledge, benefit and harm:
pain of birth, again and again, control of earth
Adam's sweat, child of that union
Kayin-property, who says
This land is mine for farming, brother
Till elsewhere
War is born
could not be
but enmity
is born, seed
growing tree
of property
Mine, thine

I, thing
War!

And there was one who loved openness
Hevel-spaces, thought
They root to places but these sheep
are rootless, free
I'll follow them, saying
eh-eh-eh-eh,eh-ye-eh-eh-eh
Openness, sky hillocks folding out
eh-ye-eh-eh-eh
eh-ye-eh-eh-eh
God breath!
Eh-ye-eh-eh-eh
Eh-ye-eh-eh-eh
Then everyone, hearing the Soundless sound
began chanting Eheyeheheweheye

Hevel exulted, married
Beracha Lady-Run-Away-Blessing
She said:
Sheep for tents
Sheep for wool
Sheep for clothes
Sheep for . . .
Sheep for meat, Hevel said
repentant of killing
offering atonement in the killing
altar building
Eh-ye-he-he-he-ye-eh
Tears, for the

beautiful animal death makes
life free
Lady-Run-Away-Blessing saw Hevel
proud, sad, tall, stoop
to kill the calf
raising the knife. She said
Pomegranates, goat's milk, dates,
nuts, figs, fruit . . . honey from buzzing hives
seasonal spelt, wild barley, spring
flowing sap, roots, yams, golden
apples hanging ripe, succulent, pears
berries, pounded wheat stalked free standing
in sky-yellow fields!
He looked at her, and slew
Then cried Lady-Run-Away-Blessing, whispered
This animal breath breathing
makes my life free
One day, no fear of man
will bind the flesh that breathes

COMMENTARIES

till elsewhere

Delet Hamitbach: A story is told of Reb Chanun, his wife, Rebbitzen Ariellah, Reb Shmuel, and his wife Rebbitzen Dinah. Reb Chanun accused Reb Shmuel of stealing a sheep from his farm. Reb Shmuel accused Reb Chanun of stealing a goat from his farm. Rebbitzen Ariellah came to borrow some cheese from Rebbitzen Dinah. Reb Shmuel forbade her from offering it. Rebbitzen Dinah feared she would be beaten if she disobeyed him. In the darkness of the night Rebbitzen Dinah and Rebbitzen Ariellah met at the border of the two farms. Rebbitzen Dinah gave Rebbitzen Ariellah the cheese. In the next evening meal, Reb Chanun tasted the cheese in the casserole. Where did you get the cheese? he demanded to know. Is this cheese from one of Shmuel's goats? She had to tell the truth. No, she said, this cheese is not from one of Shmuel's goats. Whose goat is this from, then? he imperiously asked. From one of God's goats, she answered.

Ezrat Sarah: The passage makes explicit what is implicit in the expulsion from Eden reference to the "punishment" of farming, "Because you listened to the voice of your wife and ate of the tree about which I commanded you saying, 'You shall not eat of it,' accursed is the ground because of you; through suffering shall you eat of it all the days of your life . . . by the sweat of your brow shall you eat bread" (Gen. 3:17.) There is a general reference to suffering first, and then another specific reference to the labor of farming. But the hard work isn't sufficient to justify *"itzavon,"* suffering. What is the curse of farming? Farming can be a curse not only because it is labor-intensive, but also because it is spiritually dangerous and causes deep psychological suffering. The farmer is prone to become exclusively preoccupied with his own plot of land, and from such boundaried notions come enmity and war. Of special note in this is the view that affectionate kinship among distantly related people is the natural condition of the human species. It is only, or at least especially, under conventionalized relations governed by elaborate property codes that tribal rivalries occur.

Eheyeheheh

Safah Berurah: In our traditional works, yod yod, yod heh, and yod heh vav heh are alternate spellings of the ineffable name. In Exodus, 3:14-15, Moshe asks for a name, and the answer given is Eheye, aleph heh yod heh. These spellings show that originally the name was understood to have no distinctive spelling and to be given in chanted sound.

TEXT: THE UNMAKING OF THE WORLD

Naomi Mara Hyman

When, in the end, we saw what we had done,

and that we couldn't heal the breach we'd made,

those of us who could

returned to Eden.

None of us were left who feared the fiery, ever-turning sword.

We'd seen and done and lost too much to care.

Some came as penitents and some with arrogance,

dreaming dreams of New Las Vegas.

When we arrived, the guardians stood waiting at the gate.

Naomi Mara Hyman is the editor of *Biblical Women in the Midrash*, the co-editor (with Ari Elon and Arthur Waskow) of *Trees, Earth and Torah: A Tu B'Shvat Anthology* and a student in the professional development *(smicha)* program of ALEPH: Alliance for Jewish Renewal.

Much to our surprise they let us in; the fiery sword was sheathed. We failed
    to see the sadness and the pity in their eyes.
Some set about to build their castles on the choicest lakeside spots, but
neither earth nor tree would yield themselves to such. The
    penitents
knelt humbly, murmuring prayers, asked for little and were granted less.
When we had all assembled in the breezy time of day,
we heard the voice of God amidst the trees.
"Where are you?" cried the Voice. "What have you done?"
We answered with our tears. No words would do.
"I called you here to witness on this day the thing I swore I would not do.
I, yes even I, could not foresee what you have done
to one another, to my earth, to my Delight!
I cannot bear to watch the One I love
die such a death. Having made her,
it is only right that I should give to her the gentlest good night.
Unsaving remnant,
I have called you here to witness the Unmaking of the World."
And there was evening, there was morning,
one less day.
We felt the snuffing out of human life, saw family trees fade out like wisps
    of smoke as Future carried with it Past into oblivion.
Returned to dust were we,
once blessed as partners of the Lord.
Yet conscious dust were we—no mercy granted here, and none deserved.
We stood,
mute Golems, left to witness the Unmaking of the World.
The creeping things, the swarming things, those that had survived
the worst that we could give,
slipped silently back into mud and dust.
Gone the iridescent wing, the dew-jeweled web.

Gone the peeper's song on summer nights. The squirrels sat up, alert,
then vanished into mist.
House cat, bobcat, giraffe, coyote, monkey, milk cow, gone.
And there was evening, there was morning,
one less day.
The birds sang out their warnings, took wing and disappeared.
Herons stopped their hunting, looked up and shimmered into fog.
Bright cardinals and tanagers winked out mid-flight like small red stars.
How loud the silence that they left behind!
We did not see, but felt, the disappearance of the fish.
Shark and octopus, dolphin, eel and whale abruptly ended their ballet.
Coral reefs stood empty,
Seaweed drifted like torn curtains blowing in the breeze.
And there was evening, there was morning.
One less day.
As morning came, out faded moon and stars
and though there was a light, the sun we did not see.
Gone the fiery paintbrush of the dawn,
gone the brilliance at the closing of the day.
No more the silvery gilding of the moon, ended now the mystery of stars,
and yet
there was evening, there was morning,
one less day.
With the dawning of that day we saw the bleakest sight of all. No green
was left, no living thing at all. Mighty redwoods fallen back to dirt,
seas of grass turned suddenly to deserts of gray dust,
no fern, no fruit, no scented breeze, no color to delight the eye.
The water rose, imperceptibly at first and then
like balm
it covered up the wounded, naked earth.
And there was evening, there was morning,

one less day.

A deluge opened up and rain poured down; heavens met the earth and
    then

there was no earth at all, just wind upon the water and a silence black and
    deep.

One last evening, one last morning

One last day.

God said "Let there be darkness"

and there was—

a darkness deep, unformed and void,

a darkness in eternity for all those called to witness the Unmaking of the
    World.

TEXT: HAFTARAH FOR THE RAINBOW COVENANT

Arthur Waskow

[**B**lessed are You, the Breath of Life, Who makes of every human throat a shofar for the breathing of Your truth.]

> *You, My people, burnt in fire,*
> *still staring blinded*
> *by the flame and smoke*
> *that rose from Auschwitz and from Hiroshima;*
> *You, My people,*

Rabbi Arthur Waskow founded and is director of The Shalom Center and is a Pathfinder of ALEPH: Alliance for Jewish Renewal. He is co-editor of *Trees, Earth, and Torah: A Tu B'Shvat Anthology* (Jewish Publication Society). His other books include *The Freedom Seder; Godwrestling; Seasons of Our Joy; Down-to-Earth Judaism: Food, Money, Sex, and the Rest of Life;* and *Godwrestling—Round Two: Ancient Wisdom, Future Paths* (Jewish Lights), winner of the Benjamin Franklin Award.

Battered by the earthquakes
of a planet in convulsion;
You, My people,
Drowning in the flood of words and images
That beckon you to eat and eat,
to drink and drink,
to fill and overfill
your bellies
at the tables of
the gods of wealth and power;
You, My people,
Drowning in the flood of words and images
That—poured unceasing on your eyes and ears—
drown out My words of Torah,
My visions of the earth made whole;
Be comforted:
I Who spoke at Sinai have for you a mission full of joy.
I call you to a task of celebration.
I call you to make from fire not an all-consuming blaze
But the light in which all beings see each other fully.
All different,
All bearing One Spark.
I call you to light a flame to see more clearly
That the earth and all who live as part of it
Are not for burning:
A flame to see
The rainbow
in the many-colored faces
of all life.
I call you:
I, the Breath of Life,

Within you and beyond,
Among you and beyond,
That One Who breathes from redwood into grizzly,
That One Who breathes from human into swampgrass,
That One Who breathes the great pulsations of the galaxies.
In every breath you breathe Me,
In every breath I breathe you.
I call you—
In every croak of every frog I call you,
In every rustle of each leaf,
each life,
I call you,
In the wailings of the wounded earth
I call you.
I call you to a peoplehood renewed:
I call you to reweave the fabric of your folk
and so to join in healing
the weave of life upon your planet.
I call you to a journey of seven generations.
For seven generations past,
the earth has not been able to make Shabbos.
And so in your own generation
You tremble on the verge of Flood.
Your air is filled with poison.
The rain, the seas, with poison.
The earth hides arsenals of poisonous fire,
Seeds of light surcharged with fatal darkness.
The ice is melting,
The seas are rising,
The air is dark with smoke and rising heat.
And so—I call you to carry to all peoples

the teaching that for seven generations
the earth and all her earthlings learn to rest.

I call you once again
To speak for Me,
To speak for Me because I have no voice,
To speak the Name of the One who has no Name,
To speak for all the Voiceless of the planet.
Who speaks for the redwood and the rock,
the lion and the beetle?
My Breath I blow through you into a voicing:
Speak for the redwood and the rock,
the lion and the beetle.
I call you to a task of joy:
For seven generations,
this is what I call for you to do:
To make once more the seasons of your joy
into celebrations of the seasons of the earth;
To welcome with your candles the dark of moon and sun,
To bless with careful chewing
the fruits of every tree
For when you meet to bless
the rising juice of life
in every tree trunk—
I am the Tree of Life.
To live seven days in the open, windy huts,
And call out truth to all who live beside you—
You are part of the weave and breath of life,
You cannot make walls to wall it out.
I call you to a covenant between the generations:
That when you gather for a blessing of your children

as they take on the tasks of new tomorrows,
You say to them, they say to you,
That you are all My prophet
Come to turn the hearts of parents
and of children toward each other,
Lest my earth be smashed in utter desolation.
I call you
To eat what
I
call
kosher:
Food that springs from an earth you do not poison,
Oil that flows from an earth you do not drain,
Paper that comes from an earth you do not slash,
Air that comes from an earth you do not choke.
I call you to speak
to all the peoples,
all the rulers.
I call you to walk forth before all nations,
to pour out water that is free of poison
and call them all to clean and clarify the rains of winter.
I call you to beat your willows on the earth
and shout its healing to all peoples.

I call on you to call on all the peoples
to cleanse My Breath, My air,
from all the gases
that turn My earth into a furnace.
I call you to light the colors of the Rainbow,
To raise once more before all eyes
That banner of the covenant between Me,

and all the children of Noah and Naamah,
and all that lives and breathes upon the Earth—
So that
never again,
all the days of the earth, shall
sowing and harvest,
cold and heat,
summer and winter,
day and night
ever cease!
I call you to love the Breath of Life—
For love is the fire
That blazes in the Rainbow.

[Blessed are You, the Breath of Life, Who makes of every human throat a shofar for the breathing of Your truth.]

JUDAISM AND NATURE: THEOLOGICAL AND MORAL ISSUES

Eilon Schwartz

S ince the advent of the modern environmental movement some forty years ago,[1] dozens of articles have been written exploring the relationship of Judaism and the environment, attempting to articulate a Jewish response to the environmental crisis.[2] Many of the articles came in the wake of the environmental movement's attack on the Judeo-Christian ethic, whose Biblical injunction to "fill the earth and master it" was seen by many in the environmental movement to be the theological and ethical source for an anthropocentric and

Eilon Schwartz is director of the Heschel Center for Environmental Learning and Leadership and teaches at the Melton Center for Jewish Education of the Hebrew University. He is currently writing a doctoral dissertation on the connection between human nature and the natural world, and its implications for educational philosophy. He lives in Tel Aviv with family and friends.

ultimately exploitative relationship to the natural world.³ Articles came to defend the tradition, often by presenting Judaism's environmental credentials in the growing cultural debate.

Although usually such translations of Jewish culture into terms acceptable to the larger cultural milieu have sacrificed authentic Jewish perspectives at the altar of cultural relevance,⁴ in the case of Judaism and the environment it seemed as though no trade-off was necessary. Finding "green" traditions within Jewish sources is not difficult. Such traditions are strongly anchored in normative Judaism. *Ba'al Tashchit, Tsar Baalei Chayim, Shnat Shemita, Yishuv HaAretz,* to name a few of the Jewish value concepts⁵ most often quoted by environmentally concerned Jews, are all pointed to as representing authentic Jewish environmental perspectives.⁶ As they are. Still, the need to validate a Jewish environmental ethic, to show Judaism's credentials, as it were, stifled a true airing of Jewish positions. Judaism's relationship with the natural world is far more ambivalent than that with which many Jewishly committed environmentalists would feel comfortable. Too few have delved into the complex and intricate relationship which exists between Judaism and the natural world, a relationship which, while containing the "green" traditions often quoted, also contain the admonishment in *Pirkei Avot* that "He who forsakes Torah for the contemplation of trees forfeits his life." For Jews to confront the environmental crisis as part of a rich and complex Jewish tradition, it is necessary to come to terms with both sides of the tradition and to understand the interrelationship between them. Only by understanding the theological, philosophical, and moral concerns which are an integral part of the Jewish relationship with nature can Jews offer a voice which will not simply mimic already articulated perspectives but offer unique attitudes which will help guide the task of *tikkun olam* ("repair of the world") while confronting issues too long avoided by Jewish thought.

What follows is an attempt to organize the discussion by surveying the literature previously written on Judaism and the environment as the point of departure. I hope to influence the direction of future writing on Judaism and the environment by pointing to places which need exploration. My not-so-hidden agenda is a reasserting of the Jewish perspective in the meeting between Judaism and the environment, believing that a Jewish contribution to the growing debate on environmental ethics can only come from a response strongly rooted in all the ambivalences and ambiguities of the Jewish relationship to the natural world. Perhaps even more important, I believe that the reevaluation by the environmental movement of our modern cultural relationship to the natural world, a reevaluation which challenges some of the basic values of our modern culture, challenges deeply ingrained trends in Jewish thought, as well.

Confronting the points of tension and not only the points of confluence will facilitate a "deep"[7] dialogue from within the tradition, a dialogue which can lead to a reawakening of the natural world as a central category in our Jewish understandings of what we mean by both the human and the Divine.

PAGANISM AND JUDAISM

Any serious confrontation of the Jewish relationship with the natural world must confront the Jewish relationship with paganism. The conventional wisdom of modern Jewish thought maintains that Judaism came about as a radical distancing of the Holy from immanence within the world.[8] In this account, idolatry is defined theologically as viewing God as being contained within the material world, whereas Judaism came to assert the transcendental, wholly other nature of the Holy. Paganism, both in its Biblical and Hellenistic manifestations, understood God as being contained within Nature. Jewish monotheism distanced the Holy from paganism and its concept of nature.

Such a presentation of the Jewish relationship to nature by way of its polemic against pagan idolatry suggests an antagonism to nature and an acute theological affinity between paganism and Nature. Indeed, the modern environmental movement is filled with writings which have picked up on such a reading, calling for a rejection of monotheistic approaches to the world and a rebirth of paganism. Lynn White sees paganism as the alter ego to the Judeo-Christian theologically sanctioned exploitation of nature;[9] some eco-feminists have called for a renewal of pagan customs of May Day, celebrations of the moon, witchcraft;[10] one of the more radical biological theories of our day holds that the earth is a living organism, and has named her Gaia, the name of the Greek earth goddess.[11] This reassertion of pagan theologies, customs, and language understands paganism as a worldview which sees Nature as Holy. Eastern religions are often included in the list of religions of Nature, as well, with the many significant theological and cultural differences between the various historical cultures glossed over. These are juxtaposed with an archetypal monotheism which sees God as transcendent of nature, apart from her. The operative conclusions are clear: paganism, seeing Nature as sacred, respects the natural world; monotheism, desanctifying nature, abuses it. The rebirth of paganism is a call for the assertion of the natural over the supernatural. Mother Earth over Father King, holistic Nature over the hierarchical dichotomy of Heaven and Earth.

Aharon Lichtenstein,[12] writing about Judaism's approach to nature, accepts this typology as well. While not reaching the operative conclusion that Judaism abuses nature while paganism respects it, he certainly accepts the theological distinction of monotheism seeing God apart from nature and more important, the linking of paganism with present environmentalism. Much of the environmental movement, viewing nature as Holy, Lichtenstein indeed holds to be idolatrous. And while there might be some practical commonality in action conceivable for a time between the two in order to respond to the practical manifestations of the environmental crisis, the theological (and what may be assumed, moral) gulf between them is no different than that between Judaism and Greek-Roman paganism.

Everett Gendler[13] can be seen as representing the other end of the continuum of modern Jewish responses to the "pagan" critique by the environmental movement. Gendler holds that there is a latent nature tradition within Judaism, a tradition suppressed because of the ancient polemic with paganism, exile from the land of Israel and subsequent historical forces. Gendler sees this tradition expressing itself in the nature motifs of Jewish festivals, in female rituals surrounding the blessing of the New Moon, and in the reassertion of connection to nature in the Zionist movement. Judaism has spiritually suffered as a result of its exile from the natural world; it is time to reassert the role of nature in our understanding of the human spirit.

Gendler is, in effect, asserting a place for an immanental religious tradition within Judaism. Both he and Lichtenstein accept the idea that a relationship with the natural world has tremendous implications for the life of the spirit: Lichtenstein holds Jewish religious life to be transcendental and apart from the natural world, while Gendler believes Jewish religious life has always had a place for a complementary model[14] of spirituality contained within the relationship of the Jew to the natural world.[15]

Lamm elaborates on the content of our continuum by presenting a range of authentic Jewish relationships to nature whose poles

he defines by the Hasidic/*Mitnagdim* controversy.[16] *Hasidut,* while
"utterly different" from pagan thought, nevertheless also had manifestations which affirmed the holiness of nature. Such views, most
pronounced in *Beshtian* Hasidism, but present throughout the Kabbalist tradition, held that the spirit of the Creator is immanent in the
Creation, and thus God can be approached through the natural
world. While this is different from saying that God *is* the natural
world, a pantheistic/paganistic approach, it does suggest eliminating
the hierarchical differences between sacred and profane, and recognizing the theological possibility of the sacred in the profane. From
here it is a short distance to antinomian beliefs and behavior, seeing
Holiness in the most profane of actions. Nevertheless, *Hasidut* remained safely within the Halakhic structure, perhaps partially because of realizing the dangerous antinomian tendencies inherent in
such belief.

The Mitnagdic school of the Vilna Gaon, also rooted in the
Kabbalist tradition, believed that *Hasidut* had indeed begun to cross
outside of the normative Halakhic framework, following the implications of their belief system. The *Mitnagdim* re-emphasized the
transcendence of God from the point of view of the human being,
and separated holiness from the world, "allowing for the exploitation of nature by science and technology."[17] *Halakha,* on this side of
the pole, acts to prevent ecological abuse in a philosophical system
which otherwise legitimates it. In short, the Hasidic tradition came
dangerously close to turning the world into the sacred, the *Mitnagdim* dangerously close to removing Divine presence from the
world.

For Lamm, there is a dynamic tension between the two approaches: created in God's image, the human being is part of the
natural world but also transcends it. Living with the paradox of the
two approaches without compromising either is what it means to be

human. Extrapolating from such a view, paganism and its environmental supporters err on the side of the natural in the human; modern Western culture on the side of the transcendent. Judaism has traditionally offered a plurality of approaches, each flirting dangerously close to the extremes, but with safeguards to ensure remaining within acceptable boundaries. Gendler, using Lamm's terminology, represents the Hasidic tradition; Lichtenstein, the Mitnagdic tradition.

Lamm never addresses the question of where Judaism's modern variations stand on his continuum, perhaps suggesting that such a creative tension continues to exist between various modern Jewish approaches. Schorsch contends that, in response to intellectual currents in the larger cultural setting, modern Judaism was pushed beyond Lamm's Mitnagdic pole:

> We must dare to reexamine our long-standing preference for history over nature. The celebration of "historical monotheism" is a legacy of nineteenth century Christian-Jewish polemics, a fierce attempt by Jewish thinkers to distance Judaism from the world of paganism. But the disclaimer has its downside by casting Judaism into an adversarial relationship with the natural world. Nature is faulted for the primitiveness and decadence of pagan religion, and the modern Jew is saddled with a reading of his tradition that is one-dimensional. Judaism has been made to dull our sensitivity to the awe-inspiring power of nature. Preoccupied with the ghosts of paganism, it appears indifferent and unresponsive to the supreme challenge of our age: man's degradation of the environment. Our planet is under siege and we as Jews are transfixed in silence.[18]

For Schorsch, modern Jewish historians projected a distance between Judaism and the pagan world, a distance which is overstated because of their historiographical biases. This modern version of a "one-dimensional" Judaism is a distortion of the reality of pre-modern Jewish thought and life.

If Schorsch is correct that the pagan taboo has contributed significantly to the lack of a healthy Jewish relationship with nature, and I believe he is, then only by coming to terms with the content of the conflict can we avoid "throwing out the baby with the bathwater," as it were. In order to rethink our relationship to nature, or to re-search our traditional relationship with nature without committing the same transgression of interpreting Judaism solely according to the cultural milieu of the day—historical monotheism then, the emerging environmental movement[19] now—the Jewish relationship with paganism needs to be reexplored. The taboo against paganism in Jewish thought is so deep, and the linkage between paganism and nature is so taken for granted, that distancing from paganism has meant distancing ourselves from nature, and conversely, any attempt to reconcile Judaism with nature flirts with paganism. Only by exploring the content of the anti-pagan Jewish polemic can we hope to understand what is truly at stake.[20]

Living in fear of paganism has not only exacted a heavy price on the Jewish relationship with nature. Feminists have argued that the cultural linking of nature with female has meant that a distancing of culture from nature is linked to a distancing of culture from its feminine components.[21] Judaism's fear of paganism, therefore, has potentially led to a distancing of Judaism from its feminine components. The dominance of male God-imagery and masculine formulations of theology over the centuries can be viewed as one outcome of the fear of paganism. Loss of humility through the loss of our ability to wonder and experience awe at the beauty and vastness of the natural world is another. And losing our sense of place, a feeling of being a part of the world, and not existentially estranged from all that surrounds us, is still another. To confront the byproducts, it is essential that the root of the debate between pagan and Jewish culture be confronted. And that debate has much to do with how we understand morality.

TIME'S ARROWS, TIME'S CYCLES

The Jewish polemic with paganism was not only a theological one; it was primarily a moral one. The theological conflict had deep moral implications. Nature worship was seen not simply as a theological/philosophical mistake, but a worldview which has deep immoral consequences. The pagan and monotheism debate is a debate about morality. And Schorsch's corrective of not blaming nature for pagan excesses notwithstanding, it seems essential to explore what the moral conflict was while we are renegotiating our relationship with the natural world.

Mircea Eliade offers a helpful distinction between historical religion's and nature religion's different notions of time.[22] Eliade maintains that religions focusing on history have a linear view of time, those focusing on nature a cyclical view—what Stephen Jay Gould calls time's arrows and cycles.[23] Eliade holds that Judaism was responsible for contributing a linear sense of history to the world, that is, a progressive sense of history.[24] While offering a possibility of change to history—in fact, while creating the very possibility for history—when not counterbalanced with the repetition of time, such a perspective can lead to history without a sense of purpose. So Eliade sees our modern period.[25] Linear history, with its beginning and end, needs to be understood in terms of cyclical history, with its transcendent and repeating truths. Or in *Jewish* terms, the march forward from Egypt to Sinai to Zion must be understood in terms of our continual return to Egypt, Sinai, and Zion in each generation. Time has both its arrows and cycles.

While Eliade believes that the modern period lives in the moral danger of losing sight of the purpose of history through losing a sense of time's cycles, the moral critique works in the other direction, as well. An overemphasis on time's cycles can lead to a history without change. Time is understood in terms of rises and sets; change is illusory. Time stands still. A sense of history demands that human beings break out of the cycle and accept the responsiblity of a history which can move forward and backward. Time's cycle is connected with what is; time's arrows, with what can be. Focusing on a religion of nature, one focuses on the cyclical nature of time. A religion of history offers the moral responsibility that is the meaning of its arrows. While Eliade holds that arrows without cycles leads to a history without meaning, an emphasis on arrows has often been understood to mean an emphasis on human responsibility.

Schwarzschild[26] understands the pagan-Jewish debate as exactly one of differing views of nature coupled with different views of morality. Nature represents what is. Morality is born in the question of what ought to be. Judaism is profoundly at odds with the natural world, a world which functions according to certain laws to which history is then subjected. Judaism sees the human being as transcending those laws, with the power to impose a moral order on an otherwise amoral reality. Through human reason, that which makes the human "in the image of God," moral thought can impose its order on the natural disorder, completing the process of creation.[27] Schwarzschild recognizes that the tradition is not monolithic in this regard. The "heretical, quasi-pantheistic tendency" found expression in medieval Kabbalah, *Hasidut,* and modern

Zionism.[28] However, such a stream remained a tangential idea, contrary to the traditional Jewish perspective on nature.

Wyschogrod follows Schwarzschild's argument.[29] The heart of the pagan-Jewish controversy is the moral question of whether what is should be. And Wyschogrod, like Schwarzschild, sees the modern environmental movement as resurrecting the pagan notion of morality being equated with the world as it is. While there are certainly many environmentalists who understand the need for change in anthropocentric terms—the need to protect our health and the earth's resources for future generations—deep environmentalists subscribe to what Wyschogrod calls "the higher ecology," an environmentalism which attempts to shift our culture from an anthropocentric to a geo/biocentric worldview.

Wyschogrod contends that Adolf Hitler and the Nazi movement were deeply influenced by such a perspective.[30] Borrowing heavily from Nietzsche, Hitler believed that nature teaches us the basic laws of morality: that the strong kill the weak and through such a process, nature moves forward. Wyschogrod writes:

> Evolutionary morality is the right of the stronger to destroy the weaker. Nature wants the weak to perish. The weak contribute to the march of evolution by perishing; and when they refuse to perish, then the weaker have triumphed over the stronger.[31] Judaism (and Christianity)[32] interferes with the natural order by letting the weak survive. A morality which changes the natural order prevents nature from taking its rightful course. Such a perspective on morality Wyschogrod sees shared by Plato, as well. In his ideal state, modeled after an organism, there is no place for protection of the weak. Imperfectly born infants are to be disposed. Of course, attempting to understand morality as an outgrowth of the natural order does not necessarily demand understanding morality as "survival of

the fittest"; Nature's lessons were interpreted in radically different ways by its social Darwinist interpreters.[33] But, regardless of
the particular interpretation of nature's morality, there is a cate-
gorical difference between morality based on the natural order,
however that "natural order" is understood, and a morality
based on values whose source is outside of materialist understandings of the world. And in the confrontation between the
morality of "the world as it is" and "the world as it should be,"
both Wyschogrod and Schwarzschild understand Judaism as the
flagship of a morality which imposes itself on the natural order.

Yet, in spite of his antagonism for such a "higher ecology,"
Wyschogrod accepts that the moral philosophy of Judaism, which
demanded the desacralization of nature, has contributed to the destruction of nature. Returning to a religion of nature is profoundly
dangerous, yet, given that, a reconsideration of the human intercon-
nection with the natural is demanded by the ecological crisis.

Wyschogrod's articulation of the link between a religion of nature and an ethics in which "what is" is defined as "what ought to
be" finds expression in the environmental movement. Indeed, the
burgeoning field of environmental ethics continues to confront the
question of whether ethics are learned from the natural order. In the
debate between animal protectionists and deep ecologists, one of
the main points of conflict is whether the interests of the individual
should take precedence over the needs of the community. For example, should a herd of deer which overpopulate an area because of
the extinction of its local predators be hunted in order to protect
the flora which they eat, which as the primary producers in the energy chain maintain the health of the ecosystem as a whole? Animal
protectionists abhor the idea of hunting as the unnecessary suffering
of sentient beings. Deep ecologists have supported hunting as part
of the laws of nature, which maintain the health and well-being of

the ecosystem. Some have tended to idealize hunting as a return to the primal state of the human being, a return to the natural world, and have criticized what is popularly called "the Bambi syndrome"—the projection of a human code of morality onto the workings of the natural world.[34] Aldo Leopold, a forerunner of deep ecology, taught the need to learn to "think like a mountain," to think like nature.[35] The implications for all of this in terms of human existence has been one of the most sensitive subjects of environmental ethics. Parts of the deep ecology movement, notably the Earth First! movement, have expressed what Schwarzschild and Wyschogrod's interpretation would suggest:

> Some Earth First!ers, who are supposedly motivated by deep ecological ideals, proposed Draconian birth control measures, spoke approvingly of AIDS as a self-protective reaction of Gaia against an over-populating humanity, used social Darwinist metaphors, and displayed apparent racist attitudes. Earth First! cofounder Dave Foreman even stated that humans "are a cancer on nature."[36]

While in no way should the ideas expressed by a particular part of a movement be chosen to reflect the thoughts of the movement as a whole, the predictive ability of Schwarzschild and Wyschogrod's thesis forces us to recognize the danger inherent in philosophies currently prevalent in the environmental movement, moral questions which have been part of the internal environmental debate for over a decade.[37]

The response to such a morality of nature need not be a denial of the place of the natural within Jewish worldviews. Ehrenfeld and Bentley,[38] for example, while understanding Judaism as a human-centered philosophy, maintain that the great chain of being[39] does not place man at the pinnacle, but rather God. The human place in the God-given scheme of things is caring for God's creation, the role of steward. It is the secularization of the world, the removal of God from the hierarchy and placing the human being at its pinnacle, which leads to what Ehrenfeld calls "the arrogance of humanism."[40] The stewardship argument is heard often in the environmental ethic debate, changing the perspective from anthropocentric to theocentric.[41] It is but one attempt to deal with the tension between a hierarchical model of creation and an egalitarian model, models which see the human being as primarily a spiritual being standing apart from the natural world and models which see the human being as a material being existing as part of her. Reducing our understanding of human purpose to a material, deterministic view of the world has been shown to be a problematic option. But the environmental movement has suggested that a view of human purpose which ignores the material base of human existence is equally problematic. The dualistic notion of the world which sees human purpose in that which differentiates the human from the rest of creation implicitly devalues the material, natural side of human existence. Boyarin claims that such a spiritual/material dichotomy was never part of normative Rabbinic Jewish thought.[42]

The Jewish emphasis on the body as a category of spiritual existence suggests the need to describe a far more complex understanding of what is the interrelationship of the material and spiritual. Any reassessment of the Jewish relation to nature demands a reevaluation of the interrelationship of the spiritual and the material, including the possibility of forgoing such a dichotomy altogether.[43] In answering Disraeli's question whether the human being is ape or angel, emphasizing our affinity to the world of the ape need not by definition distance us from the spiritual. It might even bring us closer.

The environmental crisis offers both a challenge and an

opportunity to modern Judaism. A challenge, because all cultures will be judged in future generations by the depth of their response to modernity's rape of the planet. A Judaism which refuses to respond through its unique language to modernity's spiritually bankrupt relationship to God's world will be judged for its silence. An opportunity, because far too often Judaism has been forced to speak within the narrow confines which modernity offered. The environmental crisis challenges modern culture, and offers the opportunity for other voices, long delegitimized, to reassert themselves within the larger culture. Speaking from within the tradition, and confronting the manifold challenges which a reappraisal of Judaism and nature demands means a renewal of our relationship with our world. It means evaluating how we relate to the world around us, but no less important, how that world around us touches our lives. The environmental crisis is not only a crisis of technology, nor a crisis of human values, but most assuredly also a crisis of the human spirit. How we respond to the challenge and opportunity which the environmental crisis presents has implications not only with how we deal with our world but also with how we deal with ourselves, our fellow human beings, and our God. This is the context in which a Jewish articulation of an environmental ethic must be considered.

ON THE JUDAISM OF NATURE

Everett Gendler

Each of us, I think, approaches the official tradition of Judaism with a particular set of inherited tendencies and lived experiences: archetypes, somatotypes, infantile impressions and childhood visions, adolescent agonies and all the rest. For each of us, surely, the living tradition of Judaism must be somehow distinct, different, individual. If not, what is the meaning of our religious being?

I was born in Chariton, Iowa, and lived there eleven years: a small town surrounded by open country. Nature was omnipresent. Des Moines, the "city" of my adolescence, also enjoyed her presence. So did I.

Not that I was conscious of it at the time. It seems to me

Rabbi Everett Gendler was born in Iowa and served congregations in Mexico, Brazil, and Princeton, New Jersey, before spending nearly twenty-five years as the rabbi at Temple Emanuel in Lowell, Massachusetts, and nearly twenty years as chaplain and instructor at Phillips Academy in Andover, Massachusetts. He is an organic gardener and an avid proponent of nonviolence, social justice, peace, and the environment.

now, in retrospect, that not until after ordination from seminary and a period of time spent in the valley of Mexico did nature as such come more fully to my awareness.

The realization of this awareness took time, its relation to my religious outlook more time still. The entire process, I now know, was furthered by graduate academic studies and by poetry. J. J. Bachofen, Johannes Pedersen, Erich Neumann, Erwin Goodenough, Mircea Eliade, D. H. Lawrence, e. e. cummings, William Blake, Saul Tchernichovsky, Lao Tzu, Kenneth Rexroth, the Besht, Reb Nachman: these, finally, were among my latter day teachers, and I mention them for others more than for myself. It is true, their names do constitute for me a doxology of sorts, and their effect on me is mildly magical. But perhaps it might be that for a few others as well, with similar sensibilities, these men might serve too as the good companions, those who, however indirectly, help make our selves known to ourselves.

From this, then, the re-evaluation of official Judaism, and the pained perception of its present plight: sea-sited synagogues with sea-views bricked over! Tree-filled lots with windowless sanctuaries! Hill-placed chapels opaque to sunsets! The astonishing indifference to natural surroundings!

Was Judaism always this way? I very much doubt it.

However powerful the Biblical assault on ancient nature cults, elements of those cults persisted, however purified and sublimated, for centuries thereafter among loyal Jews. This much I think is convincingly established by the evidence in Raphael Patai's *The Hebrew Goddess*. This underground stream, flowing from the most ancient of times down to the present, re-emerges strikingly at times—in Kabbalah, Hasidism, and recent Hebrew poets such as Saul Tschernichovsky—as the re-assertion of both the Natural and the Feminine components of religion.

Further, whatever merit there may be to the claim that post-

Biblical Judaism is very much an urban development, it must be remembered that cities until quite recently were rarely so totally cut off from natural surroundings as are our present megalopolitan sprawls. However removed from landholding by legal disabilities, the Jews of Eastern Europe were nevertheless constantly aware of it and often envious of those who were privileged to have direct proprietary contact with it. Many are the reminiscences of Hebrew and Yiddish writers which focus on *heder* memories of their natural surroundings. And a perusal of the very moving photos in the Polish volume *Wooden Synagogues* (by Maria and Kasimierz Piechotka) makes quite vivid the rural locations (at least by our standards) of so many of these incomparably expressive structures.

Important, also, is the evidence from the persistence of various folk customs into recent decades. An especially telling instance concerns *Shavuot*, the least nature-oriented of the three pilgrimage festivals.

> It is a custom to put trees in synagogues and homes on *Shavuot* . . . and to spread grass about in the synagogue . . . to recall that at the giving of the Torah the Jews stood upon a mountain surrounded by foliage. The *Maharil* used to spread fragrant grass and flowers on the floor of the synagogue in celebration of the holiday and if *Shavuot* fell on Sunday, the *Maharil* would bring them in before *Shabbat* . . . On *Shavuot* the *shamash* used to distribute fragrant grass and herbs to every worshipper in the synagogue. . . . (Eisenstein, *A Digest of Jewish Laws and Customs*)

And what of the *Seder* traditionally celebrated by the Sephardim on *Tu B'Shevat,* when some thirty varieties of fruits, nuts, grains, and wines are consumed with special *kavanot* (intentions) and accompanied by readings from the Bible and the Zohar?

Most significant of all, however, has been the faithfulness of the folk to the rhythms of the moon throughout the ages.

In the biblical period, *Hodesh* or *Rosh Hodesh* (New Moon) was a holiday at least comparable to the Sabbath. Commerce was prohibited (Amos 8:5), visits to "men of God" were customary as on Sabbaths (II Kings 4:23), and New Moon is grouped with Sabbaths and festivals as a major holiday in the Jewish religious calendar (Hosea 2:13; II Chron. 2:3, 8:12–13, and others). It is interesting to note that, quantitatively speaking, the New Moon offerings prescribed in Numbers (28:9–15) and Ezekiel (46:37) exceed those prescribed for Sabbaths.

> The moon was, of course, the most visible heavenly marker of the passage of time. As such, she was essential to the determination of festivals and sacred celebrations. At the same time, however, her numinous quality constantly tempted people to worship her (Deut. 17:2–7; Jer. 7:18, 44:15–19).
>
> Schauss, *The Jewish Festivals*

It seems likely, then, that Hayyim Schauss is correct in suggesting that the prevailing rabbinic attitude toward the moon was also hostile, and that in so far as *Rosh Hodesh* survived at all, it was due to the loyalty of the folk; not the representatives of the severely anti-pagan official tradition.

This folk feeling for the moon should not be hard to comprehend even in our own terms. As Mircea Eliade has pointed out:

> The sun is always the same, always itself, never in any sense "becoming." The moon, on the other hand, is a body which waxes, wanes and disappears, a body whose experience is subject to the universal law of becoming, of birth and death. The moon, like man, has a career involving tragedy, for its failing,

like man's, ends in death. For three nights the starry sky is
without a moon. But this "death" is followed by a rebirth: the
"new moon." . . . This perpetual return to its beginning, and
this ever-recurring cycle make the moon the heavenly body
above all others concerned with the rhythms of life . . . they re-
veal life repeating itself rhythmically . . . it might be said that
the moon shows man his true human condition; that in a sense
man looks at himself and finds himself anew in the life of the
moon. *(Patterns in Comparative Religion)*

Small wonder, then, that a folk desirous of maintaining some significant connection both with cosmic rhythms and with the self
should preserve its lunar festivities despite official frowns. Nor is it surprising that women, whose bodily functioning includes built-in, peri-
odic natural rhythms, were most closely related to the lunar rhythms.

Work on Rosh Hodesh is permitted . . . but women are accustomed not to work on Rosh Hodesh . . . weaving and sewing
were especially avoided on Rosh Hodesh. (Eisenstein, *A Digest
of Jewish Laws and Customs*)

Other observances on *Rosh Hodesh* include these:

It is a mitzvah (recommended practice) to have an especially
ample meal on Rosh Hodesh . . .
    In some countries, Yemen, for example, it is a custom to
light candles on the eve of Rosh Hodesh both in the synagogues and on the tables at home, just as on Sabbaths and Festivals. Some people prepare at least one additional special dish
in honor of Rosh Hodesh and wear special festive garments.
(Eisenstein, *A Digest of Jewish Laws and Customs*)

Of all this and more, how much is practiced today? Except
for the announcement of the new month in the synagogue on the

Sabbath preceding—and I do mean new month, not new moon; it is all very calculated, calendrical and non-lunar—very little, from what I have noticed. As for the ceremony of *klddush hal'vanah* (the sanctification of the waxing moon), an out-of-door ceremony dating from Talmudic times which requires visual contact with the moon between the third and fifteenth days of the lunar month, and which also includes dancing before the moon—except for a few Hasidim, how widely is this practiced or even known today? Yet it is prescribed even in the *Shulchan Aruch,* the classical sixteenth-century code of Jewish law.

These few examples do, I trust, establish that the present Jewish institutional alienation from nature was not always the case, and that it is, in fact, a comparatively recent development.

An attempt to analyze why this has happened would take us far afield and lengthen this essay beyond its appointed limits. More important are some of the psycho-religious consequences of this estrangement from nature.

Two or three poetic formulations are among the best brief statements on this subject that I know.

> *Great things are done when Men & Mountains meet;*
> *This is not done by Jostling in the Street.*
>
> William Blake

> *They know not why they love nor wherefore they sicken & die,*
> *calling that Holy Love which is Envy, Revenge & Cruelty,*
> *Which separated the stars from the mountains, the mountains*
> *   from Man*
> *And left Man, a little groveling Root outside of Himself.*
>
> William Blake

179

Oh, what a catastrophe for man when he cut himself off from the
rhythm of the year, from his union with the sun and the earth.
Oh, what a catastrophe, what a maiming of love when it was a
personal, merely personal feeling, taken away from the rising
and setting of the sun, and cut off from the magic connection
of the solstice and the equinox!
That is what is the matter with us.
We are bleeding at the roots, because we are cut off from the earth
and sun and stars, and love is a grinning mockery, because, poor
blossom, we plucked it from its stem on the tree of Life, and
expected it to keep on blooming in our civilized vase on the table.

D. H. Lawrence

Nor should one overlook the important lament by Tcherni-chovsky over

the distress of a world whose spirit is darkened,
for Tammuz, the beautiful Tammuz is dead.

It seems increasingly clear that whatever the penalties which man may have suffered when he was subjugated to nature, his "liberation" from nature has become, in fact, an alienation which is truly a dreadful freedom. No longer attuned to the cosmic rhythms about him, increasingly entombed by the contrived, man-made elements of his environment, he neither knows himself as microcosm nor has any felt, enlivening connection with *chei ha-olamim*, the Life of the Universe (a term for the Divine which twice occurs in the traditional morning service).

Where, today, does one find that confirmation of being expressed in this rabbinic statement?

*Whatever the Holy One, blessed be He, created in the world, He
    created in man . . .*
He created forests in the world and He created forests in man . . .
*He created a wind in the world and He created a wind in
    man . . .*
A sun in the world and a sun in man . . .
Flowing waters in the world and flowing waters in man . . .
Trees in the world and trees in man . . .
Hills in the world and hills in man . . .
*Whatever the Holy One, blessed be He, created in His world,
    He created in man.*

(*Abot d'Rabi Natan,* version A, Ch. 31)

The self shivers in solitary confinement, and each detached attempt to discern one's true being seems to catapult the self into an abyss or finds the self facing sets of mirrors which merely cast further and further back, in dizzying regress, that very image of the self which was seeking its substance.

Without grounding in felt being, what of relating, of love? The ever-shifting, estranged-from-the-universe subjectivity often means simply a mutual sense of being lost together—hardly a solid basis for a lifelong relationship which should help children also gain some orientation in this world.

Also, what does it mean to grow up, as increasing numbers of children do today, with so little contact with other growing things? How does it affect personal growth when almost all easily observed, rapid developmental paradigms are of other-determined end products, not self-determined growth? What does it mean to have numerous examples of making and processing all around one, but few if any examples of that slow, deliberate, self-determined unfolding of inner potential which is so amazing to watch in the transformation of seed into plant? The separation from the vegetation cycle may have consequences for the spirit that we have hardly begun to comprehend.

And what may be the effects of this estrangement from nature on the environmental crisis which we face? It is hard to imagine that there is no connection between the devaluation and disregard of nature on the one hand, and her maltreatment and shameful exploitation on the other.

These considerations, for the most part historical and theoretical, are meant to suggest that a vital and relevant Judaism for this age must begin to reclaim seriously its nature heritage. Such a suggestion has, I think, much to support it, as evidenced by the way that people do, in fact, respond to such nature elements. Let me cite a few examples.

For some four summers, we held Friday evening services out of doors at the Jewish Center of Princeton, weather permitting. The setting itself was the attractive lawn behind the sanctuary, flat but ringed by shrubs and bushes, with a number of older, substantial trees in view. The hour of the service was advanced somewhat (from 8:15 to 7:45 P.M. to take full advantage of sunset, twilight, and in late summer, the dusk. Nature elements in the traditional service were emphasized; special readings appropriate to a nature setting were included in the service; periods of silence and meditations on trees and shrubs were part of the worship; and the varying qualities of the "twilights" *(aravim)* were also a focus of attention.

I can report that the reaction to this, among adults as well as young people, was almost universally favorable and often enthusiastic. In fact, except for a few occasions when the bugs were especially bothersome (no, we did *not* spray!), the out-of-doors services were deeply appreciated by nearly all involved.

Another practice which received a generally favorable response was connected with the morning service of Sabbaths and festivals. When there was no *Bar Mitzvah* and our numbers were not increased by people unfamiliar with the building, on bright days, temperature permitting, we would leave the sanctuary immediately after the *Barchu* and head out-of-doors. There, under the skies and in the face of the sun, we would chant together that part of the service which celebrates the gift of light and the radiance of the luminaries. And on days when it was not possible to go out-of-doors, this part of the service was prefaced by a focusing of attention on the light streaming in through the many windows in the sanctuary. In both cases, the added power of this part of the service was quite perceptible.

Speaking to various groups, I have found that, for the most part, people have responded with considerable interest as nature elements in Judaism were brought to their attention. They often seemed eager to relate to more of these elements in their own lives and were also extremely appreciative of the nature poetry which I might read on such occasions. Such examples as these could be multiplied if space permitted.

I make no claim that such findings constitute a "scientific" survey of the total scene today. I am convinced, however, that they do represent the expression of a profoundly felt need among many people for a renewed relation to *chei ha-olamim,* the Life of the Universe. I am also convinced that contemporary Judaism, if it is to be a living religion, must respond to this need by a renewed emphasis on those many nature elements which lie dormant, neglected, sublimated, and suppressed within the tradition.

At one period of history it may have been the proper task of Judaism to struggle against nature cults insofar as they represented man's subjugation to nature. Over the centuries, however, the reverse has occurred, reaching a frightening climax in our age: man's almost total alienation from nature. Consequently, one of the crucial religious tasks of our age is to work toward man's integration with nature, with all that implies societally, psychically, and theologically.

The elements of religious renewal are many, and the paths to the Divine various. But for at least some of us in this age the following expresses, far better than we could ourselves, how it appears to us:

> And if you ask me of God, my God,
> "Where is He that in joy we may worship Him?"
> Here on earth too He lives, not in heaven alone,
> And this earth He has given to man.
> A striking fir, a rich furrow, in them you will find His likeness,
> His image incarnate in every high mountain.
> Wherever the feeling of life flows—in animals, plants,
> In stones—there you will find Him embodied.
> And His household? All being: the gazelle, the turtle
> The shrub, the cloud pregnant with thunder;
> No God disembodied, mere spirit—He is God-in-Creation!
> That is His name and that is His fame forever!

(Saul Tchernichovsky, c. 1900)
trans. R. Cover, E. Gendler, and A. Porat

NADIE LA TIENE: LAND, ECOLOGY, AND NATIONALISM

Aurora Levins Morales

¿Puedes venderme tierra, la profunda
noche de raices; dientes de
dinosaurios y la cal
dispersa de lejanos esqueletos?
¿Puedes venderme selvas ya sepultadas, aves muertas,
peces de piedra, azufre
de los volcanes, mil millones de años
en espiral subiendo? ¿Puedes
venderme tierra, puedes
venderme tierra, puedes?

Aurora Levins Morales is a Puerto Rican Jewish writer, historian, and activist. She grew up in the mountains of western Puerto Rico and learned ecology from her biologist father, her bird-watching, bromeliad-loving mother, and the children of coffee workers. She lives in Berkeley, California, with her daughter.

La tierra tuya es mía.

Todos los pies la pisan.

Nadie la tiene, nadie.

Can you sell me the earth, the deep night

of roots, dinosaur teeth and the scattered lime

of distant skeletons?

Can you sell me long buried jungles, dead birds,

fishes of stone, volcanic sulfur, a thousand

million years rising in a spiral? Can you

sell me land, can you

sell me land, can you?

  The land that is yours is mine.

  Everyone's feet walk it.

  No-one has it, no-one. [1]

(African-Cuban poet Nicolas Guillen, from *¿Puedes?*)

Spring 1995. I sit on the shoulder of our family mountain, one of the highest in this part of the Cordillera Central of Western Puerto Rico, in the pine forest that rises abruptly off the smooth deforested slope to the east, making a profile easy to recognize from miles away. From the red forest floor I look out between the straight trunks of Honduran pine over rolling miles of cleared land planted in bananas, coffee, oranges and drenched alternately in full tropical sunlight and the quick moving rain showers of the season. Each time my brother Ricardo or I return to this farm where we spent our most important childhood years, we make pilgrimage to this exact place where, after the fire in the early sixties, the forestry service paid our family to plant pine seedlings. They wanted to start a small timber seed industry and our farm became part of the test acreage. In fact, it was Lencho Perez who planted the trees, not us. Hundreds of seedlings in black plastic bags spaded into the blackened hillside.

Lencho had been doing odds and ends of agricultural and other work for my parents for several years. In the midst of the Korean war my communist parents called the land Finca la Paz, "peace farm," but Lencho called it Monte Bravo, "fierce mountain."

In 1966, for political reasons my father was denied tenure at the University of Puerto Rico, where he had been teaching biology. So he accepted a job in Chicago and we moved there.

The day we left, the pine trees were still spindly seven-foot saplings, but somehow the knowledge of how they grew without us, how the farm continued to flower and decay, sustained my brother and me. The memory of it, the smells and sounds and colors, was one buoyant piece of driftwood in the shipwreck of our intense culture shock. We sent our spirits there for imaginary refuge from the harshness of our new lives and invoked it at night so we could sleep among the alien noises of Chicago. I dreamed of walking up the path into the farm every night for years.

Now we return to it as if checking on a buried treasure. Our ownership of these thirty-four acres preserves the land from clear-cutting, and the fact of that ownership is balm for exile. The colonial economy, the lack of the kind of social and political community we now need, the structures of our personal lives all keep us from coming here to live. But we need the knowledge of that deep valley full of rain, protected from bulldozers. Ownership is a foothold in a slippery place of identity and longing, of necessity and choice.

From my bedroom thousands of miles from here, this piece of earth and the land stretching out around it become a kind of amulet against dispossession. I imagine the rain falling on it, the hawks circling above it, the lizards skittering across it, its continued aliveness an affirmation of my roots there. That in spite of generations of shifting nationalities and loss behind me, in spite of the unpredictable changes of jobs, relationships, rented houses, I have a home on earth. In my imagination the land makes me safe.

But whenever I sit here listening to the wind in the trees, the haunting cry of lizard cuckoos in the valley proclaiming the coming downpour, smell the sunbaked ferns and decaying banana leaves and feel the dense clay under me the symbol begins to unravel. Slowly, as I listen to it, the land becomes itself again. Not mine, not anyone's. Talking to me, yes, but not any more than it talks to the fire ants building their nests or the bats' bones becoming humus or the endlessly chirping reinitas twittering among the señorita flowers.

I am an ecologist's daughter. I grew up in a house where the permeable boundaries of other worlds crisscrossed our own. At night you could hear the termites munching inside the walls and the slow trickling grains of digested wood. Rats ran in the attic, and if we ventured into the kitchen after hours they stared offended at our intrusions. Lizards hunted daily on the glass fields of our windowpanes, stalking moths and wasps. Hummingbirds, momentarily stunned from crashing into those windows, would lie in our hands, then shoot back into the hibiscus bushes. Around the ripening bunch of bananas that hung from the kitchen ceiling, clouds of fruit flies rose each time we pulled off a piece of fruit. Autumn evenings of rain, a single tree frog would sing from the moist crevices under the sink. In my parent's bedroom, a long tendril of jasmine that had crept between roof and wall wound sinuously across their shelves of paperbacks. A rat lived inside the washing machine, and my mother always had to hit the side of it before she started it up. It was never our house.

My father would take me walking sometimes, show me the last fading scar of the old road, the Camino Real, poke into the holes of rotten tree trunks, peer into the cups of flowers to see the teeming insect life. I grew up in a place where a tree might fall and, within a week, new seedlings sprang from the dead wood. The mountain slid and shifted under the heavy autumn rainfall, the garden left untended grew lush and tangled overnight, and it was never the same place for long. How can you own something that changes under your hands, that is so fully alive? Ecology undermines ownership.

My parents bought this farm for $4,000 in 1951, ninety acres of abandoned coffee plantation that had fallen back into wilderness after the coffee market crash of 1898, the hurricanes of 1899 and 1928, and the economic devastation of Puerto Rico in the '30s and '40s. Near the house I grew up in were the ruins of cement washing tanks and a wide drying platform where we rode our bikes: the last remaining evidence of the coffee boom of the last century when immigrants from Corsica and Mallorca and coastal towns carved up the mountains into landholdings and turned the subsistence farmers who had for centuries cultivated where they pleased into landless laborers. The laborers, the climate, and the soil combined to produce the best coffee in the world for wealthy patrons in Paris, Vienna, and New York.

When my parents bought it, the coffee had gone wiry, wild ginger choked the pathways, and bitter orange, grapefruit, and bananas flowered untended under the imported shade trees, brought in to protect the precious crop. My father, unabashedly speaking Brooklyn High School Latin, would stand at the counter of the tiny roadside *colmado*[2] drinking beers with the coffee laborers until he had enough Spanish to talk politics and begin organizing. My mother used the Agricultural Extension Club to get women out of their houses and learning about leadership and organization at the same time that they learned how to sew, make lard cans into stovetop ovens, cook, and do small carpentry projects. After a couple of years my parents sold off half the land at prices the landless or nearly so could afford, and for years people would come around trying to buy from the Americano who didn't know better. But how else do communists own land?

They raised chickens and the vegetables that my father peddled from their battered red truck. He worked as a lab tech at the hospital in Castañer and taught in San German while my mother took science courses, farmed, raised me and my brother, washed all the diapers and sheets and work pants by hand, cooked, cleaned, and tended the machete wounds and cooking burns of the neighbors at the first aid station. The week my parents were married the Korean War had broken out. They had come to Puerto Rico to await my father's arrest for refusing the draft, uncertain what the consequences would be. But he was declared unfit for service, and they stayed, raised children, made a life, and loved the land for its beauty and peace.

For my ancestors, land had different potency. When Eusebio Morales died in 1802, the lands that were measured for division among his heirs stretched between landmarks like "the old *ceiba* on the slope above the river." But what lay between those markers was money. Wealth extracted from the land by slave labor and the so-called free labor of the landless. They raised cattle and grew coffee and tobacco, sugar cane and rice. Land and slavery stood behind the petition of Eusebio's grandson Braulio to found a new town, behind the club of wealthy men who rotated among themselves the offices of mayor and militia captain, marrying their children to each other so obsessively that I am descended from the same patriarch by six different lines of descent.

Land and slaveholding still stood behind my grandfather in the Depression. When he worked as a janitor and then as a stock clerk in a New York City public school cafeteria. When he fed his family on food the supervisor pretended not to notice he was taking home. It was there in his certainty of his own rightness, in the phrase *"por lo derecho"*[3] that meant that he lived righteously, with dignity and correctness, not like all those wrong-living *títeres*[4] that surrounded them in Harlem.

My grandmother Lola expressed that pitying sense of superiority even more overtly than my grandfather. She would speak of some African American neighbor who was "so nice, poor thing." Although she complained that the Moraleses thought her not good enough, her own ancestors had all taken their turns administering class power. It was the service of her ancestors, the Díaz brothers, leading the local militia against the English invasion of 1797 for which her family was rewarded with lands in Barrio Anones. Although her father had gambled away the family store and she did garment work in New York, although she distanced herself from her relatives and liked the bustling anonymity of New York, she still wore her *"buena familia"*[5] like an especially nice perfume and was sorry for those who didn't have it, until at the end of her life it became a weapon against the staff of one nursing home after another where she reduced the dark-skinned, working-class workers to angry tears.

My great grandfather Abraham Sakhnin also grew up on a farm his family owned. This was in the southern Ukraine, up the railroad line from Odessa. In his old age he painted it: the horses, the cellars full of pumpkins, the harvesting of wheat. The Sakhnins had come from Lithuania in the days of Tsar Nicholas I when Jews were promised draft exemption if they settled on the borders as a buffer against the Turks. They were given land and taught to farm it by German settlers imported for the task. For five generations they did so. But land, for Jews in Eastern Europe, was not the foundation it was for Catholic *hacendados* in Puerto Rico. My great-grandfather fled the farm in 1904 rather than fight in the war against Japan. Pogroms were on the rise along with revolutionary violence, and although the family was Bolshevik sympathizers and some stayed to take part in the revolution, Abe left for Canada and then New York; his first cousin Alter went to Buenos Aires; and his sister married and left for Siberia. In 1941 the entire settlement, known as Yaza, was destroyed by Nazis. Land was no guarantee.

Land is no guarantee, but in the mythmaking of exiled and dispossessed nationalisms it becomes a powerful legitimizing force. The central symbol of Puerto Rican nationalism, the phrase most often used to mean that which is struggled for, is *madre patria,* usually translated as "Mother Homeland." Just as the enthusiastic propagandists of the 1898 U.S. invasion feminized and sexualized the land, describing "her" as well endowed, fruitful, and docile, a young girl who "surrenders herself graciously to our virile marines," so too nationalists have portrayed the colonized country as a captive mother, the *madre tendida en el lecho* ("stretched out upon the bed") in the hands of foreigners who rape her.

The idea of "patria" is deeply rooted, like patriotism itself, in both patriarchy and its *raison,* patrimony—the inheritance passed from father to son. And the basis of that inheritance is land. Under the rhetoric of *madre patria* lies that which is most despised and exploited in practice, most ignored in nationalist programs, most silently relied on as the foundation of prosperity for the future republic, the basis for its industrial development and for a homegrown class of owners. The unpaid and underpaid labor of women, mothers or not. The labor of agricultural workers so often characterized as "backward sectors." The generous and living land itself. These, in nationalist rhetoric, become purely symbolic sentimental images, detached from their own reality.

Nationalism has tremendous power. It mobilizes just rage about colonial oppression toward a single end. It subordinates all other agendas to that end. It silences internal contradictions among the colonized, postpones indefinitely the discussion of gender, sexuality, class, and often "race," endowing nationalist movements with a kind of focused, single-minded passion capable of great force. But although that force draws its energy from the real pain and rage and hope of the colonized, nationalism does not attempt to end all forms of injustice. Nationalism is generally, both in the intent of its leaders and in its results, a one-point program to capture patrimony for a new group of patriarchs.

In nationalist rhetoric, land does not move. No wonder it is so often portrayed as a mother. Eternal, loyal, and patient, it waits for its exiled children to come home. It would know them anywhere. But the real land, the soil and rocks and vegetation, is never still. In the United States the average acre of land loses five tons of soil every year, blown by wind across property lines and fences, municipalities and national borders, washed by rain into river systems that drain a thousand miles downstream. Even massive shapes like the Grand Canyon shift and collapse and move continually. Each autumn in Puerto Rico the water running off our mountain turns a heavy orange and flows away downhill, leaving the silt of our property spread over hundreds of square kilometers of flatlands and leagues of sea.

This movement of land has occasionally been used as part of imperial reasoning. In the late nineteenth century, one U.S. statesman claimed that Cuba was literally U.S. soil because it must have been formed by mud washing out of the mouth of the Mississippi. But "national soil" is a nonsensical statement. Places have history, but soil does not have nationality. Just as the air we breathe has been breathed by millions of others first and will go on to be breathed by millions more; just as water falls, travels, evaporates, circulates moisture around the planet—so the land itself migrates. The homeland to which Jews claim to have returned (land of the Canaanites before them and many others after) is not the same land. The earth that lay around the Temple could be anywhere by now. So what exactly is it we've been dreaming of for so long?

Land and blood. Mystical powers that never change their identity so that a speck of Mississippi mud and an individual red blood cell are both seen as carrying unalterable identity, permanent membership in human cultures. This is the mysticism that allows fascist movements to call up images of long dispersed and recombined ancestral peoples like the ancient Aryans and Romans or entirely mythic genetic strains like The White Race, and scream for genocide to return them to a state of purity.

The reality is that people circulate like dust, intermingling and reforming, all of us equally ancient on this earth, all equally made of the fragments of long-exploded stars, and if, by some unlikely miracle, a branch of our ancestors has lived in the same place for a thousand years, this does not make them more real than the ones who have continued circulating for that same millennium. All of us have been here since people were people. All of us belong on earth.

So what about the stealing of land? What about all the colonized places on earth? What of indigenous peoples forcibly removed by invaders? The crime here is a deeper and more lasting one than theft, akin in some ways to enslavement. Before land can be stolen, it must become property. The relationships built over time between the land and the human members of its ecosystem must be severed just as ties of family and village and co-humanity were severed so that slavers could enslave. The indigenous peoples of the Americas did not own land in the European sense. They lived with and from the land and counted it as a relative. The blow that cracked Hawaiian sovereignty was the imposition of land ownership. At gunpoint, Hawaiians were forced to divide sacred and common land, to commodify it, price it, allot it. In Europe itself, it was the enclosure of the commons, the grazing lands and great forests from which people subsisted, that created a massive class of landless laborers to fill the factories and transport the goods of industrial capitalism. Earth-centered cultures everywhere held our kinship with land and animals and plants as core knowledge, central to living. The land had to be soaked with blood and that knowledge, those cultures shattered, before private ownership could be erected. It wasn't just theft.

And yet owning has seemed like such a good defense. With the common lands gone, strive to own. With land commodified and confiscated, struggle to enforce treaties. If you are driven away, fight to return. For Jews, barred for centuries from landholding, how legitimating, how healing, what a chance to strike back at history it is to acquire land. Why should we alone be excluded? When Baron Rothschild sought to help the Jews of Eastern Europe to escape the pogroms, he bought them land: in Argentina, in New Jersey, in other places, and settled them there to farm. Landlessness had been a central feature of Jewish oppression. Having land became a symbol of resistance. Our own connections with land have been severed time after time. We would come to know and trust a particular landscape, to understand Babylonian weather, to know the growing seasons of Andalucia, to recognize the edible wild foods of the woods around Rouen, the wildflowers on the Dnieper or the Rhine or the Thames, and it would be time for another hurried departure. To have land, to farm, became one of the most emotionally powerfully images of Jewish freedom, even when getting land meant severing someone else's ties to it. Even when it meant tearing the olive trees and the fragrant dust and the taste of desert spring water out of the lives of Palestinians whose love for the land was hundreds of generations deep.

In the 1930s my father's family sang this song, translated from the Yiddish of Russian Jews:

On the road to Sebastopol,
not so far from Simfaropol
Just you go a little further on.
There you'll see a collective farm,
run by sturdy Jewish arms
and its called Zhankoye, Zhan.
Aunt Natasha drives the tractor,
Grandma runs the cream extractor
as we work we all can sing this song:
Who says Jews cannot be farmers?
Spit in his eye who would so harm us.
Tell him of Zhankoye, Zhan.

Land ownership was only a hundred years old in my community of Indiera when I was growing up. Its hold on people's imaginations was still tenuous. It was not until the 1860s that the Massinis and Nigaglionis, Agostinis and Pachecos began filing title claims to large stretches of mountain lands. That there were already people living on and from that land was irrelevant, because none of them had surveyed it, fenced it, paid a lawyer to draw up deeds to it. Since at least the 1570s, the mountains had been worked by wandering subsistence farmers who would clear and burn off a bit of forest, cultivate it for a few years and move on while the land renewed itself. Descendants of Arawak and other indigenous people enslaved by the Spanish, runaway slaves and poor Europeans, the people of the mountains didn't *own* the land. They moved across it and lived from it.

The new settlers owned and profited. Our own farm was carved out by a Corsican named Massari who, like the others, planted the new boom crop, *arabiga* coffee for faraway markets. Then it was owned by Pla, who was Mallorcan. Then by my parents. But

the neighbors who held small plots and worked other people's land
for cash never seemed to take boundaries seriously the way my
neighbors in New England did. Everyone harvested bananas, root
vegetables, oranges, and wood from the farms of the Canabals, the
Nigaglionis, or Delfín Rodriguez, who only kept Hacienda Indiera
as a tax write-off to protect his sugar profits. Our neighbor to the
north, Chago Soto, was always moving the fence between our prop-
erties. On one visit we found that Cheito Agostini had built pens
for his pigs on our side of the road. Another time, exploring the
deep overgrown valley on the back side of our land, my sister-in-
law and I stumbled across a cement holding tank built over one of
the springs and plastic pipes leading the water out to a house and
garden. It was only when we introduced ourselves to the man load-
ing a truck in front of the house and saw his chagrin that we realized that the water was on our side of the property line.

So what do communist landholders do with privilege? My father says you have to get rid of it or use it for the common good. So
we tell Cheito he can keep the pigs there, but no more dumping
piles of Pampers, and no permanent structures. We let the farmer to
the north know that we understand the water came from our land,
and for now it's OK. But what are we doing with this land at all,
now that we don't live there?

Class privilege allows us this option: to see ourselves as stewards of this land. Because we don't need to live from these thirty-
four acres we can resist the pressure to sell. Our neighbors keep
asking: can't you sell us a piece of the farm to expand my coffee, my
bananas, to build a house? After all, you're not using it. Poverty does
not allow them the luxury of thinking twenty or thirty years ahead,
but we know the land they want now for farming cash crops will
pass through their hands and into other uses and that in thirty years

this place would be lots for cement houses. My mother says the rich ruin the poor and the poor ruin the land.

From up here in the *cordillera* you can see where the rich ruin land directly. We grew up with the smudge of poisoned air over Guayanilla, where the oil refineries used to make such a stench we would always buy sweet *mavi* to drink before we got there so we could hold the cups over our noses as we went by. There are puffs of dust where the limestone hills are being bulldozed and ground into cement for more housing developments, shopping malls, factories. So much of the land has been paved, in fact, that the drenching rains of autumn have nowhere to soak in. The water runs off into the sea now, and the water table has dropped so much that last year some neighborhoods in San Juan went without water for weeks at a time. But up here it hasn't yet been worth their while. Here it's the desperation they've created in the lives of the poor that does the work for them.

Between the land hunger of the poor to turn acreage into a little money and the commodification of the earth into real estate, only privilege seems able to preserve the land. The Rockefellers, buying up islands, keep pockets of wildness alive in the Caribbean while deforestation and massive shopping malls destroy the fresh water supplies of Puerto Rico, leaving everyone thirsty.

This is what we want our privilege to buy, my brothers and I. Because of how we lived there, because of the ways our parents cherished and nurtured our intimacy with the land, we know we're kin to it. We don't want it to die. But we also want to give the land a chance to tell its story and the story of the people who have worked it. On that overgrown abandoned coffee farm in the middle of increasingly cleared and pesticide-soaked lands, we want to build a cultural center and museum of the history and ecology of Indiera, where the community can participate in retelling its past. We hope that in this process of storytelling, the people of Indiera will rediscover pride in their heritage of work and a new sense of their connection to this land. By drawing tourist dollars from the nearby Panoramic Highway, we also want to model another way of living from the land, in which livelihood comes not from extracting the land's wealth but from telling, in as much detail as we can, the complex story of our relations with it.

I imagine a museum filled with family photographs, letters from migrant children who moved away, and recorded voices of elders testifying. I imagine showing the people who grow coffee the faces of the people who drink it and vice versa. I imagine a narrow pathway winding down into the rain valley through the forest of tree ferns, South American shade trees, wild guavas, and African Tulip trees. I remember how my father used to take his microscope down to the schoolhouse and how the children would crowd around waiting for a turn to be amazed at what the world looks like close up. I imagine the children of the barrio walking among the photographs and voices and trees that way, renaming their place on this land and in the world.

Because the land is alive, our relationship with it is real. We are all kin to the land, love it, know it, become intimate with its ways, sometimes over many generations. Surely such kinship and love must be honored. Nationalism does not honor it. Nationalism is about gaining control, not about loving land. But it wears the cloak of that love, strips it from its sensual and practical roots and raises it into a banner for armies. The land invoked as a battle cry is not the same land that smells of sage, or turns blue in the dusk, or clings thickly to our boots after rain. That land is less than nothing to the speechmakers. The land invoked to the beating of nationalist drums is what lies at the linguistic roots of the term "real estate," meaning royal property. It is the land my *hacendado* forebears kept in the bank, ransacked, used to pay the bills. The land bristling with "No Trespassing" signs, the land the lords of Europe enclosed against the peasants in the infancy of capitalism, the land as symbol of power over. It is the land we can be mobilized to recapture because with its fences and mortgages and deeds, it has been the symbol of our dispossession.

Ownership shatters ecology. For the land to survive, for us to survive, it must cease to be property. It cannot continue to sustain us for much longer under the weight of such merciless use. We know this. We know the insatiable hunger for profit that drives that use and the disempowerment that accommodates to it. We don't yet know how to make it stop.

But where ecology meets culture there is another question. How do we hold in common, not only the land, but all the fragile, tenacious rootedness of human beings to the ground of our histories, the cultural residues of our daily work, the individual and tribal longings for place? How do we abolish ownership of land and respect people's ties to it? How do we shift the weight of our times from the single-minded nationalist drive for a piece of territory and the increasingly barricaded self-interest of even the marginally privileged toward a rich and multilayered sense of collective heritage? I don't have the answer. But I know that only when we can hold each people's particular memories and connections with land as a common treasure can the knowledge of our place on it be restored.

TO WORK IT AND GUARD IT: PRESERVING GOD'S WORLD

Arthur Green

As we seek to articulate a Judaism appropriate to a new era of Jewish history, we cannot fail to note that this period begins in the same decades when the human race realizes it has achieved the gruesome possibility of destroying the planet on which we all live. The rabbis tell us that shortly after Adam was created, God walked him around the Garden of Eden and told him to take care to guard the world that he was being given.[1] "If you destroy this world," he was told, "there is no one to come and set it right after you." Such an *aggadah* has a level of intense meaning in our age that the early rabbis could hardly have foretold.

Dr. Arthur Green is a professor at Brandeis University and former president of the Reconstructionist Rabbinical College. His books include *Seek My Face Speak My Name,* and *Tormented Master: The Life and Spiritual Quest of Rabbi Nahman of Bratslav* (Jewish Lights). He is also the translator/editor of the works of two major Hasidic rebbes.

Telling the tale of Creation is itself a statement of love of the natural world. It needs to be accompanied by actions that bear witness to that love—without these it is false testimony. The ethic that proceeds from this tale is one of strong commitment to *ahavat habri'ot,* the love of all God's creatures, and a sense of absolute responsibility for their survival.[2] (For us Jews, after all, love and responsibility always go hand in hand!) This is a worldview in which the love of God and love for the world, including both the natural and the human dimensions, are in no way separable from one another. A piety that proclaims the love of God, without showing it by a love for world, is theologically self-contradictory. It is the natural world that embodies the only God we know. The tale of Creation achieves its fulfillment in acts we undertake to make our appreciation of divinity real by the way we live. We do so both in our individual personal lives and in the commitments we make to greater causes. The needs of the world are so great and so urgent that they cannot be adequately addressed only by a life of personal purification that creates a "holy" elite but does nothing more to help the world survive.

Here, too, the details are hard to specify, and each person and community has to find ways to fulfill these commandments. By way of example, it surely seems right that we achieve a high level of consciousness and action regarding the ways we live, the products we use, and the ways we dispose of them.[3] We must stop being callous and excessive users of earth's resources. We must become aware and share with others the realization that a small minority of the human race consumes far more than its appropriate share of earth's resources. We need to concern ourselves with the continued availability for generations to come of pure air, pure water, and good earth that will yield untainted produce. As good Jewish parents, concerned always with providing for our children, we must not allow ourselves to consume the legacy that belongs to future generations. The many areas in which to become active in ways helpful to the world's survival hardly need enumerating here. Each of us must find significant means to become partners in giving attention to such concerns. The fact that we band together in such activities with persons of good will who relate to the divine through other traditions (or without the language of traditional religion), is all for the good. There is an authentic *kiddush ha-Shem* in expressions of our Jewish faith that can be shared in such a way with others. The example of Abraham and Sarah, who fulfilled their love of God by making God beloved to others, is the starting point of our renewal of the Jewish moral life. The open tent of our first parents, into which all were welcomed and where all were fed and taught by example, must once again be open to others in our old-new home.

Another series of *mitsvot* that proceeds directly from a relationship with this Creation tale is that which is called in Hebrew by the general term *tsa'ar ba'aley hayyim* ("the suffering of living beings"), or sympathy with pain caused to animals. Our story of Creation tells us that we humans were created on the same day as were the land animals. Here again, even within the Genesis tale, we are being told that we are less separable from the animal kingdom than other aspects of that story may lead us to think. The Creation tale also makes us rulers over the animal kingdom, but only as God's viceroy who bears responsibility to the ultimate Ruler. This role demands of us that we be sympathetic to the suffering of other creatures, and that we not cause them needless pain. A commitment to preserving the earth also means a commitment to preserving the great and wondrous variety of life species in which the One is manifest.

Vegetarianism:
A Kashrut for Our Age

In this spirit, I believe the time has come for us to reconsider the question of whether we should continue to consume animal flesh as food.[4] Our tradition has always contained within it a certain pro-vegetarian bias, even though it has provided for the eating of meat. In the ideal state of Eden, according to the Bible, humans ate only plants; we and the animals together were given the plants as food. Only after the expulsion from Eden, when the urge overwhelmed humans and led them toward evil, did the consumption of flesh begin. The very first set of laws given to humanity sought to limit this evil by forbidding the flesh of a still-living creature, placing a limit on acts of cruelty or terror related to the eating of animal flesh. The Torah's original insistence that domestic animals could be slaughtered only for purpose of sacrifice, an offering to God needed to atone for the killing, was compromised only when the Book of Deuteronomy wanted to insist that sacrifice be offered in Jerusalem alone. Realizing that people living at a great distance could not bring all their animals to the Temple for slaughter, the "secular" slaughter and eating of domestic animals was permitted. Even then, the taboo against consuming blood, and later, the requirement to salt meat until even traces of blood were removed, "for the blood is the self" of the creature, represent a clear discomfort with the eating of animal flesh. Most significantly, the forbidding of any mixing of milk and meat represents a proto-vegetarian sensibility. Milk is the fluid by which life is passed on from generation to generation; it may not be consumed with flesh, representing the taking of that life in an act of violence. The fluid of life may not be mixed with that of death. As the Torah says of the hewn-stone altar: "For you have waved your sword over it and have profaned it."

The reasons for acting upon this vegetarian impulse in our day are multiple and compelling, *just as compelling, I believe, as the reasons for the selective taboos against certain animals must have been when the Community of Israel came to accept these as the word of God.* This is what we mean, after all, when we talk about a *mitsvah* being "the word of God" or "God's will." It is a form of human expression or a way of acting that feels compellingly right. This rightness has both a moral and a spiritual dimension; it is an expression of values we choose, but it also makes a more profound statement about who we are. We then come to associate it with divinity, and it becomes a vehicle through which we express our spiritual selves. With the passage of time, origins are shrouded in mystery, and the form becomes the "will of God." Israelites of ancient times felt that way about the taboos widely current in their society against the consumption of certain animals that they saw as repulsive, against the eating of blood, the mixing of milk and meat, and so forth. They associated this series of taboos with the God of Sinai. Over the centuries, *kashrut* as we know it became a *mitsvah*, a way in which Jews are joined to God.

Our situation has certain important parallels to this one. We are urgently concerned with finding a better way to share earth's limited resources. We know that many more human lives can be sustained if land is used for planting rather than for grazing of animals for food. We are committed also to a healthier way of living and are coming to recognize that the human is, after all, a mostly vegetarian species. But for us as Jews, the impulse is largely a moral and religious one. We have a long tradition of abhorring violence. Cruelty to animals has long been forbidden by Jewish law and sensibilities. Our tradition tells us that we must shoo a mother bird away from the nest before we take her eggs so that she does not suffer as we break the bond between them.[5] We are told that a mother and her calf may not be slaughtered on the same day.[6] The very next step beyond these prohibitions is a commitment to a vegetarian way of living.

We Jews in this century have been victims of destruction and mass slaughter on an unprecedented scale. We have seen every norm of humanity violated as we were treated like cattle rather than human beings. Our response to this memory is surely a complex and multitextured one. But as we overcome the understandable first reactions to the events, some of us feel our abhorrence of violence and bloodshed growing so strong that it reaches even beyond the borders of the human and into the animal kingdom. We Jews, who always looked upon killing for sport or pleasure as something alien and repulsive, should now, out of our own experience, be reaching the point where we find even the slaughter of animals for food morally beyond the range of the acceptable. If Jews have to be associated with killing at all in our time, let it be only for the defense of human life. Life has become too precious in this era for us to be involved in the shedding of blood, even that of animals, when we can survive without it. This is not an ascetic choice, we should note, but rather a life-affirming one. A vegetarian Judaism would be more whole in its ability to embrace the presence of God in all of Creation.

Wilderness in Time, Sabbath in Space

Evan Eisenberg

The Mountain and the Tower are the poles between which human culture has shuttled for the past six thousand years. One can learn a great deal about a culture, or piece of a culture, by asking which claim it accepts. Does it follow the Canaanites—and Israelites—and consider that the center of the world is wilderness? Or does it side with the Mesopotamians in judging that the center of the world is the city?

Both sides are right. Both city and wilderness are sources of life, sources of weal, centers from which human waves have moved outward. The question is whether one looks to the proximate

Evan Eisenberg is the author of *The Ecology of Eden* and *The Recording Angel*. His writing on nature and culture has appeared in *The Atlantic Monthly, The New Republic, The Nation, Natural History,* and other publications. A sometime cantor and former gardener for the New York City parks department, he lives in Manhattan with his wife, an urban planner, and their daughter.

source or the ultimate source. Looking to the proximate source is useful in many ways and may leaven the growth of civilization; but in the long run it is dangerous. Convinced that our well-being springs from our own cleverness in reshaping the world around us, we are tempted to reshape more and more of it, extending the reach of the Tower into every corner of the world. And that is biting off more than we can chew.

For the myth of the Mountain is rooted in ecological fact. Manmade landscapes survive only at the sufferance of the wildness around them, or the wildness that remains in them. The flow of energy, water, nutrients, and genetic information; the maintenance of temperature and the mix of atmospheric gases within narrow limits; the fertility of the soil: all these are achieved by wild nature in ways we do not fully understand. As we do not know how the job is done, we cannot do it ourselves. Even if we could, we would end up spending most of our waking hours working for something that we used to get for free.

In other words, humans and their allies are able to conquer the world, but they are not able to run it all by themselves. If the waves of human advance go too far or run too deep, they may finally bring about their own undoing.

Whatever else Eden may be, it is first of all an avatar of the Mountain. And the main lesson of the story of Eden is that we cannot live there. Although it is the source of human life, it is not a place for humans to live. A place for gods and animals, but not for us. As soon as we become fully human, we begin to destroy Eden, and thereby expel ourselves. Only by keeping our distance from some of the wilderness that remains can we keep from fouling the wellspring of our own life. The fiery sword (whatever it is: our awe of wilderness, our fear of its dangers, our dismay in the face of its grueling beauty) is the best friend we have.

If the first lesson of Genesis is that we cannot live in Eden, there may be some comfort in the second lesson: we can yet enjoy Eden's benison, if only we let it flow. That is a big if, however. The four rivers of Eden are ensigns of the flow of wildness. Dam that flow, and the manmade world must dry up and blow away; and so, at last, must wilderness itself. Even the biggest wilderness preserves are not big enough to stay healthy if migration, gene flow, and the circulation of energy and nutrients are blocked beyond their borders by highways, dams, development, ranchers' fences, the dredging of wetlands, and the poisoning of waterways. Wilderness is the heart of the world, but a heart is not much good without arteries and capillaries that touch every cell of civilization with wildness. There must be Mountains on every scale, from the Amazon rainforest and the Arctic tundra to the vest-pocket park in the inner city and the thicket in your backyard: swathes and patches and pockets of wildness, representing not only literal mountains but ecosystems of all kinds.

A HABIT OF MINDFULNESS

Wes Jackson, the Kansas geneticist who is trying to breed an "edible prairie," has proposed a moratorium in the deployment of new biotechnologies.[1] If you can call a time-out in a basketball game, he asks, why not in this game on whose outcome so much hangs? A more sweeping idea has been put forward by the Jewish philosopher Arthur Waskow.[2] Let every seventh year, he says, be set aside as a sabbatical in which no new technology is deployed, no new houses are built, no raw land is developed. Let people stop and think about what they have already done and what they might do in the future.

Such an idea is unthinkable in modern society, which is a good sign that it deserves serious thought. In fact, some of us already set aside every seventh day in roughly this way. For many Jews, Christians, and Muslims, the sabbath is a time when we do no work, and reduce our dependence on technology. On that day we meddle with nature as little as we can and enjoy nature as much as we can.[3] The sabbath, the sabbatical year, and the jubilee year are puddles and ponds of wildness in time, fed by the rivers of Eden. In the rhythm of Earth Jazz, they are times to lift the reed from your lips and just listen.[4]

Unfortunately, the secular weekend is often just the reverse: a time to shop for and play with the toys you worked all week to afford. But even secular society has kept alive the tradition of using weekends and vacations as a chance to live more simply, to get closer to Mountain and achieve some brief detachment from the Tower. Hiking, camping, and weekend or summer homes are not without cost to nature, but the cost to nature will be less if we respect the simplicity that closeness to nature demands, and really try to do without modern technology—if we backpack instead of taking a forty-foot trailer, or build a rude cabin instead of a plush second home.

Anyway, the cost to nature is amply repaid if people end up thinking harder about what they are costing nature the rest of the year. When the television ads tell you what you need, and the politicians tell you what the economy needs, it is good to have firsthand experience of needing less. In this respect, a vivid alternation between town and country may be more useful—as well as more satisfying—than the usually futile search for a middle landscape that is perfect all year round.

But to become mindful, to detach oneself from the rush of technology, may not always require that one venture into the wilderness, or even into the countryside. The sabbath, or something like it, can allow one to step back from the Tower without actually leaving it: to be in the modern world but not of it. Instead of moving toward wildness in space, one allows wildness to well up in a particular volume of time. To the receptive soul, a walk in the park can be as restorative as a trek in the wilderness. Even the city streets wear a new face when you carry no money or credit cards and travel only on foot.

This last example refers to the traditional Jewish sabbath, when Jews are commanded to do no work. Though the Bible does not specify what it means by work, the rabbis interpreted the word to cover all the activities involved in the building of the tabernacle in the desert, which later became the Temple on Mount Zion. So while the need to build the Tower is acknowledged as a part of human nature, from the very start there is a counterweight: a reminder not to take our Towers too seriously.[5] God is a wild creature, a creature of the Mountain, who cannot be cooped up in humans constructions, no matter how grand. And humans are very much like God is this respect.

A habit of mindfulness, I said, may be more important than either rigid habits or rigid beliefs. A habit of setting aside a time or place for mindfulness can be part of this. Such a habit may help to overcome the spoiled-child greediness, broken by spasms of rejection, that now marks our dealings with technology. The habit should be applied, though, not only to technology in the narrow sense, but to economics, land use, lifestyle—the whole breathless march of civilization.

TSIMTSUM

The sixteenth-century kabbalist Isaac Luria of Safed, known as the Holy Lion, taught that in order to create the world, God had to draw himself inward—to take a step back, as it were. Since God was everywhere, he had to retract himself in order to leave a space where other things could exist. This self-retraction Luria called *tsimtsum*.[6]

The time has come for a human *tsimtsum*. The present lord of creation, humankind, must take a step back and give the rest of nature room to breathe. Man must tighten his belt so that the rest of creation (by which I mean both the object and the activity) can go on.

In saying this, I am calling neither for a return to primitive living, nor for a "decoupling" of humans from nature.[7] Even as we make more room for wilderness, we must collaborate with the rest of nature in new and creative ways.

In the Lurianic system, *tsimtsum* is only the first stage in the process of creation. While the universe takes on a life of its own, it is formed and nourished continuously by the emanations of godhead. To speak of a human *tsimtsum* is not to deny our creative partnership with nature, but to admit that true creation begins with self-limitation: with the acknowledgment that there is something in the world other than the self, and that this something has its own creativity. Only with such an other is partnership possible—not with a mere reification of our needs, desires, and fears.

What is nature's creativity? A poet could give a thousand answers, but I will give just one. Nature's creativity lies in the ecological and evolutionary processes that give the planet its thousands and millions of faces, as well as the single, remarkably consistent face that some call Gaia. Since we are dependent on those processes for our very survival, *tsimtsum* has an urgency far stronger than the courtesies of "I" and "Thou."

The ecologist Barry Commoner argues that the notion of carrying capacity is meaningless when applied to a planet run by clever humans. "In an abstract sense, there is a global 'limit to growth,' but this is determined not by the present availability of resources, but by a distant limit to the availability of solar energy. . . . That distant limit is irrelevant to current policy. . . . The question is whether we can produce bountiful harvests, productive machinery, rapid transportation, and decent human dwellings sufficient to support the world population without despoiling the environment."[8] The answer, of course, is yes—provided we take Commoner's advice.

His view of population growth is not quite so cavalier as that; he takes the line that economic development will at some point (the "demographic transition"; see later) stabilize population more or less automatically. Still, I am troubled by his denial of limits, by his vision of a planet wholly humanized: a vast organic garden spangled with appropriate machines. For an ecologist, Commoner is oddly silent here about such matters as species extinctions and the loss of wilderness. With the best intentions and the best technologies, large numbers of humans weigh heavily on the ecosystems they invade. Farming, even the organic farming that Commoner favors, takes up space. If there is one thing ecologists have learned in recent years, it is that wilderness cannot be kept in boxes; and the smaller the boxes, the more frantically they must be managed to retain even a semblance of life. Today, many wilderness areas are being managed very frantically indeed. Wildlife biologists now speak of wilderness areas as "megazoos" in which endangered species are tagged, tracked, and provided with mating services.

People involved in such projects, and in the many other projects managers get involved in, may think they are collaborating with nature. But management is not collaboration. Few humans can do creative work with the boss looking over their shoulder, correcting each dubious move. In this regard, human and nonhuman nature are very much alike. Before we can hope to collaborate with nature, we must give her some elbow room.

Would a human *tsimtsum* mean rolling back the waves of human-led change? If so, the notion might seem as facetious as King Canute's when he sat on the shore and commanded the tide to turn back. But the truth is that the tide of human advance has ebbed many times, in many places. War, famine, and plague have been responsible most of the time, but not always. For the kind of rolling back we need, a decrease in human population is not essential, though it would certainly help. While the sheer number of people on earth matters, where they are and what they are doing matters just as much.

Oddly enough, the waves of human-led change may in effect be rolled back or annulled by new waves of human-led change. Industrialization can often bring about a "demographic transition" that lowers the rate of population growth to something very near zero. As wealth and health increase, people switch from an *r* strategy (having as many kids as they can) to a K strategy (having a few kids in whom they invest heavily). (In ecologists' patois, *r* and K are similarly used to describe the difference between annual and perennial grasses, or between frogs and rhinoceri. The terms come from the basic ecological equation in which *r* is the intrinsic rate of a population's increase, K the highest stable population its territory can sustain. In other words, the *r* strategist trusts in sheer numbers of offspring, hoping that some will survive; the K strategist invests heavily in a few offspring, a number appropriate to the resources available, and works to ensure that all or most of them survive.)

While the switch is far from automatic—hinging on the specifics of economic security, the position of women, and other social factors, as well as the availability of contraception—it has been thrown in a number of newly industrial nations.

Industrialization's older sibling, urbanization, can concentrate people in a smaller area and so, in theory, leave more room for wilderness. More productive farming can squeeze more food from less land: in India, high-yield grains are reckoned to have spared for nature's own use more than a hundred million acres that would otherwise have been plowed. In all these ways, the expansion of humans and annual grasses may be reversed.

In practice, it is not easy to know whether a real *tsimtsum* is taking place. Though people of industrialized nations may have fewer offspring, each one uses much more of nature—both as larder and as dump—than preindustrial people do. Squeezing people into cities does no good unless their needs for energy, sanitation, and so on are met sustainably, a condition few Third World cities are set up to meet. As we have seen, the effective base of the Tower generally extends far beyond the city limits. And modern agriculture does not cut nature any slack if it depends on overuse of chemicals and abuse of soil, and so is unsustainable in the long run. Nor does nature gain much if the retraction of civilization leaves only a wasteland. Sometimes, it is true, nature heals itself, spontaneously reclaiming its lost realm; more often, perhaps, humans must help it along by the practice of "restoration ecology."

For nature's sake and our own, we must give nonhuman nature space in which to go about its business. On the simplest level, this means preserving wilderness. But it also means arranging our own, human space in intelligent ways.

A Spatial Sabbath

Probably the most sweeping vision of *tsimtsum* yet proposed in any detail is the North American Wilderness Recovery Project, known to its friends as the Wildlands Project.[9] Under this plan, at least half the land surface of the lower forty-eight would be devoted to core reserves and the inner parts of corridors between them. Within these areas all roads, dams, power lines, and other prying fingers would be dismantled. Outside these areas, like a bulky parka keeping off the chill of civilization, would be buffer zones of limited human activity. But the parka image is not quite right, for civilization would no longer be the outside and wilderness the beleaguered inside; instead, civilization would be confined to pockets within the matrix of wilderness. In a way, the buffer zones would be more like the lining of the stomach, keeping acids and toxins away from the rest of the body.

The Wildlands Project speaks deeply to my wilder self. It may even flow logically from some of the premises I have set out. Given the political realities of the moment, though, I want to propose something slightly more modest.

Earlier I said that as the rivers of Eden distribute wildness in space, so the septenary cycles of jubilee, sabbatical, and sabbath distribute wildness in time. They make ponds and puddles of wildness on every scale, from which the rules and uses of human economy and technology are excluded, or in which they are mirrored softly, lazily, and upside-down.

The analogy, too, can be turned on its head. If the sabbath is a wilderness in time, then wilderness is a sabbath in space. Why not use the serried cycles of sabbath, sabbatical, and jubilee as a model for the way wildness ought to be distributed in space?

Take any geographical unit—country, state, province, county, town, borough, precinct, block, backyard. Let each unit devote one seventh of its land to wilderness, or something as close to wilderness as circumstances permit. If the wilderness is there already, let it be preserved; if not, let it be created.

The result, you might think, would be that one seventh of every country would be wilderness. You would be deceived, for two reasons. First, what I have in mind is not a simple fraction, but a sum of fractions—something like the sum of an infinite series in integral calculus. A county, for example, would add its own wilderness to the wilderness set aside by the state, just as each week adds its sabbath to the sabbath that comes every seven years.

Secondly, on the continental scale the portion of wilderness could and should be much greater than a seventh, at least in some cases. Thus a continent such as North America, South America, or Eurasia (to say nothing of Antarctica) would ideally preserve vast tracts that either resist settlement and exploitation, or are thought to be vital to the workings of the biosphere. At the risk of stretching the analogy past the breaking point, such tracts might be compared to the Edenic or the messianic era, "the time that is all sabbath." As these stand beyond the geometry of time, so the great wildernesses of the world stand beyond the normal geometry of human space. They are the Mountain itself.

A cynic might ask: Why all this *tsimis* (Yiddish for a stew, metaphorically a fuss, not to be confused with *tsimtsum*) about the number seven? Should a question of great ecological weight rest on the slender reed of a Chaldean superstition? Is this notion any less arbitrary than, say, the recent insistence of a Republican Congress that the federal budget be balanced in exactly seven years—an insistence based, as the Speaker himself admitted, on a hunch?

Well, it is *somewhat* less arbitrary. Ecologists estimate that at a bare minimum, 5 to 10 percent of an ecosystem must be preserved if it is to stay at all healthy. Make it a seventh, and you have a margin of error. (While trying to set aside one seventh of every "original" ecosystem might raise more problems than it solves, it is plain that in choosing which parts of a state or county or town to set aside, we should make sure that key ecosystems are represented—just as we should take into account all the questions of spatial relation, connectivity, and so on that were previously mentioned.) Besides, it is hardly arbitrary—or it is arbitrary in a useful way—to join a culture's sense of space to its sense of time, and to ground both in the bedrock of ancient symbols. Even those self-styled conservatives who despise conservation might warm to the idea of a network of wildness, were it presented to them in these terms. Many of them claim to know what the temporal sabbath is all about; should not a spatial sabbath be right up their alley? If we can set aside sevenths of our time for holiness—that is, for purposes higher than human aggrandizement—why not sevenths of our space?

TSIMTSUM IN
YOUR OWN BACKYARD

On so large a scale, bringing about a healthy spatial relation between Mountain and Tower, between the network of wildness and the network of civilization, takes political action. Without shrinking from this, some of us may be forgiven if we wonder what we can do with our own two hands, in our own backyards. How can we set aside a seventh—or if we choose, more than a seventh—of our own turf for nature's use?

In her marvelous book, *Noah's Garden: Restoring the Ecology of Our Own Backyards,* Sarah Stein gives the beginning of an answer.[10]

Slowly and with many missteps, Stein has transformed her own six acres in New York's Westchester County from the museum of invasive exotics typical of suburbia to something an Indian might have recognized. By bringing back native trees, grasses, and wildflowers, she has brought back as well such native Americans as the bluebird, the meadowlark, the great blue heron, and numberless butterflies.

Not everyone with a backyard has so many acres to work with, or the time and resources (including a son who is a plant molecular biologist) to work with them so well. But if all the hours and dollars now spent on suppressing native plants (above all by lawn-mowing) were spent instead on encouraging them, a fairly spectacular *tsim-tsum* could be achieved in a fairly short time.

Many people, told that their grounds must be one hundred percent native and natural, rebel—and rightly. They like their tulips and tea roses, their tonsured hedges and lawns. But the fact is that one can have such things and still be ecologically correct. The key is to keep them in their place.

Ancient Roman estates could have tousled meadows and groves as well as formal topiary gardens. Renaissance villas could have sylvan *boschi* as well as formal parterres. In thinking that his naturalistic lawns had to run all the way to the door—that every thread of knot garden had to be ripped up, every boxwood fancy lopped down—Capability Brown was, at best, confused. And some advocates of the wild garden may be said to share his confusion.

Every lived-on property, whether an estate of ten thousand acres or a brownstone lot with a backyard a few yards square, has its progression from inside to outside, from hearth to wilderness. Metaphorically it has that progression; it ought to have it in practice, too. Close to the house, artifice is in order: the well-tended garden, the stretch of lawn for children to play on. Farther out (and generally, farther from the road) wildness should be invited to make itself at home.

In all this, one rule must be respected. Exotic plants are fine, but only if they are a lot of trouble. The kinds of exotics that garden stores and catalogues are most eager to push, and many people are most eager to buy—hardy, spreading perennials, eagerly self-seeding annuals, "low-maintenance" plants in general—are exactly the kinds that out-Herod Herod and must be avoided, because they may be invasive. They may escape into the wild.

By and large, this means that exotics belong in the high-maintenance, relatively formal part of your garden. If a nonnative plant needs cossetting to stay live in your climate, it is not likely to survive in the wild. If, on the other hand, a nonnative plant can be "naturalized" in a naturalistic setting, it does not belong there: it is invasive enough to be shunned.

Is it only for reasons of mythic convenience that I put the formal garden near the house, the wild stuff farther off? Not at all. Other sorts of convenience also come into play. There is your own convenience in having things that need tending close at hand, as well as a relatively controlled environment for sitting, reading, playing, eating. There is the convenience of wild things, many of which are shy of houses and people. And there is the convenience of wild things in a larger sense: the convenience of connection, of flow. The back of your property may border a woods or a meadow; more likely, it borders the back of someone else's property, which—for reasons of mythic or personal convenience—is likely to be the wildest part of that property. In many very ordinary suburbs, the result is a series of woody or shrubby corridors that stretch most of the length of a neighborhood and link up with larger, often public wild patches.

Mostly, this happens by accident. If people did it mindfully—

making an effort to restore native ecosystems and maximize the flow of wildness—the result would be that much better. Stein suggests a way of doing this with little or no palaver or prearrangement. Let us suppose you live in a suburb of squarish lots in a region like the eastern United States, which naturally wants to be forest. You preserve or restore a margin of woods and thicket along the back and sides of your property, with as large a patch as possible in one corner. If everyone in the neighborhood does this, the effect is a network of corridors with large nodes at many of the intersections—a suburban version of hedgerows and woodlots. A tiling of the suburban plane, in which each lot is a tile. The more tiles in place, the more complete, beautiful, and useful the pattern.

LAND, COMMUNITY, AND SPRAWL

Ellen Bernstein

H appy new year!

As you know, today is Tu B'Shevat, the fifteenth of the month of Shevat, the trees' new year.

Today I want to talk with you not only about trees but also about the landscape they belong to, their place in our communities, and what our tradition has to say about them.

Trees compose our landscape, and so they make their way into our minds and hearts without our doing anything. We open our eyes and they are there. They are imprinted on our imaginations. Think of times when you let loose and felt the most playful, times

Ellen Bernstein founded Shomrei Adamah/Keepers of the Earth and edited *Ecology & the Jewish Spirit: Where Nature and the Sacred Meet* (Jewish Lights). She is director of community building at the Jewish Federation of Greater Philadelphia. She was a member of Philadelphia's mayoral transition team in 2000, and is a member of the board of the Natural Lands Trust.

when your love was kindled, times when you've had an experience of the spiritual.

I imagine that you associate these moments with special places. Perhaps there was a particular tree there that marks the moment in your memory. Trees are the beginning of art and poetry; they are the symbol of life and renewal.

Composing our landscapes, trees comprise our culture. It's probably not surprising, then, that trees held a special place in the Jewish imagination. They are the symbol of life and sustenance. The Torah is described as a "tree of life" to those who hold her dear; the Garden of Eden is noted for its two trees in the center, the Tree of Life and the Tree of Knowledge of Good and Evil. Significant biblical events are marked by the trees which stood by as witnesses. God appeared to Abraham by the terebinths of Mamre (Gen. 18:1). The greatest biblical love poem, the Song of Songs, is filled with images of trees. So are the psalms. There are trees clapping hands, trees providing food and shelter for all the animals. There are willows, palms, myrtle and *etrog,* whose branches and fruits are required to celebrate Sukkot.

Trees are special in and of themselves, but they were even more significant in the context of the ecosystems of which they are a part. Ezekiel's description of a rebuilt, Edenic Temple gives a magical sense of this rich and diverse ecosystem with trees at the center. His paradisic vision of the Land transformed (Ezek. 47:1–12) included a riparian habitat with gigantic trees growing along the banks. "All kinds of trees for food will grow up on both banks of the stream. Their leaves will not wither and their fruits will not fail; they will yield fruit each month. Their fruit will serve for food and their leaves for healing."

Ecologically speaking, trees are the heart of this paradise ecosystem. They shape the stream, holding the banks in place. They shade the stream, keeping temperatures constant and providing food for fishes and other water creatures. They bind the soil and build the soil. Without trees, the land is subjected to the eroding forces of wind and water. The soil blows away leaving a dry and wasted land, and it runs off into streams causing turbid, murky water, and limiting plant productivity.

In the rabbinic imagination, paradise was associated with trees. The rabbis said that God created paradise on the third day of Creation, the same day God made trees and green growing things. They said that there were eighty myriads of trees in every corner of Paradise and that the Tree of Life had fifteen thousand tastes and it stood in the middle. The rabbinic paradise was the picture of biological diversity.

In our tradition then, trees are evocative of the diversity of life, of the exuberance of life, of the dignity of life. In their verticality, with roots reaching into the depths of the soil and branches stretching towards the sky, trees symbolize the connection of the heaven and earth.

It was not just the trees that evoked a power in Jewish imagination; it was the land itself. The Bible tells us, "For the Lord your God is bringing you into a good land, a land with streams and springs and fountains issuing from plain and hill; a land of wheat and barley, of vines, figs, and pomegranates, a land of olive trees and date syrup, a land where you may eat food without stint, where you will lack nothing."

Land is a central theme of biblical faith. The land is a blessing that God promises our ancestors over and over in return for their faith and adherence to the covenant. God could give no greater gift; nor provide a greater challenge—the people were being asked to live consciously on the land in community; to live an ethical life. The land was never actually the Israelites' to own, because the land belonged to God. The land was not to be sold in perpetuity. The people were not given ownership; rather they were afforded the right to inhabit the land and use it for proper purposes, to live a way of life guided by the covenant.

The land was in a sense alive and the people were expected to treat it sensitively. There was a sense of intimacy with the land. The land took on God's emotions; it laughed and mourned and vomited out and swallowed up.

Keep the covenant and the land would be fruitful and the people would be provided for; violate the covenant and the land would grow dry and barren, and the people would suffer epidemics and invasions, and eventually would lose the land.

I share these images and attitudes with you because I want you to hold on to them as we talk about the most serious environmental problem that confronts Pennsylvania today—that is, suburban sprawl. Throughout Pennsylvania and specifically in Montgomery, Bucks and Chester counties, once rolling farmlands and woodlands—gigantic trees bordering pristine streams—are being gobbled up to make room for what are commonly called McMansions. Such development entails a profound violation of the land and its creatures. It requires bulldozing hundreds of tons of soil, ripping out trees and rerouting streams. It means paving over paradise for highways and parking lots, and developing new water systems, new sewage systems, and new schools. It means taxes going to support the new infrastructure.

It means too many cars on already congested roads, air pollution, and the depletion of precious natural resources. For the last twenty years, Pennsylvania has been losing farmland, forest, and other open space at a rate of one acre an hour, a rate that is second only to Texas, a pace that is twice that of the rest of our nation.

Pennsylvania has lost more than four million acres of farmland since the '50s, an area larger than Connecticut and Rhode Island combined. What's stunning is that while population has only increased by 13 percent since the beginning of the 1960s, land development has increased by 80 percent. In other words, land development is surpassing population growth by six to one. You might expect this kind of sprawling development in Florida and California where population growth has increased by 400 and 600 percent, respectively, but not in Pennsylvania where we've hardly grown at all. What we've done is spend billions of dollars for a new infrastructure to take our existing population of once urban dwellers and spread them around in the exurbs. As industries and jobs and taxpayers and their dollars make the exodus to once rural farmlands, there's less money left to support the cities and the inner ring suburbs.

There are many unspoken tragedies that come in the service of the new subdivisions. The new suburbanites are entirely car-dependent; they have no other option. In terms of air pollution, environmental degradation and global warming, nothing has been more harmful to Pennsylvania's environment in the past 50 years than suburban sprawl. With our dependence on cars, we've forsaken the most energy-efficient system of overland transportation known—that is, the train. While European countries are developing vast networks of high-speed rail and some, like the Swiss, have put a moratorium on the development of highways, in Pennsylvania in the last thirty years we've abandoned 6,000 miles of rail lines.

Water pollution is another consequence of sprawling developments. Vast lawns of industrial parks and acres of blacktop do not drain water effectively, and the water runs off into nearby streams carrying toxic lawn chemicals and soils. Today the Chesapeake Bay, the drainage area for the Susquehanna and all of the streams from our region that feed it, faces ecological extinction. According to the

Chesapeake Bay Foundation, uncontrolled development is the Bay's worst enemy. It is the leading catalyst for pollution in our streams and rivers.

The ability of native plant and animal species to survive is severely threatened with sprawling development as well. You can't make it in this life if your natural habitat is wiped out, and that's what happened to eighty different species of plants and animals in Pennsylvania—we've lost them. Thirty more are threatened by sprawling development.

While our lands are suffering, so is a whole way of life. Though developers call their subdivisions "communities" and give them idyllic names like Thornton's Woods, these are not traditional communities by any stretch of the imagination.

Once we had towns or suburbs like towns, vibrant with shopping districts and streets humming with pedestrians, and children playing in centrally located parks. The physical design of the town itself brought together people of all ages and backgrounds to socialize and share ideas. Residents felt a sense of place, a sense of belonging, a sense of pride in their communities.

Unlike the people-friendly suburbs of the 1920s, in most postwar developments there are no town centers; no Main Streets, no sidewalks, no people out walking, no corner stores, no places to congregate naturally. You have to plan your encounters with people. The exurbs are too often characterized by strip malls, corporate centers, and office parks surrounded by huge expanses of treeless parking lots, which are in turn surrounded by multilane highways. In flattening our landscapes, we're flattening our culture. A pattern of life has evolved that turns us inward, isolating us in our homes and our cars instead of encouraging our communities.

How did we arrive at this place? The problem can be traced in large part to the marketing of the American dream—an image that we have that happiness comes with big homes, bigger lawns, and a three-car garage. Size, privacy, and security seem to be the values that people hold sacred as we enter into the twenty-first century. From 1983 to 1997 the average square footage for privately owned homes has increased by 26 percent in the Northeast.

Government has supported the American dream. For decades after World War II, the Federal Housing Authority and Veterans Administration enthusiastically promoted suburbia at the expense of cities, giving preferential ratings to suburban homes. Federal and state government poured millions of taxpayer dollars into new highways that encouraged industries and people to move out from the cities, yet they spent little on the public transportation that cities depend upon.

Add to this situation the land planning ideas that were fashionable around World War II. The zoning codes of that time required that buildings with different functions be segregated from each other so that homes were in one area, stores in another, factories in another and so on. According to Thomas Hylton, author of *Save Our Lands,* "the traditional character of Pennsylvania towns with narrow streets and small lots and mixtures of homes and stores was basically outlawed." Today, suburban America is designed for cars, not people.

The values that shape our worldview have also shaped our new subdivisions. The aesthetic, spiritual, and environmental value of the trees and land which carry so many layers of meaning in the Jewish tradition have been lost on our world today. We take land and trees for granted. We grow up in the midst of all these riches and we grow accustomed—habituated—to them. Green fields and trees are so common that we think them ordinary.

We approach land and trees as something we can use for our own private satisfaction, rather than as a treasure for the public good. "We treat nature as a toolbox," wrote the great rabbi, Abraham

Joshua Heschel. We have lost touch with the Jewish ideas that the land is good and has value and integrity in and of itself, that land has the potential for holiness if we make it so, and that true riches lie in rejoicing in what we have—our communities, our calendar, a rich and meaningful way of life—not in our acquisitions.

What can we do?

There's nothing that we can do that will help our environment more than staying put in our cities, villages and towns and first-ring suburbs, and cultivating the simple pleasures of walking and talking. We need to make our neighborhoods fashionable again and take pride in them. Jenkintown is a good example of this—the community has just received a $35,000 grant to set up a series of public meetings to talk about reviving the shopping district. We need to become acquainted with the precious natural and historic treasures in our backyards—and invest ourselves in our place.

Urban and suburban blight happens when people get seduced away from what they have; abandoning the old in search of the new; blight happens when people don't care anymore.

Preserving our diverse neighborhoods is consonant with a Jewish way of life; indeed some might say that the preservation of our neighborhoods is essential to the preservation of Jewish life. A Jewish way of life thrives on close-knit neighborhoods, where people can walk to shul and walk to visit their friends and neighbors, where community-building is effortless because people gather together naturally on the streets and on the train and in the park and at public places and in the synagogues.

A Jewish way of life requires us to do *mitzvot* for each other. It calls on us to visit the sick, comfort the bereaved, to open our hearts to those less fortunate, to take care of those in need. It is difficult for us to remember to do *mitzvot* and to teach children to do *mitzvot* when we don't see and feel the need any more, when we live so far away from our neighbors that we're unaware of the goings-on where we live, when all we know is affluence.

From a Jewish perspective, there's plenty you can do here in Elkins Park to make your community an even more wonderful place to live. In addition to the values that our tradition teaches concerning the sanctity of all life, there are specific Jewish laws that require bands of green space to surround cities. According to the Talmud, every city must have around it a ring of green space called a *migrash,* about one-fourth mile where trees and vegetation grow without any help from people. And beyond that was required another one-fourth mile ring just for animals to graze. You can make the idea of a *migrash* a reality in your neighborhood. Join a lands trust or get on local township commissions and lobby for green space. You might call The HighSchool Park—the eleven-acre site that has been transformed into a park within walking distance from here—a kind of contemporary *migrash*—it's a wonderful testament of what concerned citizens can do to make their neighborhoods a better place to live.

You can give *tzedakah* to preserve and beautify your own neighborhood. You can engage your kids in giving *tzedakah* to local environmental causes that they can feel and touch. Take them on field trips to Curtis Arboretum or Awbury Arboretum or High-School Park and the various lands trusts. Let them decide where to give *tzedakah.* You can support the Kehilla of Old York Road, a program initiated by several of the women of this congregation, who were concerned about strengthening this neighborhood and insuring a Jewish future in Elkins Park.

You can plant trees and other growing things. There's a Jewish law that forbids people to live in a town without green growing things and there's the *midrash* that tells us that if you're out planting a tree and you hear that the Messiah is coming, just keep on planting.

You could consider planting native species around the perimeter of your yard and suggesting your neighbors do the same. Once you've established your own green space, you'll find native species of birds and butterflies coming home to roost as well.

You can start a garden at the synagogue and watch the Jewish year come alive. You can grow wheat and harvest it during Shavuot, which was originally the harvest festival for spring wheat. You can have a vegetable garden and gather in the fruits of your labor during Sukkot. (Gourds and grasses make for great sukkah decorations.) I've even heard of people in America growing *etrogim,* but you probably need to be further south for this. A garden also provides an ideal way to help people who are less fortunate than you. You can give the produce to soup kitchens.

There are as many ways to help out our communities and save our natural beauty and the legacy of our lands as there are people in this room. That is up to you. So I recommend that on this New Year's Day you make a commitment to remember that nature matters and to take whatever steps make sense to you to express your caring. I'm sure that as you help to make your community a better place to live, you will feel your own life expand and grow richer.

Transforming Shabbat, the Earth, and the Jewish People

Michael Lerner

The earth needs a Shabbat, so God instituted the Sabbatical Year. "But the seventh year thou shalt let [your land] rest and lie fallow" (Exodus 23:11). Let the earth replenish itself. One year out of seven we have no right to exercise mastery over it. Instead, we will eat whatever the earth puts forth without our intervention or exercise of power over it.

This is not a metaphor.

One year out of seven we should stop working the earth, dedicating this year to replenishment of the earth. The seventh

Rabbi Michael Lerner is the editor of *Tikkun* magazine and the author of *Surplus Powerlessness* and *The Politics of Meaning.* This article is based on ideas further developed in his books *Jewish Renewal: A Path to Healing and Transformation* (HarperCollins, 1996) and *Spirit Matters* (Hampton Road, 2000).

year becomes our joint commitment to working on the ecology of the planet together. The earth needs a rest from all our pollutants and from all of our complicated efforts to master and dominate it.

The result, Torah tells us, will not be mass starvation. The earth will continue to produce food, and we can gather it and distribute it. In fact, during the seventh year it might be a very valuable experience for all those who dwell in cities to spend at least part of the year doing some of that gathering and distribution.

Torah clarifies that the food that is produced in this way does not have any owner—it is *hefker* ("ownerless") and available to everyone. By insisting that the food has no owner, Torah institutes a regular process of reminding us of a truth that today we are reminded of only by earthquakes, floods, and hurricanes—that we are not really in control, that we are really dependent on God for the sustenance that we think *we* have created.

The Sabbatical Year becomes an important instruction to the human race: you don't run things, you are stewards, and you can have power to run your lives only if you do it in accord with the higher purpose that you are here to serve.

Imagine the human race taking off one year out of every seven.

Imagine a society, or even a world, in which everyone would have one year off out of every seven, and for about 85 percent of the population, it would be the same year. Those who wished to participate in the Sabbatical Year would commit themselves to use the time to:

- Immerse themselves in some form of learning (which could include courses designed to provide them with the basic skills to start a whole different profession or life path in the next seven-year cycle, or just be courses on topics that they had always wanted to pursue).

- Participate in community discussions about how to re-structure local communities and the larger society in the coming seven-year cycle.
- Participate in some community service activity.

Time for these activities would be arranged so that at least half of people's time was unstructured and allowed for play, artistic activity, relaxation, reading, meditating, resting, camping, picnics, and fun. Kids would not attend ordinary school but would have other child-oriented activities.

For the 15 percent who had to run essential services (food growing and distribution, energy services, communication services, and health services), there would be a rotating sabbatical over the other six years, plus a guarantee that they could take off the next Sabbatical Year. (We would train personnel who could take their place.)

There would be, of course, a dramatic slowdown in most people's lives. For at least one year, we would forgo some of our frenetic production of goods and services. There would be a worldwide closure of stock markets and investment firms, most government services and activities, and most of the buying and selling in the society.

Implementing this biblical idea would be a powerful reminder that there's more to life than the frenetic accumulation of money and power.

Slowed down in this way, the human race could catch its breath and begin to think seriously about what we have achieved, where we want to go, and what we really value. It would be an opportunity for a spiritual renewal of the entire society. And it would also show us how much of what is being done in this society could be done without—an important step toward reduction of the total amount of production as a way of saving the environment and eliminating needless work.

It will take intense and empowering struggle to get this proposal considered and adopted. On the one hand, people from a wide variety of spiritual approaches will immediately see the importance of the Biblical command for a Sabbatical Year. On the other hand, cynics and technocratic pragmatists will argue that the barbarians would smash the gate, should we try for a moment to stop our furious-paced pursuit of more and more and more.

The debate itself will clarify the real values that people hold, and whether they are willing to begin a planning process for carrying out the Sabbatical Year. (It might take five to ten years of planning after the initial proposal gets societal sanction.)

Of course, we will be surrounded by people who think the very process of imagining such a possibility is inviting the sky to fall in and the earth to collapse beneath our feet. There will be plenty of hysteria.

But I know many city planners, health care professionals, technocrats of every sort, and pragmatic visionaries who believe that this could be made to work in ways that would not lead to a destruction of all the good things we get from contemporary technology (to be spiritual is *not* to be a luddite wishing to destroy all technology), and would not lead to crises in the availability of food, shelter, clothing, health care, energy, transportation, or education.

I believe that this proposal could become a major focus of public debate sometime in the next hundred years, as more people become open to the danger of an earth shattered by material greed and the value of a world shaped by spiritual concerns.

The Sabbatical Year will reduce the total number of goods and services available, a hardship which, if distributed fairly, people would quickly come to accept.

The Sabbatical Year would place a lot of time on our hands, time in which we would be able to reconnect with the earth and with one another. The question of how to organize our society, what goods need to be produced, and how best to provide for the continuation of the planet could be looked into with the seriousness that it needs but does not currently obtain.

The Sabbatical Year will also provide us with an opportunity to rethink what we are doing with our own individual lives and how much we are serving our own understanding of the common good.

Actually carrying out the Sabbatical Year may be generations off. Yet it would certainly make sense for the Jewish renewal movement to paint a picture of what a world might look like that committed itself to this concept, and then struggle to achieve it. The Sabbatical Year provides both a halt to ecological danger and a moment to organize new directions. It is a statement on the part of every person on the planet that we are in this together, that we care about one another and the future of humanity, and that we are dedicating this time to finding ways to take our stewarding responsibility seriously.

It should be noted that a Sabbatical Year would *not* be a revolutionary elimination of capitalism. It would, rather, be a significant restraint on capitalist relations. It would challenge the fundamental ethical basis of ownership, and it would eliminate that ownership for one year, but would not eliminate it permanently. This is a reformist measure. But it would be the kind of reform described by Andre Gorz as a nonreformist reform, because it would increase human beings' total amount of power to struggle for the kind of world in which they want to live, while actually being itself the embodiment of that conquest of power, a massive saying no to all those who tell us that what we must do to be adults or mature or realistic is to spend all of our adult years working.

Revolutionary? No. It's merely renewing the tradition, going back to the sources, taking it from the point when Jews "got" it and understood what was at stake in God's revelation.

But if this was always there in the Jewish tradition, why didn't you know about it? The answer is that the tradition itself turned away from the plain meaning of the text and transformed it to fit the times. Whenever people tell you that some modern is trying to twist the text to fit contemporary needs, just remind them of the way that was done by the mishnaic rabbis who transformed the Sabbatical Year into something much tamer.

The classic step that the rabbis took refers to one of the important concomitants of the Sabbatical Year: the Biblical injunction that all debts should be canceled every seventh year. The elimination of debt was a way of saying to everyone that the ultimate important thing was not our money, but our caring for one another.

But by the time of the Mishnah the Jews no longer lived in that kind of society. They had been conquered, first by the Greek imperialists, then by Romans. Within class-dominated societies, the rule of selfishness always appears to be common sense or human nature. Lenders feared they would lose their money if they made loans to the poor, who might hold off on repaying them till the Sabbatical Year, in which they would be absolved of responsibility. So lenders stopped making loans, and the poor or near-poor suffered. And thus the rabbis who shaped the Mishnah and Gemara backed away from the radical meaning of the Torah text and created a legal fiction, which they called the *prozbul,* an arrangement which allowed loans to be made directly to the court, rather than to another individual, and the court would then lend to the borrower, with the stipulation that loans from the court were not subject to the Sabbatical Year injunction.

The *prozbul* is indicative of the "realistic" accommodation that the rabbis began to make to the world of imperialism and oppression. I raise the issue not to condemn them, but to understand how the spirit of Shabbat and Sabbatical Year could slowly become subverted so that future generations would no longer recall the meaning that these institutions had, a meaning that challenged the world of domination.

Nor should we lose sight of the fact that Jewish law, even while becoming more and more "realistic," has retained its strong commitment to the notion that moral claims of the community supersede any property rights. When private property rights are used in a selfish way, the rabbis believed, they would almost certainly lead to the destruction of the community. They made this point most forcefully by declaring that the sin of Sodom was its inability to share its wealth with the stranger, with the weak, and with the poor, and its insistence on the absolute right of each individual to his own property.

SAVING THE PLANET

The bottom line for saving the planet is this: We need to develop a worldwide plan for how to use the world's resources and how to distribute the world's wealth.

If we let each individual corporation or each country decide how to do this, we will get the following picture: The wealthy countries will buy up the resources of the poorer countries, and buy "rights" to dump the world's garbage there. Those resources will then be shaped into products that can "find a market" in the wealthy countries. On this path lies the exhaustion of the world's resources, the continuing increase of planetary pollution, and the escalating destruction of the ecosystem.

The justification corporations use—that the market shows what people want more effectively than anything else—misses the point that the market has no mechanism for people to show their desire for planetary survival and no mechanism to show their desire for a morally and spiritually grounded universe. The market can show only what choices we support within the logic of limitless consumption: a logic that has caused profligate destruction of the world's resources.

A worldwide plan would have to address what goods we want to have produced, what resources need to be preserved for future generations, what restrictions on production are necessary to protect the environment, and what we can do with our toxic wastes. Such a plan needs coercive power, the product of a serious decision on the part of the entire human race to give priority to saving the planet.

Won't this require a massive change in the way we do business?

Yes, it will. And that's part of the reason why Shabbat and the Sabbatical Year are such important contributions, because they are practical ways of building and reinforcing a new attitude toward the world.

A strategy to save the planet will have to address the question of social justice, just as the Bible did in instituting the Sabbatical Year. We will have to make it in the self-interest of Third World countries to participate, and the only way that can be done is for us to rectify the tremendous imbalances of wealth between the developed and underdeveloped world. In the past, this concern has been framed entirely in terms of justice. But now there is an equally compelling reason: the need to save the planet. If we understand that the future of the human race depends on a whole new orientation to the use of the resources of the world, then we need to create the conditions under which those resources will be wisely used. That will require significant redistribution of the world's wealth so that poverty no longer generates abuse of the environment.

Of course, it would be ridiculous to focus primarily on ecological destruction in the Third World without noting that it is the advanced industrial societies that are responsible for most of the misuse of the world's resources and the bulk of its pollution.

"But," you may object at this point, "surely if people did not choose to purchase environmentally destructive products, the corporations wouldn't produce them. Similarly, if people did not choose to spend hundreds of billions of dollars on wasteful weapons systems or other environmentally hazardous governmental projects, they could elect different representatives, who would choose different priorities. So it's really people's attitudes that have to be changed."

True enough, as far as it goes. And for this reason, Shabbat and the Sabbatical Year become central precisely because they are vehicles for introducing a different kind of consciousness, one that reconnects us with the earth's rhythms and challenges the priority of making, conquering, subduing, shaping the world to our immediate needs. It is from a standpoint of reverence and wonder that we can begin to develop attitudes that would make us put the survival of the planet above other desires.

Yet there is something misleading about the logic of any argument that focuses so much on the need to change individual consciousness without understanding the economic and political realities that daily help shape our choices. Take, for example, one of the heaviest polluters—the automobile. The immense power of the auto and oil industries around the world has been mobilized to block the development of a rational system of mass transportation.

In Los Angeles, for example, a public train system was bought and dismantled by automobile manufacturers so that people would become more dependent on cars. Using their resources to encourage the election of sympathetic legislators, the corporations got government to build a massive highway system. In circumstances such as these, it makes sense for people to choose to live far away from the areas in which they work, and to rely on automobiles to get there. It misses the point to blame the individual consumers for making this choice or to ask them to raise their environmental consciousness. What is needed is systemic change.

But the moment people recognize that those larger changes are needed, they become overwhelmed. Transforming the world economy? Creating a worldwide system of rational planning for use of the world's resources? "It's too big for me to handle," is a typical response. "I have enough trouble keeping my own life together. Let me do what I can do—recycle my garbage or vote for a candidate who says he or she will deal with a few of the worst environmental hazards."

Yet if this larger transformation is necessary to save the planet, then this feeling of powerlessness becomes a major environmental issue. Environmentalists cannot afford to simply address environmental issues—they need to look at the emotional and ideological sources of this sense of powerlessness.

Jewish renewal can be an important ally in this process. Jewish renewal confronts the ideologies of powerlessness and tells us unequivocally: the God that rules the universe is the Force that makes possible the transformation of that which is to that which ought to be. And Shabbat becomes the moment in which we reconnect to that Force.

For these reasons, the environmental movement needs Jewish

renewal, and it needs to learn how to encourage people to become involved in Shabbat.

Jews and Money

Saving the planet cannot be done without a fundamental revision of our attitude toward money. There is nothing intrinsically evil or dirty about money. Money can be used to serve God and to serve the highest goals of our human community.

But there is some problem with the current distribution of money and the ways that those who have disproportionate amounts of it tend to use it. They often hide from themselves any knowledge of how their disproportionate access to money was achieved—at what cost to other human beings.

Traditional Judaism challenged the attitude that people with money have a "right" to use it in any way that they please. Money was always seen as a gift from God, and the possessors had responsibilities to the community, which would govern how it was used. It was these very limitations that the early capitalists sought to overthrow, and their attempts to reform or abandon Judaism were in part motivated by a desire to be free of any such ethical constraints.

Jews can use the economic power available through the Jewish community, and more importantly through individual Jews who have money and who can be influenced by a moral vision projected by a Jewish community committed to healing and repairing the planet.

But even to begin to get to these issues, Jews are going to have to heal some of the pain that they feel around money issues. Jews have been accused of being cheap (though in fact Jews are more generous with their money than most other ethnic communities in the United States when it comes to charitable giving), fixated on making money, and willing to be dishonest or manipulative to secure and retain it. These anti-Semitic stereotypes have made wealthy Jews very reluctant to engage in any serious discussion about the responsibility of money.

Fearful of offending those with money, many progressive Jewish organizations have avoided raising any questions that might potentially suggest conflict with the capitalist market system. Unfortunately, to avoid that issue is also to avoid any serious grappling with saving the planet.

Jewish family funds and foundations have developed a racket in which liberal staffpeople spend their energies making the funders feel good about themselves so that the money keeps flowing. To create that feel-good atmosphere, the staff avoid exposing the donors to projects involved with ideas that might challenge fundamentals, develop society-wide strategies for transformation, or generate radical activism. Instead, the projects that are funded delineate limited areas, avoid "ideology," and are concrete and practical rather than visionary and transformative. So we get a Jewish health center, educational center, or some video project, but what we don't get is funding for strategies aimed at the creation of transformative movements. The funders can feel good that they can see something practical and concrete (the late-twentieth century equivalent to having their names on plaques, or on buildings they helped finance), and everything works fine until someone asks, "Exactly how is all this activity likely to change the fundamental dynamics that have created the problems we are facing?" But since those who ask these kinds of questions get escorted to the door, the racket works just fine. The racket concludes with gatherings in which the fundraisers bring the recipients together with the donors, the donors get lauded for the great work they have been funding, and everyone leaves feeling smug and self-satisfied.

Jewish renewal must challenge these dynamics. It should insist that those with money begin to take their stewardship of the money more seriously. If saving the planet is first on the agenda, then how we transform the market economy is necessarily part of the discussion. And if transforming the market economy is relevant, then how we build a movement that can challenge the ethos of selfishness and me-firstism comes next. And if we talk about trying to challenge the ethos of selfishness, then we must discuss how to challenge the cynicism and defeatism that make most people unwilling to think about attempting to change any fundamental aspects of reality. And this in turn leads to Jewish renewal as one of the venues that gives people hope and faith in the possibility of transforming something fundamental. These are the kinds of issues that would transform Jewish money from a venture in feel-goodism to a force for real healing and transformation.

Recovering the Sensuous through Jewish Ecofeminist Practice

Irene Diamond and David Seidenberg

There is no defense against an open heart and a supple body in dialogue with wildness. Internal strength is an absorption of the external landscape. We are informed by beauty, raw and sensual. Through an erotics of place our sensitivity becomes our sensibility. If we ignore our connection to the land and deny our relationship to the pansexual nature of earth, we will

Irene Diamond teaches in the political science department at the University of Oregon, where she is co-director of the Rockefeller Humanities Fellowship Program, "Ecological Conversations: Gender, Science, and the Sacred." She lives in Eugene, Oregon, with her nine-year-old daughter, Maya Chaya Sarah.

Rabbi David Seidenberg is completing work for a Ph.D. degree in ecology and Kabbalah at the Jewish Theological Seminary, where he was ordained in 1994. A founder of the Hasidic egalitarian minyanim in New York and Los Angeles, and former congregational rabbi in British Columbia, he works on peace and economic justice issues as well as ecology. He teaches and writes in Seattle.

render ourselves impotent as a species. (*An Unspoken Hunger,*
Terry Tempest Williams)

We come to the questions of ecological practice as politically
committed Jews whose passions, and search for truth, tell us that at
this juncture, neither feminist theory nor Jewish theory can rest on
an understanding of humanity, sexuality, or carnality which does not
take account of the life of the planet that nourishes our spirit and
flesh. Like Terry Tempest Williams, we find ourselves compelled to
examine human desiring bodies within the context of the earth.

Our work together is part of a conversation in process in
which we are exploring understandings of human embodiment
through a specifically Jewish sensibility. We believe that such a project is important not only in terms of transforming Judaism but also
in terms of the alternative models it might suggest to the disembodied approach to knowing and being that has prevailed in the West
since the time of Hellenism.

We will suggest that embedded within Judaism is an understanding of sensuous minds that points to a path beyond human/
animal, culture/nature/mind/body dualisms. That's the promise. At
this point in the conversation we'd like for each of us to speak in dialogue with the other, tracing our own individual paths into these
questions.

Irene: As a fairly typical Jewish intellectual for much of my
adult life, I lived through daily practices that had nothing to do with
the intricate Jewish rituals that mark virtually every aspect of bodily
life. My reading and writing was focused on rethinking the feminist
philosophical assumption and political strategy that freedom for
women was to be achieved through gaining control over our bodies. This work was primarily informed by the ecofeminist insistence

on women and men's dependence on the earth and by Michel Foucault's analysis of the operation of power/knowledge in societies governed by the human sciences. In my book *Fertile Ground,* I explored how the production of what I termed the sexuated body through technologies of control diminishes our access to the sensuousness of life.

To the extent that my life had anything to do with the world of ritual, it was through rituals that are a part of ecofeminist political and cultural activities. In my limited and intermittent involvement I found these rituals interesting and meaningful primarily as opportunities for frivolity, camaraderie among humans in the here and now, and tools for creating political unity and effective political strategies. A shift occurred with the passing of my mother, when I found myself immersed in the intricacies of Jewish burial practices.

Suddenly Judaism, with its emphasis on bringing the dead body in direct contact with the earth, appeared to have important ecological traces. I began to see that Judaism was a repository of ritual practices whose character starkly contrasted with those of a dominant culture bent on staving off the decay and withering integral to the cyclical nature of life on earth. This disrupted for me the indigenous/nonindigenous and monotheistic/pagan dualisms that frame much of contemporary ecofeminism.

Something was amiss with the dominant ecological narrative that railed against a so-called "Judeo-Christian" ethic. Attention to the actual Hebrew of the Jewish Bible pointed to an understanding of embodiment and sentience in which body and mind are one and intimately related to and dependent on the elemental force of breath. I discovered an understanding of bodies that was far more corporeal and involved with a sensuous living earth than is commonly understood through the lens of most Hellenistic and Western Christian thought. For example, the body and mind, which are one, are called by the one word *nefesh* in the Torah. These insights led me directly to formulating an idea of "the sensuous mind" in my latest work, a concept which I use to explore the openness of the human body as a disciplined formation of awareness. The sensuous mind is the sensuous body.

Searching for paths for my own grounding, I discovered the Jewish concept of Shabbat, when we let both ourselves and the earth rest while engaging in the sensual pleasures of learning, eating, and sexual play. In the process of immersing myself in Jewish texts and practices I began to see that feminist discourse is primarily focused on the sexed openings of the body. My immersion in Jewish rituals generated an enriched understanding of the many ways human bodies open to the world—the diverse creatures, plants, and elemental forces that nourish all flesh. I learned to pause for blessings for eating foods that came from the ground and those that came from trees, for the wonder of a rainbow, for hearing thunder, and, most amazingly, even for the proper opening and closing of the holes that allow for elimination. What I had written about as the limitations of the sexuated body standardized by genital sex became grounded in a set of practices in which my body was palpably connected to the earth.

Looking back, I would now argue that Foucault's account of how sex became the truth of ourselves is inadequate because it is derived primarily from an analysis of human institutions vis-à-vis human bodies. His polemics are directed at the human sciences; he takes little note of how new models of the natural world in the physical and biological sciences had rendered the earth into an inert machine, a process ecofeminism has sometimes described as "the death of nature."

Foucault's analysis only pertains to shifting inscriptions on bodies understood as surfaces. If however we understand human bodies as constituted by a multitude of openings that provide for orientation, pleasure, and communion with the life-world, then the intensified focus on the specifically gendered openings of human bodies which Foucault analyzes must be understood to have resulted in a deprivation of opening or awareness of the nonhuman natural world, in effect diminishing the body and not just reinscribing its surface.

Foucault's short-sightedness with respect to the natural world is recapitulated in most feminist critiques of gender. Contemporary feminism has surely complicated our understanding of bodies and human desire in profound ways. However, between the prevalence on the one hand of poststructuralist theorizing that undermines any truth of the body, and on the other hand the popularity of Catharine MacKinnon's radical feminist science of domination which reifies sexual desire, the central debates of feminist theory have little to say about the vitally important relations between body and earth. For example, when Judith Butler writes that "gendering is, among other things, the differentiating relations by which speaking subjects come into being" (*Gender Trouble,* p. 7) the speaking subjects to which she refers are clearly human subjects, and gender emerges strictly from a constructing of human differences.

Ecofeminist theory and practice is one of the most important places where such ideas about the body are challenged. Simply put, it is not just human relationships that enable us to become aware, speaking, consciously alive subjects, but our relationships with all beings and all dimensions of being. While feminism in general regards gender, sex, standpoint, and embodiment from within a strictly human context, ecological theory suggests a much broader context. For example, Carol Bigwood and David Abram both focus on Merleau-Ponty's phenomenology of the body in order to map out new directions in feminism and ecology which would allow us to understand sensuous embodiment and go beyond the idea of the body as a self-enclosed container. For Bigwood, "The phenomeno-logical body is not fixed but continually emerges anew out of ever-changing weave of relations to earth and sky, things, tasks, and other bodies. The living world . . . is not merely external to the body. The world-earth-home is the ever-present horizon latent in all our experiences" (*Earth Muse,* p. 51).

David Abram expresses a similar idea when he writes,

[T]he boundaries of the body are open and indeterminate; more like membranes than barriers, they define a surface of metamorphosis and exchange. The breathing, sensing body draws its sustenance and its very substance from the soils, plants, and elements that surround it; it continually contributes itself, in turn, to the air, to the composting earth, to the nour-ishment of insects and oak trees and squirrels, ceaselessly spreading out of itself as well as breathing the world into itself, so that it is very difficult to discern, at any moment precisely where this living body begins and ends. (*The Spell of the Sensu-ous,* p. 46)

David: I'd like to flesh out what this means by using one ex-ample: the ritual of living in a booth during the fall harvest festival called Sukkot. Traditionally Jews construct a simple booth, called a sukkah, which we live in for seven days starting with the seventh full moon after Passover. This ritual is done in remembrance of two things: that the Jewish people wandered through the desert living in temporary shelters for forty years, and that the "roof" which pro-tected them during their wandering was the presence of God or Shekhinah in the form of "clouds of glory."

The practice of constructing a sukkah with a roof of leaves or branches on the full moon after Yom Kippur, a place where we eat, sometimes sleep, and even make love, is a lesson in creating a sense of place:

- Two-and-a-half or three or almost four walls (minus the door).
- The space under the roof, big enough to cover "a person's head and most of the body," because the sukkah is like a body.
- The roof itself, precisely defined as one which is more shade than light, without a gap larger than a hand's breadth, but through which one can see stars.

The sukkah is a precise physical form for the way we sense the world, through a latticework of sense and interpretation, through openness and limitation, through the "interweaving" of the senses. The profound depth of this ritual, like all rituals, is found in the physical experience of it, sharing meals with friends, watching the moon through the leaves, feeling both protected and open to the world. And finally, this framework of a body, like all bodies, must break down, turn back to its parts.

To dwell in a sukkah with this openness of body and mind is to experience real joy. Halakhah in an ideal sense then becomes a tool which guarantees the intersubjective depth of each ritual by precisely defining what must be experienced: a sukkah must embrace the earth, its walls must reach down to the ground and up to the roof, and its roof must be made of living things cut from the ground. These definitions teach us to bind the inside and the outside, the internal and the external, the physical and the spiritual, the sensible and the sensual.

Such a phenomenological understanding of Jewish ritual is not foreign to the tradition. For example, the sukkah is interpreted as an

expression of God's own reaching by the Hasidic Rebbe Meshulam
Feivush, Rebbe of Munkatch. He writes:

> Embrace is hinted at in the sukkah: Just as a person embraces
> his child in love, encircling him with his arms, and sheltering
> him with his head, so here for the arm there are the two [walls
> according to] their rule/halakhah, plus a third [wall at least as
> wide as a] handbreadth, and the third, the handbreadth, is the
> hand, and all of it is a parable for the situation of being em-
> braced, [i.e.] our being drawn near to Hashem in joy and pu-
> rity. (*Yosher Divray Emet*, p. 36a, sec. 57)

The sukkah becomes an incarnating of God's presence shelter-
ing each of us, because it manifests this moment of ingathering of
sense and meaning and smell and sight, earth and wind and starlight,
which is the embrace of our consciousness and sense of home and
self. The sukkah captures and manifests the interfacing of body and
earth, divinity and history, creation and redemption.

Irene and I are collaborating as Jews and not just as theorists.
We know that there are many other paths besides Judaism which
may teach the discipline of a sensuous relationship to the world.
However, Judaism is privileged for us by arbitrary facts of birth,
family, and culture. Furthermore, it is these very elements of identity, history, and place which constitute the ethos and eros of being.

In Judaism, from a liberal perspective or anthropological perspective, it is clear that sacredness is constructed by ritual actions
which mark the sacred as different from the common. Each time we
learn Torah sacredly, we reinscribe the text as sacred and at the same
time create new openings in the text for sacredness. Each time we
withdraw from creating on Shabbat, we create the possibility for re-
visioning the world on new terms, outside the law of labor and
production.

This is not so different from what Butler calls "performativity." She writes, "Performativity is thus not a singular 'act,' for it is always a reiteration of a norm or set of norms . . . " (*Gender Trouble,* p. 12). But where for Butler such an act is simply a repetition which deceptively conceals its conventions, within a living ritual system an act which repeats norms can also create meaning. An act of ritual can therefore become a transformative way of knowing and constituting knowledge. More than this, the nature of learning and knowing as constituted by Jewish ritual practices is one which completely circumvents the usual binary construction of rationality which is of such great concern for feminism.

The physicality of ritual provides a kind of screen or vortex through which divinity, humanity, and nature are drawn into a single embodiment. The phenomenology of ritual can help us understand something about the nature of our consciousness and self. Rituals in Judaism are firstly physical, not spiritual; moments of awareness, rather than ideas. Ritual can teach us to open our thinking to this intertwining, to think "sensuously." If our body is destined to the world, then somehow we can understand the world through our bodies. The human body, as we have understood it, is really a form for awareness, a form which connects rather than contains. We open out to touch other creatures, other forms, and most importantly, the earth itself.

For us in a Jewish context, ritual has been one of the primary ways we encounter the opening of the body. It is only because we are animals, "packaged" to move, as it were, that we don't normally see all our fractal branching, that our bodies appear to be smooth and rounded surfaces. Every surface of the body, despite its apparent smoothness, is also a branching out, an extension of the senses, of breath and sweat and fluid, a casting out upon the world beyond the apparent boundary it represents. It is this openness, and our ability to reflect on this openness through the gift of insight and imagination, which allows us to see the infinity which unfolds within the finite. Ritual, along with science and simple meditation, is among the many ways we begin to see and continue to see the wonder of what we call nature.

Irene: We cannot enter into this discussion without acknowledging that Judaism is a tradition whose sensuality has been arbitrarily gendered according to the needs of men. Even on the most basic level, David's body is marked as a Jewish body because it has been cut ritually as part of a covenant. But my female body is not Jewishly marked. Even though only the body of a Jewish woman traditionally has the power to pass on tribal peoplehood, the covenant itself is carried out through men acting on male bodies through the ritual obligation of circumcision.

Therein lies much of the challenge for Jewish ecofeminist practice. As feminism reclaims the fullness of Jewish ritual for men and women, it awakens the possibility of a Jewish body which gives both female and male bodies their full due, but at the same time it risks the possibility of rendering the body neutered, de-gendered. How will we evolve a Jewish culture which affirms both species-being and gender-being? It is our belief that this can happen through connecting to the sacredness of life and the land; through a practice which acknowledges and gives meaning to sexedness without essentializing or codifying this meaning.

As Jews confront this dilemma which we inherited from our ancestors, we are also confronted with radical accusations about Judaism which come from outside of our experience as Jews: Among both feminists and ecological thinkers, Judaism is understood to have killed the Goddess, to have created in monotheism the foundation for patriarchy's domination over both women and the land.

This line of reasoning mimics the accusations made against Jews of being "Christ-killers." It is used by some Christian feminists to pardon Christianity or Greco-Roman culture for their patriarchal imperialism. In fact, it would be easy enough to shrug off the charge, since we know that, historically, Judaism evolved in the shadow of patriarchal polytheistic cultures; the matriarchal religions had already died out or been subverted. Nonetheless, it is true that Judaism under Greek and later Christian influence rejected the biblical conception of living nature and intensified the biblical subjugation of women.

Exile and persecutions led much of European Jewish culture more and more deeply into the written text and away from the sensuousness of the natural world. However, it was through the inner dynamics of rabbinic cultures in which the "textuated body" became synonymous with the sexuated male body that sacred learning became the domain of men. Learning became extraordinarily eroticized and sensual, equaling sexuality in both pleasure and sacredness.

David: This sensuousness, the sensuousness of minds and bodies, was saved in a kind of coded form. In the twentieth century as learning has become opened up to women as well as men it continues to be forged and reforged as sacred and sensual. But the code itself must be radically invigorated and transformed. Jewishly informed ecofeminist insights and teachings are particularly important in this regard. One might say that the code must be decoded, unraveled, and rewoven. The ritual of *mikveh* provides a particularly stark example.

The rituals concerning fertility and sexuality, especially *mikveh,* the immersion in "living water," are among the most difficult for many liberal Jews. Yet these rituals have the potential to bring the most powerful transformation. A *mikveh* is a "gathering" of "living waters," waters which flow from a spring or river, or from the ocean, or which are gathered directly by rainfall. *Mikveh* water must always be flowing in and out, it cannot be left standing; in other words, it must be connected to the cycle which joins water to the intimate process of life, evolution, and birth.

Immersion, in which every surface of the body must come in simultaneous contact with the water, returns a person to a state of bodily wholeness by connecting to the flow which began at creation. Our texts teach about an ancient ritual which was in constant use by men and women to help them cope with the disruption of the body through normal contact with life processes in the world. Centuries of practice, however, have confined the ritual of immersion to a process for making women sexually available to their husbands after menstruation. The physical state which brings a woman to the *mikveh* is associated with sin and impurity by the Prophets, and by normative strands of rabbinic and medieval Jewish culture.

Irene: This gender difference in ritual practice happens to correspond with most modern models of sexuality, which portray fertility as primarily a concern of women's bodies and interiors and male ejaculation as a straightforward machine-like process. The idea of the male body as an hydraulic machine accepts male seed as inert, lifeless, and therefore full expendable. From an ecofeminist perspective, we can easily see this as a deprivation of sensuousness and aliveness to the body. Biblical stories and rabbinic injunctions against the spilling of seed could help us to complicate the idea of male sexuality, but in cultural contexts where the fullness of human sensuality has atrophied and the sexuated body permeates consciousness, the notion of not wasting seed as one would not waste any element of life is associated with an increase in sexual fear rather than an increase in sensuality.

It is important to remember here that the *mikveh* ritual was once applied to both men and women after contact with either semen or menses. If men were to reclaim the *mikveh* as a ritual for restoring their relationship to fertility, it could help Jewish culture to go beyond a drive model for male sexuality, freeing men and women to experience fertility as a divine blessing which encompasses both male and female.

This cannot happen as long as the *mikveh* ritual is carried out exclusively under the determinations of medieval halakhah. It is the same halakhah that guarantees the profound integrity of other rituals like sukkah which also guarantees that women's bodies will oscillate between the categories of permitted and forbidden, depending on a woman's going to the *mikveh,* and that a male body, once circumcised, is forever covenanted with God. So we are confronted with a ritual that has great potential to teach ecological wisdom, but only when the Jewish people develop the courage to transform the way it is "supposed" to be practiced.

A Jewish feminist practice which does not embrace ecology would seem to have only a slim possibility of achieving this. And yet the teaching of the body in this ritual, the body in contact with waters whose course traces back to the first tide, the first upwelling, is one of the most profound.

David: One is perhaps reminded of Foucault's ideas about micro-resistance to regimes of surveillance. But it is acts of resistance to the constant onslaught of technology and labor, of modernity and machine, which he contemplates. In this Judaism has the most powerful ritual, the ritual of not-doing, the Sabbath which we will enter into later today as the sun sets on another seven days. On the mythical level, Judaism commands the celebration of creation, every single week. It is one of the few particularistic Jewish rituals which has been adopted by numerous Christian sects, the only ritual law to take a place among the Ten Commandments, perhaps the only Jewish ritual that has universal significance.

The Sabbath is in fact one of the few rituals whose letter, though enormous in weight, elaborateness, and complication, cannot overcome its spirit. The Sabbath has been extolled rhetorically perhaps too often; no better panegyric exists than the simple contemplation which can come with the discipline of resting. It is this dimension of discipline which escapes so many modern Jews, who interpret rest as "relaxation" and so pursue television, shopping, and such on Shabbat if they take the time to consider it.

But the discipline of rest requires more than this: it is the discipline of refraining from human manipulation, of relinquishing the powers we accumulate through culture and human endeavor, even when it does not bring pleasure.

This brings us to the heart of the difference between being pleased by things, and contemplating the world which grants them. On Shabbat, Judaism commands that we give up the powers which make us seem so different from the other animals. This means two things: we become more like the other animals, who don't bake bread, build fire, plow fields, etc., and we become more like God, who rested after the first week of creation.

On the mythical tribal level, we allow the hierarchies which divide the theistic world to lapse, we set a limit on expansion, acquisition, aggression, domination. It seems not to be enough to prevent the destruction of the natural world of human activity, nor to prevent the retreat of humans into an artificial life-world which doesn't acknowledge the sources of civilization in nature. But if even the Sabbath is not sufficient, we cannot let the simple act of resting be beyond reach, if we are to believe in the possibility of stopping or changing the course of human development.

Shabbat and all of our other rituals of ecological righteousness, like tree planting or recycling, can't mean much if they don't change the way we live in the rest of our lives. According to the Jewish tradition, what is forbidden on the Sabbath is the work necessary to build the Tabernacle, the structure which manifested God's presence in the world. The implication is that all of our work during the rest of the week should be devoted to holiness. According to common interpretation, the Tabernacle in the desert was not just a site for ritual sacrifice, but a pattern of human activity which reproduced the structure of creation. This same Tabernacle was said not just to be patterned after creation, but to have achieved consciousness upon the completion of the first sacrifices and the lighting of the menorah—the consciousness of creation itself.

I'd like us to recognize in these interpretations not just nice sermons or ancient legends, but a practical tribal wisdom about preserving the sacredness of the world amidst all the busy upheaval of human action. Even in the contemporary practice of rituals, such as *mikveh,* there is a deep echo and trace of a wisdom about connecting to the sacred living body of the world.

To say this is to speak in parables, as it were, yet many of us believe that we must turn to exactly this kind of knowledge, which is commonly termed "indigenous," in order to chart a different path for Western and human civilization.

The Jewish people stand between being indigenous and being without a home, between sharing the ancient roots of nomadic herdsman and embracing modern industrial society, between spreading universalist ideas of truth and preserving a particular tribal knowledge of the world. Perhaps someday we, or some other people, may find within the wisdom encoded by ancient rituals and laws a language for revivifying the connnectedness with each land that must have been the starting point for every culture. Such a turn would likely endure if accompanied by the opening up of cultural wisdom which comes by looking at things, customs, relationships, through a sensuous mind that knowingly lives in the embrace of nonhuman creatures and the more-than-human world. We believe that ritual can be a teacher of this sensuousness.

Irene: The sensuous mind is none other than the sensuous body aware of what Terry Tempest Williams called "the pansexual nature of earth." We recognize it when we exert internal self-discipline in what we take from the bounty of the world and from our passion for another person. We recognize it in an awareness of the future; in seeking to balance desires of the moment with an awareness of the needs and desires of other creatures and other times; in taking pleasure in the discipline of simply being rather than needing to transcend; in loving the discipline of learning. The writer Grace Paley said, "It is essential to love the natural world before you can understand it." We submit that discipline, rigor, joy, fertility, loss, and the willingness to experience these through the matrix of ritual and cultural inheritance are critical components of this love.

Can the restraint, withdrawal and disciplining of human needs inspired by ecological questions or demanded by ritual obligations restore what has been deprived or destroyed in a world where we share neither one cultural history nor one set of cultural practices?

AND THE EARTH IS FILLED
WITH THE BREATH OF LIFE

Arthur Waskow

T he wisdom of the Jewish people alone cannot heal the earth,
but there are unique wisdoms and unique energies that we
can bring to this healing. In doing so, we can renew the deepest and
most powerful energy of Judaism, energy that has been embanked
and hidden so long that we have forgotten it's there. In the ensuing
coolness we have ourselves cooled to large areas of Torah that can
reawaken to us if we can dis-cover them, get the coverings off.

In the deepest origins of Jewish life, the most sacred relationship was the relationship with the earth. Ancient Israel got in touch

Rabbi Arthur Waskow founded and is director of The Shalom Center and is a
Pathfinder of ALEPH: Alliance for Jewish Renewal. He is co-editor of *Trees, Earth, and
Torah: A Tu B'Shvat Anthology* (Jewish Publication Society). His other books include
*The Freedom Seder; Godwrestling; Seasons of Our Joy; Down-to-Earth Judaism: Food, Money,
Sex, and the Rest of Life;* and *Godwrestling—Round Two: Ancient Wisdom, Future Paths*
(Jewish Lights), winner of the Benjamin Franklin Award.

with God by bringing food to the Holy Temple. We use an abstract term to describe this, the "sacrificial system," but it was food—all the foods of the Land of Israel. And so we affirmed, not in words but with our bodies, "We didn't invent this food; it came from a Unity of which we are a part. The earth, the rain, the sun, the seed, and our work—together, *adam* and *adamah,* the earth and human earthlings, grew this food. It came from the Unity of Life; so we give back some of it to that great Unity."

Through food and with the earth, not through words, was how biblical Jews got in touch with God. And in turn there was a way of relating to the earth that was not working the earth, or making the earth work, but resting with the earth. The tradition affirmed the earth's restfulness and the restfulness of human beings in relation to the earth. Not only the seventh-day Shabbat but the *shmitah* year, the sabbatical year. Every seventh year the earth was entitled to rest and the human community that worked the earth was obligated to rest as well.

Shabbat—not only the Sabbath day but also the sabbatical year—was one of the most powerful ways in which the community affirmed the Unity of all. That rhythm of work and rest, and that affirmation of what connects *adam* and *adamah,* the humans and the humus, the earth and the earthlings, affirmed that we live in a world of All, a world of joyfulness, spiritually together. There really was a down-to-earth Judaism.

The question is, What does it mean to us, who have lived through the Diaspora experience? It is not that we have lived only in cities—there were Jewish farmers—but that we have had a limited share of the responsibility for dealing with the earth, because we were usually not in a position of power to shape the economic or environmental policy of the communities we lived in.

What does it mean for us living in the Diaspora now? We live

262

in a modernity in which the human race has created technology and a work system that is the most brilliant act of work in all of human history—new forms of controlling the earth, dominating the earth, making, doing, inventing. We have already affected the planet in ways no human beings ever have before. We have changed the biology and chemistry of the planet. The last commensurate level of change came from a great meteor strike 65 million years ago. Now one of the earth's own species, one that evolved with the technological ability, the intellectual ability, and the consciousness to review and improve its own work, has taken so much power into its own hands as to affect the entire planet.

We must strive to understand what this means for us. We must open ourselves to the larger meaning of this event: Why is this happening to us? And we must also seek to invoke the wisdom of the landed people—shepherds, farmers, and tree-keepers—that we were a couple of thousand years ago.

First, my own thoughts on how to think Jewishly about why this is happening to us. Some Kabbalists have taught that an Infinite and Utterly unfettered God, One Who encompassed all that was and wasn't, is and isn't, contracted inward in order to leave space for a universe to emerge. But in that empty space, what was the seed of the world? It was the "left-overs" of God, the thin film, as it were, of olive oil that is left within a vessel when one pours the oil out. It was this thin film of God that grew and grew, appearing as the universe—itself indeed the universe, God disguised by folds of God into seeming something other than God. And this aspect of God grows toward revealing Itself, toward mirroring the Infinite Beyond.

This growth, this process of self-revelation and self-mirroring of the God Whose Name is Ehyeh Asher Ehyeh, "I Will Be Who I Will Be," makes up all that we may see of evolution and history. This growth appears to us as a double spiral.

In one spiral, growing self-awareness is used in the service of greater efficiency at controlling the surrounding universe—greater power.

In the other spiral, growing self-awareness is turned toward creating deeper love, broader connection.

In one spiral, my I eyes what I have just done, to do it more effectively.

In the other spiral, my I eyes the face of an Other and sees within it my own face, sees within its differentness my own uniqueness, and so can love my neighbor as deeply as my Self.

These two spirals were rooted in the living universe long before there emerged what we call life, or humankind. What we call life, and then what we call humankind, are themselves leaps forward in both spirals—the one that is more efficient, and the one that is more loving.

The two spirals are not independent of each other. They are intertwined. What Martin Buber called I–It intertwined with I–Thou. One spiral of more Doing intertwined with one of deeper Being.

Each of these comes into the world as a step in the journey of the world to become more and more a Mirror for God, more and more a fully aware being, ever more fully aware of its own Unity.

What makes each of them a spiral is the other. As each moves forward in what might have been a straight line, it reaches a point of impending self-destruction that calls forth the other into vigor. Each curve forward in the one spiral calls for a curve forward in the other. An increase in efficiency unaccompanied by any increase in a sense of connection threatens that the more efficient being will gobble up its own nurturing environment—and ultimately find itself without nourishment—unless it learns to become part of a larger whole, a deeper, fuller community. Whether the being is a proto-protein hmmming in a sweet and early sea, or an amoeba devouring all the sugar-water in the neighborhood, or a global human civilization using up all the space in which other species can survive, the discipline of learning to love, to connect—or to die—is very strict.

And the creation of a new level of community—a multi-celled creature at one level of this double spiral; at another level, a society that understands it is part of a larger, richer habitat in which grow other species—the achievement of this new level creates the context for another leap forward in efficiency and power.

One of these spirals—the one in which self-awareness gives a being the ability to "look" at its techniques for acquisition, see its shortcomings, imagine a more effective solution, and make it happen—is the "competitive natural selection" aspect of evolution. The mistake of social Darwinists is to see this as the only aspect of evolution, ignoring the I–Thou spiral.

The emergence of life was one enormous leap forward in the ability of aspects of the universe to understand and control, and then of these same aspects to pause, reflect, love, and be self-aware.

The emergence of the human race was another such great step. For the universe to continue on this journey toward self-awareness, there needs to be a species capable of self-awareness—made up of individuals who can reflect upon their own selves, and also able as a species to reflect upon itself and to see itself as part of the Unity of the universe—on which it is also capable of reflecting. That is what it means to live in the Image of God—to reflect upon the Unity, and thus to mirror God's Own Self. Among the species on this planet, the human race so far bears this Image of God—the self-awareness of Unity—most fully. That does not mean that other beings have no share in this Image, nor does it mean that the unfolding of the Image stops with us.

And within human history, the pastoral and agricultural revolutions were further leaps forward in accessing the Divine attributes of power. Each meant that human beings were able to hold and use powers that previously had been held only by Divine "outsiders"—gods, spirits, God. Each meant that some aspect of Divine power became more available to human hands. And in response to each, human beings created new forms of connective community, intended to cradle the new energy of doing in new forms of loving.

And so the thin film of God that became the universe revealed Itself more and more fully, as the universe grew toward mirroring the Infinite.

And on each of these occasions, a leap forward in power and control had to be followed by a broadening of love and a deepening of self-aware reflection. Otherwise the new intensity of power would have swallowed up the world. And each growth of broader community gave the context and the impetus for another leap forward on the Doing, Making, I–It spiral. Thus the double spiral continues.

The agricultural revolution was one such turn on the Doing, I–It spiral—and it required the emergence of biblical Israel, Buddhism, and the other great ancient traditions on the Being, I–Thou spiral. From this perspective, some scholars have suggested that what we know as Torah was the response of a community that had been gatherers and shepherds to an encroaching agricultural empire, Babylonia, and the attempt of Israelites to absorb and limit the new imperial agriculture. Thus the Garden of Eden and the tale of Cain and Abel are seen as a mythic portrayal of this leap in knowledge and its tragic aspects of alienation from the earth and from each other—a leap repeated again and again in human history since.

From this perspective, the Sabbath and the sabbatical year are ways of limiting the engulfment of the new agriculture: limiting its imperial destructiveness of Doing by pausing to become gatherers and shepherds again, pausing to love and to Be.

Another great turn on the Doing, I–It spiral came when Hellenism brought a more powerful form of economics, science, politics, and war to the Mediterranean Basin. This leap shattered biblical Judaism as well as other traditional cultural and religious forms. The I–Thou response was the creation of Rabbinic Judaism, Christianity, and Islam.

In the last several hundred years, we have been living through another such leap forward in the I–It powers of the human race. This leap is what we call modernity. It is by far the greatest of these leaps, for it brings the human race into the arena in which it is transforming the very web of planetary life from which it sprang.

That we would reach this point was probably inevitable. For to be capable of self-aware life inevitably also means to be capable of creating the technology that can wreck the planet. Human social history is simply incomparably swifter than biological evolution at applying self-awareness to technological improvement—so swift that it reaches the asymptote of possible self-destruction.

That swiftness, to some extent throughout human history but with utter urgency today, gives the human race a mandate unique among all species: to act as if it were a steward for the planet. If we fail in this task, the planet's ruination will take us with it. In that sense, we are strange stewards and the "steward" model is not fully adequate, for we remain partially embedded in the earth we steward.

Today, what is the alternative to ruination? It is another curve forward on the spiral of Being, Loving, I–Thouing. It is the renewal and transformation of Judaism, Christianity, Islam, Buddhism, Hinduism, the spiritual traditions of all indigenous peoples—a renewal and transformation that can deepen each tradition in its own uniqueness while broadening the circle of love it can encompass. It is the bringing of restfulness and reflectiveness to a deeper level, just as work has been brought by modernity to a higher level. It is extending our love to the whole of the earth of which we are a part, without denying our uniqueness in its web of life.

Now that we live in the era of high-tech industrialism, and are not shepherds or farmers or orchardists in the ordinary sense, we must learn to be shepherds, or farmers or tree-keepers again in a different sense. For shepherds, farmers, and orchardists know you must not exhaust the earth you live on. If you're a shepherd and you let the sheep eat all the grass in one year, the sheep may be fatter and the wool thicker, but you're finished off. And farmers, vintners, and tree-keepers learn the same thing.

What does this mean for us who have forgotten it, in the wild rush of making, doing, inventing, producing over the last couple of hundred years? What does it mean for us to renew that shepherds' wisdom, the wisdom which knew that consuming what comes from the earth is a central sacred act, is a way of being in touch with God? What would it mean for us to renew that wisdom?

I want to imagine a new version of the Jewish people—a new way of understanding and shaping ourselves. Imagine that we were to decide to see ourselves as having a mission, a purpose on the earth. A purpose to heal the earth—one that is not brand new but is described in the Torah as one of the great purposes of the Jewish people.

What does it mean that Shabbat is a symbol, a sign between the God of the universe and "His" once whole people? The Shabbat of Sinai comes in two different guises. In Exodus, we hear it as the moment when our restfulness connects us with the cosmic resting that imbues all of creation. In Deuteronomy, Shabbat renews the liberation of human beings and the earth. And there is also the Shabbat that comes before Sinai—the Shabbat that comes with the manna in the Wilderness, betokening our free and unlabored reconnection with the earth. This Shabbat betokens the peace agreement ending the primordial war between ourselves and earth which began as we left Eden—which came from a misdeed of eating and brought us painful toil and turmoil in our eating.

What would it mean for us to renew the sense that deep in our very covenant, deep in our covenant-sign Shabbat, is the call to be healers of the earth?

Imagine the Jewish people as a kind of transgenerational, transnational "movement," committed for seven generations, from one generation to the next and beyond, to transmit the wisdom and the practice that can heal the earth. Imagine a people that can reach out to others and can encourage others, work with others, to do that.

I want to suggest four dimensions of a Jewish people through which we could be pursuing that mission to heal the earth. These four dimensions correspond to the four worlds through which our Kabbalists, our mystics, saw Creation.

One dimension is the explicit celebration of the Spirit through the rituals, the ceremonies, the symbols of celebration that we use to get in touch with the One. Look, for example, at the second paragraph of the *Sh'ma,* the one that says, "And if you act on Torah then the rain will fall, the rivers will run, and the earth will be fruitful and you will live well. And if you don't act on Torah, if you reject it, if you cut yourself off from this great harmony of earth, then the great harmony will cease to be harmony and will cut itself off from you, and the rains won't fall [or, I would say, they will turn to acid], and the rivers won't run [or they and the oceans will flood], and the sky itself will become your enemy [as in the shattering of the ozone layer or the fouling of the atmosphere with too much carbon dioxide], and you will perish from all this good *adamah* that you grew up with."

Today we can see this as a searing truth. Yet in many of our synagogues and havurot this passage is said in an undertone or even omitted. What would it mean for us to elevate it to a central place in our liturgy, and perhaps every four weeks or so, perhaps on the Shabbat before the new moon or the Shabbat before the full moon, to read it with a fanfare: to remind ourselves that we are part of the web of life, its most conscious part, the part most aware of the Wholeness of which we and all the rest are part—but still a part of the web, endangered whenever we bring danger on the web?

We need to focus on the second paragraph of the *Sh'ma*. By racing through it, we race through a central place of our celebration and a central place in our lives; we blind ourselves to the world around us, racing through a wonderful ecosystem without pausing to see its rich intertwining.

Let me take another example. I wrote a piece that appeared in several American Jewish newspapers in the early 1990s. It began with a fantasy.

One day in the fall, all over North America, tens of thousands of Native Americans show up at the edge of rivers everywhere. They are carrying a sacred object of their own tradition, and they are also carrying willow branches. They dance seven times around their sacred symbol; they beat the willow branches on the earth; and they invoke the Holy Spirit and ask for help to heal the planet from plague and disaster and drought.

It would be on the front pages of every American newspaper and on the evening news of every television network. Everywhere students on college campuses would be demanding courses on Native American spirituality. And members of Congress and presidents of corporations would be bombarded by letters, "Something's wrong with the rivers, what are you doing about it?"

Now imagine a different fantasy—that it wasn't tens of thousands of Native Americans, but tens of thousands of American Jews who showed up on this day in the fall. Their sacred object was the Torah, and they danced around it seven times and they beat willow branches on the earth, and they prayed in English and Hebrew for the YHWH, the Breath of Life, to help them heal the earth. They too appeared on television, and they too led demands that Congress and the corporations heal the earth.

What would many of our present Jewish leaders say?—Probably, I thought, "This is primitive, this is pagan, this is radical, this is un-Jewish!"

Yet what I have just described is at the end of most traditional Jewish prayer books, because it's a description of the seventh day of Sukkot, Hoshanah Rabbah. But we don't do it anymore, we certainly don't do it that way. A few people in some traditional synagogues will gather in a small chapel and beat willow branches on the rug. Nobody ever hears about it. And they say the words of prayer to heal the earth, but they don't connect the words with any act that might be done.

Look at the prayer books, however. Look up Hoshanah Rabbah, the seventh day of the festival of Sukkot, and look at the words of "Hosha na." "Hosha na" got transliterated into the rather meaningless English word "hosanna"—it actually means "Please save us." Right there: "Save the earth, save us!" And read the words of these prayers, for many of them name the dangers that face the earth and plead with the Breath of all Life to save the earth from plague and drought. One of them ends, "Save the earth—suspended in space."

In 1998, The Shalom Center gathered about 250 Jews and 50 people from other spiritual traditions—a leader of the Lakota Nation, Catholic nuns, Pete Seeger—at the banks of the Hudson River in Beacon, New York. And on the seventh day of Sukkot, we celebrated Hoshanah Rabbah. We danced the seven dances with great bright banners, each in one of the colors of the rainbow, keyed to the seven days of Creation. We chanted "Hosha na," some in ancient Hebrew and some in English, newly written. One of the prayers we broke into, verse by verse, with shouted headlines about the pollution of the Hudson by the General Electric Corporation. Broken world, broken prayer. And as part of the liturgy, we signed petitions demanding that GE clean up the damage it had done. Ancient form, made profoundly new. Its deepest meaning, unchanged.

Those are just two examples; the tradition is rich with possibilities.

Our whole festival cycle, after all, is attuned to the rhythms of the earth. Let us imagine it alive with earth again:

- On Tu B'Shvat, the festive New Year of the Trees that comes at the full moon of deep winter, we can plant the trees that together make up the Tree of Life. (One year in the Headwaters redwood forest of California, two hundred Jews actually trespassed on the land of a corporation that was threatening to log those grand and sacred groves, so old they were living when the Temple fell. It was Tu B'Shvat; we planted redwood seedlings.)

- At Pesach we can eliminate the swollen *chameytz* ("leavening") that makes our lives swell up, and embrace instead a week of simple living. And at Pesach we can identify the pharaonic institutions that are bringing upon us the plagues that turn our seas and rivers to "red tide," that fill our cattle with disease, that infest one or another ecosystem of the earth with swarms of invasive species that destroy a habitat. We can call on these corporate pharaohs to open their hearts instead of hardening them, and to save the land they are destroying.

- And not only can we face the dark side of Pesach, the *chameytz* and the plagues, but we can also read together the Song of Songs, that lovely evocation of a spring in which humanity at last learns how to live in loving, playful peace with all of earth as well as with each other.

For us to celebrate our ancient festivals in such ways, however, to pray such "Hosha na"s, we would have to be convinced of their wisdom and their truth, of our own authenticity in so invoking them. We would have to believe that our prayerful pleas do not fall into emptiness but into a Place that hears and can respond.

In short, we would have to understand God in such a way that such prayers could be addressed not only to a distant disembodied Mystery but also to an embodiment of holiness on earth. We would have to believe, really believe, that the great Unity includes the processes of the earth.

One of the great Hasidic rebbes, the Rebbe of Chernobyl, about two hundred years ago said, "What is the world? The world is God, wrapped in robes of God so as to appear to be material. And who are we? We are God wrapped in robes of God and our task is to unwrap the robes and to dis-cover, uncover, that we are God."

So, think of the earth as one aspect of God, and think what it would mean for us to pray those prayers with that Hasidic understanding. We pray them, can we act on them? As Rabbenu Heschel, our teacher Abraham Joshua Heschel, said when he came back from the civil rights march in Selma, Alabama, "I felt my legs were praying."

What would it mean for us to pray not only with our mouths but also with our arms and legs?

Or, to put it another way: if earth is Spirit, then politics may be the deepest prayer, and prayer the deepest politics. We may realize that we are always choosing between a politics that may be prayers to idols, mere carved-out pieces of the Whole, things of partial value that we elevate to ultimates, and a politics that we may shape with such deep caring that it becomes prayer to the One.

The Kabbalists taught us that the process of Creation involved a great outpouring of Divine energy so intense that this river of Divinity crashed through each vessel intended to contain it, swept over four great waterfalls, Four Worlds of the Divine Flow, shattering Itself until it came to a shattered calmness in our world.

Each of these Four Worlds holds all four within it, like a set of Chinese boxes. In our own world, the world that from God's perspective is the world of *Asiyah,* Doing and Acting, we are able to experience and in our own lives replicate all four of the Four Worlds. When we reach toward experiencing the First World, *Atzilut,* Being, the world of Spirit, we do this by entering ritual, prayer, and celebration. That is the world we have just been exploring.

Just below *Atzilut,* on the next water-level of the Divine river, is the second of the Four Worlds, another dimension of what it would mean to shape from Jewish peoplehood a transgenerational movement to heal the earth. This Second World is *Briyyah,* Creative Intellect, Knowing, Learning. This involves learning Torah, and learning science, and learning public policy, and especially learning how all these intertwine.

Suppose we learn Torah simply because it was written down once upon a time, a matter of "religion" that teaches only about prayer and ceremonial. And suppose we learn science by going to a university department and politics and public policy from yet another university department or from the mass media. Then what do these three have to do with each other? Nothing, or very little.

But that's not in fact what Torah was. It was a celebration of the great Unity; therefore it was politics, and it was also science, the best science available to every generation of Jews who were encoded into the process. So, when the Jubilee chapter of Leviticus (Lev. 25) says, "Hey, some guy with a master's degree in Business Administration is going to say to you, 'If you let the fields lie fallow on the seventh year, what do you think we are going to eat?'" the Torah says, "Hang on! You will have more to eat, I promise you, if you let the earth rest every seventh year than if you try to work it to death."

Of course, this is a call to faith. It is "religion."

It is also "science," the science that knows the fields are more fruitful if they have a chance to lie fallow. Torah is not something separate from science. It affirms what is holy in the world, and what is holy includes knowledgeable science.

And this process did not stop with the Torah, or the biblical period. The Rabbis of the Talmud proclaimed that no one should herd "small cattle"—that is, goats and sheep—in the Land of Israel. Why? because they destroy trees and grass. The Rabbis say this even though they know perfectly well that our forebears were shepherds and goat herders. Why do they make such an amazing departure from tradition?

Because their experience, and their science, have taught them something new. Their deep sense that our relationship with the earth is sacred causes them to oppose what was normal for the early Torah period. The basic values continue; how to affirm them changes in accord with new scientific information.

Today, we might imagine saying to ourselves: "Our Torah forbids us to cut down fruit trees, even in time of war. Today we know that every tree gives oxygen to the web of life, and great forests are crucial to the life of the entire planet. Does that mean that we may cut down any tree only if it is possible to replace its fruitful supply of oxygen? That we may not cut down great forests at all? That this is now Torah because we understand the science of trees in ways our forebears did not (though they certainly knew trees were important to their lives), and we uphold the values that they held?"

We can think such thoughts and ask such questions only if we begin to interweave the knowledge that in the modern age has been separated into religion, science, and politics. What would it mean for us to take the lines of Torah in Leviticus 26, which are incredibly powerful as both a sacred and a scientific statement, not two separate things, the lines that ask, "'And what happens if you don't let the earth make its Shabbos year?'" and answer, "'The earth gets to rest anyway—on your head. The earth gets to rest through exile, disaster, desolation. The earth gets to rest, that is the law of gravity. The only question is whether you are going to rest with it and celebrate the rest and take new life, or if the earth is going to expel you from its midst into a painful exile, so that it can rest.'"

This understanding was both sacred and scientific three thousand years ago, and it still is. Today, when ecologists say, "If you insist on pouring carbon dioxide into the atmosphere and never letting the atmosphere rest from that overdose, there is going to be global warming and your civilization is going to be knocked awry if not shattered," they are simply saying what Leviticus 26 said.

What would it mean for us, both children and adults, to intertwine that learning, to shape our Torah study so that it always includes those knowledges about the web of life? What would it mean for us to reshape every Jewish curriculum and study group as if the web of life in which we live were the most important sacred fact about our lives?

The Fourth World, the fourth dimension of our imagined sacred people—I will come back to the Third World in a moment—is the world of Doing, Action, Physicality. The world of eco-kosher.

It was Rabbi Zalman Schachter-Shalomi who coined the word "eco-kosher." That word almost teaches its lesson in the word itself, if you let it reverberate in your head a little while. But let me unfold it just a tiny bit.

For people who were shepherds and farmers, celebrating food was the way of celebrating the crucial relationship between *adam* and *adamah,* because food was the crucial connection between them. And so our people generated the elaborate celebrations of that sacred nexus not only through the offerings of food at the Holy Temple but also through an elaborate pattern of what food to eat, and in what way: the kosher code. When the elaborate Temple offerings were no longer possible, the Rabbis of the Talmud compensated by making the rules of *kashrut* even more elaborate.

In the society we live in, while food is obviously important, it is not the biggest piece of our economic relationship with the earth. It's not all we eat anymore. We eat coal. We eat oil. We eat electric power, we eat the radiation that keeps some of that electric power going, and we eat the chemicals that we turn into plastic. What does it mean to eat them in a sacred way? What does it mean to say that we're eco-kosher? What does it mean to apply more broadly the basic sense of *kashrut* that what you eat and how you eat it matters?

Today our most dangerous addictive substances are not heroin or nicotine or alcohol. They are plutonium and petroleum. These are social addictions, not individual ones. I do not mainline oil or gasoline into my own body's veins, but the United States mainlines gasoline into our society's veins.

What is addiction? It is feeling unable to control or limit a behavior, especially using a substance—even one that in some limited uses may be beneficial—in such a way as to receive immediate pleasure at the high risk of long-run disease and death. And that describes the American relationship to gasoline.

Addictions are to a great extent a spiritual problem—what in ancient Jewish language was called idolatry. Carving out a small part of the great Flow of Life and worshipping that small part. Letting it take over our lives. A serious Jewish community today should see these social addictions as idolatries; we must work out ways of infusing our use of oil, coal, paper, and all the rest with holiness. We must eat them in an eco-kosher way.

Is it eco-kosher to eat vegetables and fruit that have been grown by drenching the soil with insecticides?

Is it eco-kosher to drink the wine of the Shabbat *kiddush* from throw-away nonbiodegradable plastic cups? Or would it be eco-kosher to share ceramic cups; to begin each *kiddush* with the *kavvanah,* the intentional focus, that we are using these cups to heal the earth; and to end each meal with the sacred act of washing these cups so as to heal the earth?

Is it eco-kosher to use electricity generated by nuclear power plants that create waste products that will remain poisonous for fifty thousand years?

Is it eco-kosher to ignore the insulation or lack of it in our homes, synagogues, community centers, and nursing homes, so that we burn far more fuel than necessary and drunkenly pour carbon dioxide into the atmosphere, thereby accelerating the heating of our globe?

Is it eco-kosher to use unrecycled office paper and newsprint in our homes, our synagogues, our community newspapers? Might it be eco-kosher to insist on 10 percent recycled paper this year, and 30 percent in two years, and 80 percent in five years?

I want to suggest that what makes a life-practice eco-kosher may not be a single standard, a black-and-white barricade like "pork is *treyf* (not kosher)," but rather a constantly moving standard in which the test is, Are we doing what is more respectful, less damaging to the earth than what we did last year?

What would it mean to evolve a code of daily Jewish practice for how we consume, how we eat all these things that come from *adamah*? What would it mean for each Hillel House, each congregation, each Jewish community center and nursing home to review what kind of paper, what kind of energy it uses? Do we invest money in industries that destroy the earth or in industries that heal the earth?

Most of the Jewish community is not asking those questions yet. What must we do, then, to begin the creation of eco-*kashrut*?

Let us turn back to the third dimension, the third of the Four Worlds, the world of *Yetzirah*, Relationship. For indeed the Jewish community, acting on its own, cannot heal the world. I could say to myself all day, "Hey, every time you drive the car you are polluting the planet and bringing on global warming," and yet if my society is set up so that the only way I can get from where I live to where I work is to drive, and there are no bike paths, and mass transit is rare, run-down, and expensive, then I am going to feel guilty but I am going to drive the car.

It does not help the planet if I feel guilty.

In other words, we have to act with other peoples and other communities to shape a society where we can walk from where we work to where we sleep, or we can bike, or we can take mass transit that is far more efficient and less wasteful and less likely to damage the atmosphere.

And we have to draw on the energy and clout of the Jewish people, our new ability in the Diaspora to make a difference in the societies we are a part of.

One of the notions that has arisen in American society in the last twenty years is that acting to heal the earth means acting to damage ordinary people, that there is, for example, a war between owls and timber workers, so that any action to protect the owls hurts the timber workers.

Recent American politics, however, has shown that the enemies of the owls and of the timber workers are the same—they are the institutions that see it as their task to gobble up the planet. To gobble it up biologically, to gobble it up culturally by destroying small communities which just don't fit, and to gobble up local and regional economies that just don't fit into the global market economy. To gobble up the kinds of enterprises where owners and workers felt responsible to each other, where even in the midst of struggles management and labor unions felt some kind of responsibility, a sense of limits of what profits could be, a sense of limits on whether you can fire tens of thousands of people in a prosperous, profitable company. The new corporations of Modernity Amok destroy such companies: their profits could be bigger; in this way regional and local economies are shattered along with local cultures and local bioregions, ecosystems.

Gobbling the globe means chewing up living creatures, thousands of species. It means chewing up small, odd cultures: the Jews of Eastern Europe, the natives of the Amazon Valley, the Shoshone. It means chewing up the local factory neighborhoods in Philadelphia, even the IBM towns of upstate New York. It means chewing up the family in all its forms.

The institution of Global Gobble is the global corporation, and its *torah* says that producing is what human life is all about. Producing, and of course consuming, which is not the opposite of producing, but only the other side of the coin (and I do mean coin). In the *torah* of the global corporation, resting, celebrating, reflecting, loving, being there, are all a waste of time, literally. Shabbat, a waste of time!! Think what you could be making if you were not resting!

That attitude toward the earth becomes also an attitude toward human beings. It creates a technology which pushes people in two directions: either being disemployed because the technology is better, more efficient, or keeping their jobs, but being forced to match their lives to the speed of the machine.

The result is that more and more people who keep their jobs don't work eight-hour days, but ten-, twelve-, or even fourteen-hour days. And people who lose their jobs scrabble together two, three, even four jobs in order barely to hold on by their fingertips.

In the process community is dying, divided between the disemployed and the overworked. The overworked have no time for family or neighborhood or religious life or grass-roots politics. Some of the disemployed—those who end up on the streets with no work at all or in prison because they get desperate, crazy, drugged, or alcoholic—get a perverse form of leisure, but they cannot use it for family, neighborhood, religious life, or politics. Some of the disemployed end up in ill-paid dead-end jobs with no access to health insurance, and turn themselves into the overworked—two jobs, or three—in order barely to pay their bills for rent and food.

Neither the overworked nor the disemployed can get their lives together to help shape a decent society. Neither the desperate disemployed nor the exhausted overworked can shape a loving family. In their neighborhoods, the only thing you have the energy to do after a twelve-hour day is to sit in front of the television set, which takes your depressed and exhausted self and reawakens it with jolts of your own adrenaline. And then since you are feeling jangled from being awakened that way, it calms you down with "Hey, here's something wonderful to buy." So if you're exhausted or desperate you don't create PTA's, neighborhoods, synagogues, churches, or political parties.

There is a wonderful study by Robert Putnam called "Bowling

Alone." The bowling leagues are disappearing; people still bowl but they bowl alone, because they don't have the energy anymore even to organize a bowling league. If this seems so unimportant as to be ridiculous even to mention, the point is that the seedbed of democracy, as De Tocqueville taught, is all those networks of local organizations.

We need to be serious about addressing both the issues of what we call the economy and what we call the environment. They are deeply intertwined. An economy is the way in which earthlings and the earth fit together. Economy and ecology: it is no accident that they both begin with the Greek word for household; they are both about the same processes of the human relationship with the earth. And those who want to heal the earth must also understand the institutional structures that are damaging the earth and also damaging our society. To act on either, we must act on both.

What does it mean to "act" where global corporations are concerned? Using the categories I have suggested, we can see the global corporation as another leap forward in the I–It spiral. It is a tool for Doing: efficient, effective, powerful. It carries both the virtues and the dangers of I–It. Our task may be not to destroy it, but to make of it an instrument in the service of broader community. To make it socially and ethically responsible, to humankind and to the planet. To teach it to love, and even to Be.

To do this, we need to deepen and broaden our sense of loving community by acting in all four dimensions of reality. First, the Spirit: what we call ritual, ceremony, prayer, meditation, celebration, the direct ways of getting in touch with that sense of unity, of allness in the world. Second, Knowledge: the kind of education that intertwines our ancient tradition with the constantly growing edges of tradition, with knowledge in all the spheres of relationship between human beings and the earth. Third, Relationship: reaching out to other communities and societies everywhere to join with us to heal the wounded earth. And fourth, Doing: the daily eco-kosher practice of our own self, of our households, and our community organizations.

These four need to be treated not as four separate parts but as aspects of the One. When they are split apart, very little happens. In most synagogues today, if issues of the earth are dealt with at all, they are broken up in separate spheres. Issues of the earth and ritual are discussed within the ritual committee; issues of the earth and knowledge are discussed within the education committee; issues of the earth in everyday practice are dealt with in the house committee that decides what paper is bought or who comes in to check the insulation; issues of society are dealt with by the social action committee. In each of those committees, however, the issue of how to deal with the relationship to the earth is probably third or fourth or fifth on the list of priorities. Perhaps on one committee the issue of the earth will come forward, but on the next front where the issue must be addressed, the specific committee is not interested, and the question molders.

We should not let this happen. The issue of the earth is such that in a unique way, all these in fact are intertwined. So I think perhaps the crucial strategic switch in any Jewish community, congregation, or organization comes when that community decides to create an *adam*-and-*adamah* committee, even if it has to be called the Committee on the Environment.

(The words "*adam*-and-*adamah*" say, "Hey, we ain't identical but we sure are closely intertwined." You can't say *adam* without hearing *adamah,* you can't say *adamah* without hearing *adam*. "Environment" is a word that means "in the environs, out there, something else, somewhere else. For sure, not intertwined." So even if we use the conventional English word, we should keep the sense of the Hebrew alive within us.)

But whatever we name the committee, I think the crucial change in any Jewish community or organization may be when a single *adam*-and-*adamah* body is created that has responsibility for all of those four dimensions, to report on them to the community as a whole.

From then on, judging from the places where this has already happened, things are different. The community begins to imagine itself as a piece of a broader movement to heal the earth, to imagine that that is a major aspect of what Judaism is all about.

Reframing Judaism in this way can evoke passionate commitment from the next generation of Jews in ways that few other things can. Much of what the human race is doing to the planet will have its worst effects on the planet thirty, forty, fifty years from now. Our children will have to live in what we have created. Judaism which addresses the future of the earth will evoke their passion, energy, intelligence, commitment, and spirit. Conversely, a Judaism which says, "Hey, what's this earth stuff got to do with us?" won't fly.

The passionate engagement which comes from a sense that we fit into the great Unity is profoundly necessary if the human race is to decide to stop gobbling up the earth. Those who are spiritually starving will need to fill their bellies with something—and they will try to fill themselves by gobbling the earth. Intense song, dance, Torah study, drushodrama, the engagement of the whole body, the full involvement of both women and men in shaping spiritual practice—all this spiritual intensity is crucial to a recovering addict. Spiritual vitality is necessary if we are to heal the planet.

I would encourage any of you who talk with people who talk of Jewish continuity to say, "Continuity? What is its content? Because if its content is a real, alive, down-to-earth Judaism, then I'm ready to put my passion into this. And if not, I will put my passion elsewhere, or perhaps I will cynically give up, and put my passion nowhere. For this is a question of life and death to me, a question of the life and death of my children who are not yet in this world. If you're not interested in my life or death, then I am not interested whether the empty Judaism you speak for lives or dies. Its continuity means nothing."

It does not have to be that way. Together we can create a Judaism that has a purpose for its continuity, a Judaism that answers the question, "What for?"

In this way, a renewed and renewing Judaism would become one of the elements of a great new spiral of I–Thouing in the world. We would help create the new sense of planetary community that must respond to the new fact of globalizing I–It. Not by giving up our unique symbols, languages, metaphors, ceremonies, practices, but by deepening them and connecting them to the spiritual lives of other communities.

What for? For the Breath of Life Who fills the universe. For the web of life that is the universe. And here is where we share in our depth the Breath that all peoples breathe—by whatever Name they name the One Who is always becoming.

We do the breathing, and we are the Breath. All of us. Not only do the trees breathe in what we breathe out, and we breathe in what the trees breathe out, but so do all the species, all the peoples.

Shabbat did not come to us because we were "the Jews"; we became "the Jews" because we heard the silence of Shabbat. We should be welcoming others into that hearing, even as we ourselves—some of us—have had to relearn it from the breathing of yoga and the sitting of Zen and the meditating of Buddhists and the whirling of Sufis and the chanting of those who still live on Turtle Island.

Spiraling into the Future: Sources for Learning and Doing

Imagine that for the next seven generations Jews keep wrestling with God and each other to shape an ever-evolving Torah that can help heal the wounds between *adam* and *adamah*.

As we move into that puzzling future, we will keep learning from historians and biologists, prophetic activists and gentle river guides, farmers and rabbis—from all who have journeyed amongst us these four millennia.

Many of the voices in this book will continue in that conversation, and many others are joining it.

So for me to name those who have helped me birth this book is a statement not about the past, but about the future. I intend to keep consulting these people, working with these organizations, learning these teachings. I urge others to do the same.

This book took its first shape in the process of birthing another anthology—*Trees, Earth, and Torah: A Tu B'Shvat Anthology.* In a way, these two are twins brought forth from a single womb of work—not hostile twins like Jacob and Esau, but friendly like Zerach and Peretz. My co-laborers in that first birthing were Ellen Frankel, Naomi Mara Hyman, and Ari Elon.

But the maturation and birth of the second twin took months more, and a different team of midwives gathered to help birth it—a team brought together by Jewish Lights. First, Stuart Matlins was drawn to the seed of possibility, the glimmer of a new bookshelf in down-to-earth Jewish spirituality as this volume got to stand alongside Ellen Bernstein's *Ecology & the Jewish Spirit*—and possibly, someday, others. Rabbi David Sulomm Stein, as the editor's editor, very much improved these pages with penetrating and persistent questions. Sandra Korinchak took on two tasks: first inviting me to explore new ways of unfolding and connecting these varied essays, and then pulling together all the threads of words, graphics, machines, paper, and people into a book. For me, it was a delight to have her join in the weaving.

Long before I focused on these two anthologies, I was taking part in the swirl of eco-Jewish conversation that began in the early 1970s. I learned with and from all those Jews who committed themselves to healing the relationship between *adam* and *adamah,* the earth and human earthlings. Ellen Bernstein, Barak Gale, Rabbi Everett Gendler, Mark Jacobs, Naomi Steinberg, and Mike Tabor have brought both prescience and perseverance to this work. Among the network of eco-Jewish advocates who have been crucial to me over the years are Rabbi Arthur Green, De Herman, Rabbi Margaret Holub, Rabbi Myriam Klotz, Rabbi Mordechai Liebling, John Ruskay, Rabbi David Saperstein, Rabbi Zalman Schachter-Shalomi, Rabbi David Seidenberg, Rabbi Steve Shaw, Cantor David Shneyer, and Rabbi Dan Swartz.

Since the administrative support of ALEPH: Alliance for Jewish Renewal and The Shalom Center was crucial to the completion of this book, I owe special thanks to Rabbi Daniel Siegel, rabbinic director of ALEPH, Susan Saxe, its chief operating officer, and Annette Epps, its office manager; to those who have been staff for The Shalom Center for some period during the last few years—Miryam Levy, Abby Weinberg, Laurie Schwartz, Rachel Gurevitz, Erika Katske, and for work on this book especially to Doug Heifetz; and to the Rita Poretsky Foundation, The Shefa Fund, the Nathan Cummings Foundation, the Righteous Persons Foundation, the Alan B. Slifka Foundation, the Dorot Foundation, the Walter and Elise Haas Fund, the Fabrangen Tzedakah Collective, and hundreds of ALEPH and Shalom Center members for their support of The Shalom Center.

In all my work and all my rest, I learn from my beloved co-author, co-davvener, co-storyteller, co-parent, friend, and life-partner: Phyllis Ocean Berman.

ECO-JEWISH
ORGANIZATIONS

In the United States, from year to year, a growing number of organizations and publications provide further information about Judaism and the earth.

Broadest among these is an umbrella organization, the **Coalition on the Environment and Jewish Life (COEJL),** 443 Park Ave. South, New York, NY 10016; (212) 684-6950 x 210, e-mail COEJL@aol.com; or info@coejl.org; website www.coejl.org.

COEJL works under the direction of representatives of the Jewish Theological Seminary, the Religious Action Center of Reform Judaism, and the Jewish Council on Public Affairs. Its sponsors include almost all the national Jewish organizations in the United States.

COEJL works on legislative advocacy, liturgical materials keyed to the Jewish calendar, guides to eco-sensitive living, and conferences of Jewish communal leaders, rabbis, and theologians, and annual training institutes for eco-activists. It has a growing number of local and regional affiliates. Rather than try to list these, we urge people to check with COEJL for such contacts.

COEJL sponsors an e-mail discussion group. People can join by writing listserv@jtsa.edu with the message: <sub kol-chai FirstName LastName>.

It also sponsors an advocacy network and a news distribution list. Sign up to the first by writing the same address as before, but with the message <sub COEJLAction FirstName LastName> and to the second at the same address with the message <sub L-COEJLNews FirstName LastName>.

COEJL is itself part of a broader coalition, the National Religious Partnership on the Environment, website www.nrpe.org. In the larger grouping, other components are the U.S. Catholic Conference, the National Council of Churches, and the Evangelical Environmental Network.

- **The Shalom Center,** 6711 Lincoln Drive, Philadelphia, PA 19119; (215) 844-8494; e-mail shalomctr@aol.com; website www.shalomctr.org. The Shalom Center is especially interested in developing theology and eco-kosher life-practice adequate to the present ecological crisis; in bringing together the next generation of Jews who seek to heal the earth and society; in applying Jewish communal ethics to encourage corporations to act responsibly; and in working with other religious and spiritual communities to end the pressure for overwork that now ravages the earth, shatters regional economies and cultures, disheartens neighborhoods, stresses families, and exhausts individuals.

The Shalom Center sponsors an email discussion group, "Jews Renewing Justice" (JRJ-Net@shamash.org), for those involved in Jewish action for social justice, eco-sanity, corporate responsibility, peace, and community-building. People can join by writing Rabjeff@echonyc.com.

- **Shomrei Adamah,** one of the earliest Jewish earth-oriented groups, is now mainly a support group for **Teva Learning Center,** 50 W. 17th St., 7th Floor, New York, NY 10011; (212) 807-6376; e-mail tevacenter@aol.com. Teva is especially concerned with teaching environmental ethics to young Jews, integrating direct outdoor experience with Torah.
- **Yetziah/Jewish Wilderness Journeys** is housed at Camp Isabella Friedman, 116 Johnson Rd., Falls Village, CT 06031; (860) 824-5991; e-mail yetziah@aol.com. It specializes in river and other wilderness trips that integrate Torah study with nature experience.
- **Center for Tikkun Olam,** 90 West 31st Ave., Eugene, OR 97405; e-mail YHH@aol.com. It is pursuing the creation of an ongoing guide to eco-kosher living.
- **Shalom Nature Center** offers day and residential Jewish environmental education and nature programs to Jewish day schools, households, organizations, and students. 34342 Mulholland Hwy., Malibu, CA 90265; (818) 874-1101; e-mail Shalom_Nature_Center@jcc-gla.org or Josh_Lake@jcc-gla.org; websites www.shalomnaturecenter.org and www.shalominstitute.com.

In the United Kingdom, the **Noah Project,** P.O. Box 1828, London W10 5RT, UK; e-mail environmentally.sound@virgin.net. Promotes environmental awareness and responsibility in the Jewish community through Jewish education, celebration, and action.

In Canada, there is a nascent eco-Jewish group called **Eco-Jews,** c/o Shai Spetgang, 1057 Steeles Ave. W., Suite 736, Toronto, Ontario M2R 3X1, Canada; (905) 882-7493; e-mail shai@idirect.ca.

In Israel, the most important environmental groups are:

- **Society for the Preservation of Nature in Israel** *(Haganat Hateva),* 4 Hashfela St., Tel Aviv 66183; for hikes and trails, 03-638-8677; for environmental action, 03-375-063; with an American affiliate at 28 Arrandale Ave., Great Neck, NY 11024; (212) 398-6750; e-mail aspni@aol.com.
- **Israel Union for Environmental Defense** *(Adam Teva v'Din),* 317 HaYarkon St., Tel Aviv 63504; 03-546-8099. IUED is an active legal support and challenge center for neighborhoods and towns whose ecosystems are being endangered.
- **Jewish National Fund** *(Keren Kayemet l'Yisrael),* with an American affiliate at 42 E. 69th St., New York, NY; (212) 879-9300. JNF has made tree planting in Israel one of its major programs. It has been criticized by some other Israeli environmentalists for allegedly doing this in a way that contradicts eco-sensitive requirements.
- **Heschel Center for Environmental Learning and Leadership,** Yavneh 1, Tel Aviv, 03-620-1806; e-mail heschel@ netvision.net.il. Does eco-theology, applying Torah to issues of the earth.
- **Arava Institute for Environmental Studies,** Kibbutz Ketura, DN. Hevel Eilot, 88840, Israel; 02-735-6666; e-mail arava@ netvision.net.il. Regional center for conservation and environmental protection activities; accredited program in environmental studies (taught in English).
- **EcoPeace: Middle East Environmental NGO Forum,** P.O. Box 55302, East Jerusalem, 97400, via Israel; 02-626-0841; e-mail ecopeace@netvision.net.il. Egyptians, Israelis, Jordanians, and Palestinians working together to promote ecologically sound development in the Middle East through research, education, and advocacy.
- **Neot Kedumim,** P.O. Box 1007, Lod, 71100, Israel; 08-233-3840. Nature reserve dedicated to restoring the flora and fauna of biblical Israel; publications.

SUGGESTIONS FOR FURTHER READING

Several books have appeared in recent years to address eco-Jewish concerns:

- Evan Eisenberg, *The Ecology of Eden* (Knopf, 1998). A magisterial examination of the relationship between the actual down-to-earth eco-geography of Israelite life, the evolution of biblical values and teachings about the earth, and the meaning of these for the contemporary ecological crisis.
- Ellen Bernstein, ed., *Ecology & the Jewish Spirit: Where Nature and the Sacred Meet* (Jewish Lights, 1997). Includes essays on how a number of individual Jews have been awakened to and responded to a sense of healing the earth as an aspect of Jewish life and thought.
- Ari Elon, Naomi Mara Hyman, and Arthur Waskow, eds., *Trees, Earth, and Torah: A Tu B'Shvat Anthology* (Jewish Publication Society, 1999). Since Tu B'Shvat, both in ancient days and the last century, has been intimately connected with trees and the earth, almost all the texts and essays in this collection are useful in exploring, past, present, and future.
- Marge Piercy, *He, She and It* (Knopf, 1991). A novel set alternately in the Prague of the famous Golem and in the late twenty-first century (in the newly independent Jewish city-state of Tikva, located on the hills where Boston used to be before global warming), which addresses at political, psychological, and spiritual levels the dangers of out-of control technology and the possibility of a humane technology.
- Richard H. Schwartz, *Judaism and Global Survival* (Atara, 1987).
- Arthur Waskow, *Down-to-Earth Judaism: Food, Money, Sex, and the Rest of Life* (Morrow, 1995). Looks at a number of Jewish life-path issues with special regard to the effects of the earth-human relationship.

- Matt Biers-Ariel, Deborah Newbrun, and Michal Fox Smart, *Spirit in Nature: A Jewish Hikers' Trail Guide* (Behrman House, 2000).
- Arthur Waskow, *Godwrestling—Round 2* (Jewish Lights, 1996). Puts forward a Torah-rooted theology of eco-Judaism.
- Arthur Waskow, *Seasons of Our Joy* (Beacon, 1982; 1990). Views the cycle of Jewish festivals in part as an attunement to the spiritual meaning of the sun-moon-earth cycles.
- Phyllis O. Berman and Arthur Waskow, *Tales of Tikkun: New Jewish Stories to Heal the Wounded World* (Jason Aronson, 1997). Includes "The Rest of Creation," "The Return of Captain Noah," and several other stories with eco-Jewish themes.
- David E. Stein, ed., *A Garden of Choice Fruit: 200 Classic Jewish Quotes on Human Beings and the Environment.* Available from Shomrei Adamah (see "Eco-Jewish Organizations").
- Louis I. Rabinowitz, *Torah and Flora* (Sanhedrin Press, 1979).
- Nogah Hareuveni, *Tree and Shrub in Our Biblical Heritage* (1984). Order from Neot Kedumim (see "Eco-Jewish Organizations").
- Roger Gottlieb, ed., *This Sacred Earth: Religion, Nature, Environment* (Routledge, 1995).
- *Judaism and Ecology,* a study guide produced by Hadassah and Shomrei Adamah. Available from Dept. of Jewish Education, Hadassah, 50 W. 58th St., New York, NY 10019.
- Ellen Bernstein and Dan Swartz, eds., *Let the Earth Teach You Torah.* Available from Shomrei Adamah (see preceding "Eco-Jewish Organizations").
- Martin D. Yaffe, ed., *Judaism and Environmental Ethics* (Lexington Books, 2000).
- In preparation: A series called "Torah Universe" by Noson Slifkin; Targum Press (distributed by Feldheim Publishers).
- *Operation Noah,* two pamphlets on biodiversity and protection of endangered species from a Jewish standpoint—one on contemporary science, action, and program ideas; the other on Jewish texts and sources. Available from COEJL (see "Eco-Jewish Organizations").

There are two excellent handbooks for action in Jewish communities:

- *To Till and to Tend,* published by COEJL (see "Eco-Jewish Organizations").
- *The Green Shalom Guide,* ed. Naomi Friedman and De Fischler. Available from Washington Area Shomrei Adamah, 706 Erie Ave., Takoma Park, MD 20912; (301) 587-7535.

Special issues of several journals, as well as several videos, have addressed these questions:

- *Melton Journal* of the Melton Center at Jewish Theological Seminary (Spring 1991 and Spring 1992).
- *Conservative Judaism* (Fall 1991).
- *Palestine-Israel Journal* (vol. V, no. 1, 1998), P.O. Box 19839, Jerusalem; 972-2-6282-115; e-mail pij@palnet.com.
- *CCAR Journal* (Winter 2000).
- "Visions of Eden: A Jewish Perspective on the Environment" (1997, VHS, 60 minutes). Documentary on Judaism and ecology produced by the Jewish Theological Seminary, COEJL, and ABC Television. The program follows a group of Jewish leaders, including rabbis and leading environmentalists on an overnight backpacking journey along the Appalachian Trail. JTS Communications Office, (212) 678-8020.
- "The Earth Is the Lord's" (VHS, 60 minutes). Jewish Theological Seminary of America. For all ages. Tells the Creation story and the importance of protecting all of God's creatures.
- "Keeping the Earth" (1996, VHS, 27 minutes). National Religious Partnership for the Environment (NRPE)/ Union of Concerned Scientists (UCS). Narrated by James Earl Jones. Middle school–adult. Prominent religious leaders and scientists. Order from UCS, 2 Brattle Sq., Cambridge, MA 02238-9105; (617)547-5552.
- "Green Borders," on several eco-sensitive Israeli kibbutzim and some Palestinian contacts, by Ramona Rubin, 200 Thayer Rd., Santa Cruz, CA 95060; e-mail monamoon26@hotmail.com.

NOTES

PART 1: Zionism

David B. Brooks, "The Struggle for Israel's Environment: Tougher Than Ever"

1. David B. Brooks, "Israel and the Environment: Signs of Progress," *Reconstructionist,* LV: 4 (March–April 1990), pp. 17–19.

2. David B. Brooks and Joseph Shadur, "The Sharpening Struggle for Israel's Environment," *Conservative Judaism,* XLIV: 1 (Fall 1991), pp. 51–58.

3. Shoshana Gabbay, editor, *The Environment in Israel* (Jerusalem: Ministry of the Environment, 1994).

4. The contrasts are set out in many of the growing number of articles on Judaism and ecology. For the briefest statement, see Jeremy Benstein, "Leave Nature Out of War," *The Jerusalem Report* (07 September 1995), p. 32. Other sources include: Robert Gordis, "Ecology in the Jewish Tradition," *Midstream* (October 1985); David Ehrenfeld and Philip J. Bentley, "Judaism and the Practice of Stewardship," *Judaism,* 34:3 (Summer 1985), pp. 301–11; Ellen Bernstein, editor, *Ecology and the Jewish Spirit: Where Nature and the Sacred Meet* (Woodstock, Vermont: Jewish Lights, 1998).

5. *Israel Environment Bulletin,* Special Anniversary Issue, XI:2 (Winter-Spring 1988–5748).

6. The following data are all taken from *The Environment in Israel* (Jerusalem: Environmental Protection Service, 1988) or from recent issues of *Israel Environment Bulletin.* The latter is a free English-language quarterly published by the Israeli Ministry of the Environment, POB 6158, Jerusalem 91061, Israel. It is perhaps the best single way of keeping up with environmental affairs in Israel.

7. *State of the Environment Report for Canada* (Ottawa: Supply and Services Canada, 1986); and *Human Activity and the Environment: A Statistical Compendium* (Ottawa: Statistics Canada, 1986). *Aussi disponible en français.*

8. The State Comptroller's report was summarized in English in the *Israel Environment Bulletin* (published quarterly by the Ministry of the Environment), 16:1 (Spring 1991–5751).

9. Gideon Fishelson, *Changes in Water Supply: Impacts upon the Israeli Economy* (Tel Aviv: The Armand Hammer Fund for Economic Cooperation in the Middle East, Tel Aviv University, 1992).

10. Agriculture now accounts for less than 2.5% of Israel's gross domestic product, and just over 5% of her export earnings. *Statistical Abstract of Israel, 1992* (Jerusalem: Central Bureau of Statistics). See further in Stephen C. Lonergan and David B. Brooks, *Watershed: The Role of Fresh Water in the Israeli-Palestinian Conflict* (Ottawa: IDRC Books, 1994).

11. "The Trans-Israel Highway," *Israel Environment Bulletin,* 18:2 (Spring 1995). Virtually the whole environmental movement in Israel is opposed to this highway.

12. "Life to the Rivers," *Israel Environment Bulletin,* 18:4 (Autumn 1995).

13. Valerie Brachya, "Environmental Assessment of Land Use Planning in Israel," *Landscape and Urban Planning,* 23 (1993). Ruth Rotenburg, "A Decade's Experience in Implementing a Land-Use Environmental Impact Assessment System in Israel," *Israel Environment Bulletin,* 17:3 (Autumn 1994).

14. "Focus on Air Quality," *Israel Environment Bulletin,* 16:3 (Summer 1993).

15. Special Licensing Conditions for Ramat Hovav, *Israel Environment Bulletin,* 15:1 (Winter 1992).

16. For a general review of the Peace Process and particularly the multilateral working groups, see Robert J. Bookmiller and Kirsten Nakjavani Bookmiller, Behind the Headlines: The Multilateral Middle East Talks, *Current History,* 95:597 (January 1996). Also the whole Winter 1995 number of *Israel Environment Bulletin* (18:1) is a Special Peace issue.

17. Robin Twite and Jad Isaac, editors, *Our Shared Environment* (Jerusalem: Israel/Palestine Centre for Research and Information, 1949).

18. Israel 2020: A New Vision, *Israel Environment Bulletin,* 18:2 (Spring 1995).

19. Stephen C. Lonergan and David B. Brooks, *Watershed: The Role of Fresh Water in the Israeli-Palestinian Conflict* (Ottawa: IDRC Books, 1994). Hillel Shuval, Towards Resolving Conflicts over Water Between Israel and its Neighbours, *Israel Affairs,* 2:1 (Autumn 1995).

20. Because their supplies are the first to be cut during times of shortage, as during the current drought, farmers should get water at something less than the rates to householders, who are almost assured of steady supplies. However, the difference in price is far more than is necessary to compensate for this effect.

21. See for example, Palestinian Environmental Authority, *Gaza: Environmental Profile* (1994).

22. Oslo II; Article 12:10.

23. PNGO Network, *Documents of the Palestinian Non-Governmental Organization Network* (Shu'fat, East Jerusalem: 1996). Dina Craissati, Social Movements and Democracy in Palestine: Politicization of Society or Civilization of Politics? *German Journal for Politics and Economics of the Middle East,* 37:1 (March 1996), pp. 111–36.

24. Each of the working groups is led by a "gavel holder," rather than a chairperson. The difference is apparently significant in a diplomatic sense but is otherwise irrelevant.

25. The International Development Research Centre (IDRC) is a Canadian Crown Corporation that funds research in low-income countries. When reference is made to joint projects, it should be understood that IDRC funds only the Palestinian component, though it commonly assists the Israeli component to find other sources of support.

26. Among other reports, see: EcoPeace, *One Basin; One Strategy: Symposium on Promoting and Integrated Sustainable Regional Development Plan for the Dead Sea Basin* (East Jerusalem: 1998). Eran Feitelson and Marwan Haddad, A Stepwise Open-Ended Approach to the Identification of Joint Management Structures for Shared Aquifers, *Water International,* 23: 4 (December 1998); a book to be published by Kluwer in Amsterdam by the same authors is in press. A report on the public health and environmental conditions will be published by the Israel/Palestine Centre for Research and Information early in 2000. See also the IPCRI report cited in note 17.

27. Shoshana Gabbay, editor, *The Environment in Israel* (Jerusalem: Ministry of the Environment, 1998).

28. For those familiar with the meaning of words, but not with American baseball lore, this malapropism was coined by Yogi Berra, a former manager of the New York Yankees, to suggest a series of repetitions of events.

Part 2: Eco-Judaism

Abraham Joshua Heschel,
"Text: Technical Civilization and Shabbat"

1. See A. J. Heschel, *Man Is Not Alone: A Philosophy of Religion* (New York, 1951), p. 200.

2. Exodus 20:9, 23:12, 31:15, 34:21; Leviticus 23:3; Deuteronomy 5:13.
3. *Mekilta de-Rabbi Shimeon bar Yohai,* ed. Hoffman (Frankfurt, 1905), p. 107.
4. *Pirke Abot* 110.
5. *Abot de-Rabbi Natan,* ed. Schechter, chap. 11.
6. See *Shabbat* 49b.

Erich Fromm,
"Text: The Way of the Sabbath"

1. In the following pages I draw upon the ideas and the material of a paper on "The Sabbath Rituals" in E. Fromm, *The Forgotten Language* (New York: Holt, Rinehart, and Winston, 1951), pp. 241 ff. In the same year (1951), a book entitled *The Sabbath* was published by Abraham J. Heschel, which contains a beautiful and profound analysis of the Sabbath (New York: Farrar, Straus and Giroux).
2. Cf. E. Fromm, "The Prophetic Concept of Peace," in *The Dogma of Christ.*
3. It is interesting to speculate whether the basic principle of the Jewish Sabbath might not be practiced on a day of rest (Saturday) different from the day of recreation constituted by our present Sunday, which is devoted to sport, excursions, and so on. Considering the increasing custom of having two free days, such an idea does not seem to be impractical in industrialized countries. When I speak of the principle of the Jewish Sabbath, I am not referring to all of the details of the Jewish Sabbath law, such as not carrying even a book or a handkerchief or not lighting a fire. Although I believe that even these details are important to create the full atmosphere of rest, I do not think that—except perhaps for a small minority—one could expect people to follow such cumbersome practices. But I do believe that the principle of the Sabbath rest might be adopted by a much larger number of people—Christians, Jews, and people outside of any religion. The Sabbath day, for them, would be a day of contemplation, reading, meaningful conversation, a day of rest and joy, completely free from all practical and mundane concerns.

Eilon Schwartz,
"Judaism and Nature: Theological and Moral Issues"

1. The beginning of the modern environmental movement has been traditionally understood as 1960, the year of the initial publication of portions of Rachel Carson's *Silent Spring* in the *New Yorker.*
2. Shomrei Adamah, a Jewish resource center for the environment, published a

sourcebook of readings on Judaism and the environment with a fairly thorough bibliography of the relevant literature up through 1986. See Marc Swetlitz, ed., *Judaism and Ecology 1970–1986: A Sourcebook of Readings* (Wyncote, Pa.: Shomrei Adamah, 1990). This article cites much of the pertinent literature written since then, as well.

3. Lynn White, Jr., "The Historical Roots of our Ecological Crisis," *Science* 155 (March 10, 1967): 1203–7, remains the classic presentation of this position. See Jeremy Cohen, "On Classical Judaism and Environmental Crisis," *Tikkun* 5, 2 (1990):74, for a review of the early environmental movement's polemic against the Judeo-Christian ethic.

4. One of the many examples of this phenomenon, most relevant to our topic, is the repression by early modern Jewish historians of the importance of the mystical tradition in Jewish history. Working from within the *zeitgeist* of the Enlightenment, the scholars of *Wissenschaft* were incapable of recognizing the existence of traditions within Judaism less suited to the cultural mood. Scholem's resurrection of the field of Kabbalah as a legitimate part of Jewish tradition is not simply a rediscovery of historically prominent trends within Judaism but marks a change both in the larger culture's mood and a change in the relationship between Judaism and the larger culture.

5. On the justification for extrapolating universal values from particular discussions in Rabbinic thought, see Max Kadushin, *The Rabbinic Mind,* (Philadelphia: Jewish Theological Seminary of America, 1952), pp. 1–58.

6. On *Baal Tashchit,* see David Ehrenfeld and Philip J. Bentley, "Judaism and the Practice of Stewardship," *Judaism* 34 (1985):301–11; Eric Freudenstein, "Ecology and the Jewish Tradition," *Judaism* 19 (1969):406–14; Robert Gordis, "Judaism and the Spoliation of Nature," *Congress Bi-Weekly,* April 2, 1971; Jonathan I. Helfand, "Ecology and the Jewish Tradition: A Postscript," *Judaism,* 20 (1970):330–35; Norman Lamm, "Ecology in Jewish Law and Theology," in *Faith and Doubt* (New York: KTAV, 1971). On *Tsar Baalei Chayim,* see Ehrenfeld and Bentley; Gordis. On *Yishuv HaAretz,* see Helfand. On *Shnat Shemita,* see Gerald J. Blidstein, "Man and Nature in the Sabbatical Year," in *Tradition* 8:4 (1966):48–55; Ehrenfeld and Bentley, *The Sabbatical Year—Holiness or Social Welfare?* (The Hartman Institute for Jewish Studies) (In Hebrew).

7. I use the term *deep* here similarly to the way that "deep" ecology uses it—to define an approach that explores the core issues and does not stop with cosmetic exploration of cultural assumptions.

8. See Yehezkiel Kaufman, *The Religion of Israel* (Chicago: University of Chicago Press, 1960), pp. 1148.

9. White, p. 1205.

10. Starhawk, "Power, Authority and Mystery: Ecofeminism and Earth-based Spirituality," in *Reweaving the World: The Emergence of Ecofeminism,* ed. Irene Diamond and Gloria Feman Orenstein, (San Francisco: Sierra Club Books, 1990).

11. James Lovelock, *The Ages of Gaia: A Biography of Our Living Earth* (New York: Bantam Books, 1990).

12. Aharon Lichtenstein, "Man and Nature: Social Aspects," in *Judaism in Our Modern Society* (Israeli Ministry of Education, The Branch for Religious Culture, 1971) (In Hebrew).

13. Everett Gendler, "On the Judaism of Nature," in *The New Jews,* ed. James A. Sleeper and Alan L. Mintz, (New York: Random House, 1971). See also "The Earth's Covenant," *The Reconstructionist* (November–December 1989), for a restatement of his views.

14. The idea of complementary models, mutually exclusive models which describe parts of the same reality, was originally presented by Niels Bohr. For a discussion of Bohr's theory and its implications for religious thought, see Ian Barbour, *Myths, Models, and Paradigms: A Comparative Study in Science and Religion* (San Francisco: Harper and Row, 1974), pp. 71–92.

15. Michael Rosenak has argued that theologies which emphasize creation will be focused on the miraculous nature of the world, our sense of radical amazement in confronting its awesomeness, the ultimate goodness of the world which is often hidden from our imperfect senses, and our consequent respect for God's Creation. A theology of Revelation, on the other hand, the dialogue between God and human being, rooted for the Jewish people in the experience of Sinai and manifested in the *Halakhah,* demands learning God's ways through His words. The unfathomable gap between God and human being is inexplicably bridged through the gift of Torah. Revelation allows the potentially suffering soul to transcend the vanity of existence, and to realize meaning in an otherwise meaningless world. Such a model helps to explain the larger theological tension between Gendler and Lichtenstein. Gendler is sympathetic to nature theology, whereas Lichtenstein emphasizes a theology of revelation. Such a distinction is in keeping with Rosenak's insight that nature theologians tend to be liberal in their religious outlook, whereas revelation theologians tend to be orthodox. Mike Rosenak, "On Ways and Visions: The Theological and Educational Thought of Irving Greenberg," *The Melton Journal* (Spring 1992). The environmental movement is, among other agendas, a call for the reassertion of the Rosenzweigian category of creation in theological discussion. Such a model is helpful in understanding some of the subtle ways environmentalism is in tension with traditional Jewish categories. I believe that the environmental crisis offers an

opportunity for reasserting creation theologies, while having no effect on the larger culture's openness to theologies of Revelation. Arthur Green's recently published elegant presentation of his own theology is an excellent example of such a tendency. I hold it to be largely a theology of creation, strongly influenced by environmental themes. Arthur Green, *Seek My Face, Speak My Name: A Contemporary Jewish Theology,* (Northvale, N.J.: Aronson, 1992).

16. Lamm, pp. 173–77.

17. Lamm, p. 177.

18. Ismar Schorsch, "Tending to Our Cosmic Oasis," *The Melton Journal* (Spring 1991), taken from his "The Limits of History" in *Proceedings of the 1989 Rabbinical Assembly Convention.*

19. Philosophers of the environmental movement have argued that the environmental critique of modern culture is a Kuhnian shift of paradigms. As such, the ecological manifestations of the crisis are symptoms of a failure of the current cultural model, and the science of ecology a metaphor for the new cultural model. See Carolyn Merchant, "Epilogue: The Global Ecological Revolution" in *Ecological Revolutions* (Chapel Hill: University of North Carolina Press, 1989).

20. Exploring the historical content of the Jewish polemic with paganism is complex. Our main source, the Bible, has in many ways caricatured the pagan position for easy defeat. I believe Jon Levenson was the first to point out this habit of using straw men in interreligious or intercultural debates, and its misleading character for the historical analysis of the similarities and differences between Israelites and their idolatrous Biblical neighbors. Levenson argues that the high tones of Biblical rejection of paganism, and its one-dimensional presentation of pagan theology, in fact points to close cultural affinity between the two cultures. See Levenson's challenge to Yehezkel Kaufmann's classic anti-mythical portrayal of ancient Israel in his "Yehezkel Kaufmann and Mythology," *Conservative Judaism* 36 (Winter 1982).

21. For the classic anthropological presentation, see Sherry B. Ortner, "Is Female to Male as Nature is to Culture?" in *Woman, Culture and Society,* ed. Michelle Rosaldo and Louise Lamphere (Stanford: Stanford University Press, 1974). For a variety of perspectives on the environmental movement, see Diamond and Orenstein, *Reweaving the World.* Also, Carolyn Merchant *The Death of Nature* (San Francisco: Harper and Row, 1980).

22. Mircea Eliade, *Cosmos and History: The Myth of the Eternal Return* (New York: Harper and Row, 1959).

23. Stephen Jay Gould, *Time's Arrow, Time's Cycle: Myth and Metaphor in the Discovery of Geological Time* (London: Penguin Books, 1988).

24. Eliade, p. 104.
25. Eliade, p. 151.
26. Steven S. Schwarzschild, "The Unnatural Jew," *Environmental Ethics* 6 (1984):347–62.
27. In *Midrash Tanhuma, Parshat Tizroah,* there is, for example, the exchange between the Roman Genera Turnus Rufus and Rabbi Akiva. When asked whether God's creation or human creation is superior, Akiva anticipates the challenge to the Jewish practice of circumcision, and argues for the superiority of human action, in that they complete the unfinished work of creation. Thus even the human body, perfect in Greek-Roman aesthetic perception, is born imperfect, so that the Jew through *mitzvot* can participate in *ma'aseh bereshit,* the process of creation.
28. No one articulated the pagan sympathies of some Zionist thought better than Saul Tschernichovsky. See "Before a Statue of Apollo" in *Saul Tschernichovsky* (Ithaca: Cornell University Press, 1968), pp. 97–98. See also the chapters "Proto-Judaism," pp. 36–41, and "Fusion of Judaism and Hellenism," pp. 41–52 in same volume.
29. Michael Wyschogrod, "Judaism and the Sanctification of Nature," *The Melton Journal* (Spring 1992), pp. 6–7.
30. For an elaboration of the connection between Nazism and nature, see Robert A. Pois, *National Socialism and the Religion of Nature* (London: Croon Helm, 1986). Pois sees a direct connection between Nazi ideology's pagan beliefs and Nazi Germany's policies.
31. Wyschogrod, p. 7.
32. Wyschogrod and Schwarzschild differ in their evaluation of Christianity's position on morality and nature. Wyschogrod sees Christianity as a partner in the Jewish polemic against a nature morality. Schwarzschild believes that Christianity is to be found on the pagan end of the moral divide.
33. LaVergata gives a fine bibliographic review of the many variations of the social Darwinist platform, from racist/reactionary doctrines through liberal and conservative laissez-faire positions, scientist "biologism" and eugenics, all the way to socialist and even anarchist arguments as to the lessons to be learned from nature. Antonello LaVergata, "Images of Darwin: A Historiographic Overview" in *The Darwinian Heritage,* ed. David Kohn (Princeton: Princeton University Press, 1985), pp. 958–62. In the same volume, Robert M. Young argues convincingly that all Darwinism is social Darwinism as it is ultimately an argument about the place of the human being in nature, and conversely, the place of nature in the human.
34. "The Bambi syndrome" is named for the Disney movie *Bambi,* in which the natural world is pictured as an idyllic Eden save for the encroachment of

human beings. It refers to the human misconception of nature as peaceful and nonviolent as a result of viewing nature as *Bambi* portrays her, and thus the misplaced repulsion of many people to hunting. See Matt Cartmill, *A View to a Death in the Morning: Hunting and Nature through History* (Boston: Harvard University Press, 1993).

35. Aldo Leopold, *The Sand County Almanac* (New York: Oxford University Press, 1949), p. 129.

36. Michael Zimmerman explores the link between Heidegger, his Nazi sympathies, and the deep ecology movement. Heidegger has been portrayed as a forerunner of deep ecology. Zimmerman, by acknowledging the philosophical link between Heidegger and National Socialism, confronts the need to disassociate deep ecology from those philosophical assumptions of Heidegger's thought which lead to sympathy for Nazism. See Michael E. Zimmerman, "Rethinking the Heidegger–Deep Ecology Relationship," *Environmental Ethics* 13 (Fall 1993):205.

37. The debate between social ecology and deep ecology essentially centers around this moral question. For the social ecology position, see Murray Bookchin, "Why This Book Was Written," in *Remaking Society: Pathways to a Green Future* (Boston: South End Press, 1990).

38. David Ehrenfeld and Philip J. Bentley, "Judaism and the Practice of Stewardship."

39. Arthur O. Lovejoy, *The Great Chain of Being* (Cambridge: Harvard University Press, 1964).

40. David Ehrenfeld, *The Arrogance of Humanism* (New York: Oxford University Press, 1981).

41. Wendell Berry, "The Gift of Good Land" in his collection of essays *The Gift of Good Land* (San Francisco: North Point Press, 1981), pp. 267–81. Berry's poetic piece, defending the Judeo-Christian land ethic from White's frontal attack, is a classic of environmental theology.

42. Daniel Boyarin, *Carnal Israel: Reading Sex in Talmudic Culture* (Berkeley: University of California Press, 1993).

43. Mary Midgly, *Beast and Man: The Roots of Human Nature* (Ithaca: Cornell University Press, 1978). Midgley has offered a clear presentation of the role of the nature of the human being in any discussion of morality, without reducing the moral to being synonymous with the perceived natural order.

Aurora Levins Morales,
"Nadie la Tiene: Land, Ecology, and Nationalism"

I've wanted to write some version of this essay for years. Thanks to Ruth Atkin for asking me to do so. As is often the case with me, during the writing of this piece, I had extensive conversations with my mother, Rosario Morales, and my father, Richard Levins. They contributed clarity, insights, and factual detail about our farm and their own histories. Thanks to my father for talking about the legitimacy of a wandering heritage, his comments on the mysticism of blood and soil and for always sharing with me his love of history and his delight in ecological and historical complexity. Thanks to my mother for her clearheadedness, her sharp nose for bad politics, and for our ongoing discussions of feminism and nationalism, class, writing and everything else. Thanks to them both for deciding to have me and then my brothers "so we would have someone to talk to." They continue to be my closest political, intellectual and artistic companions.

1. My translation.
2. Small grocery/general store.
3. Literally, on the straight path, living the right way.
4. Somewhere between brat and hoodlum.
5. "Good family," meaning families with long-standing privilege.

Arthur Green,
"To Work It and Guard It: Preserving God's World"

1. *Kohelet Rabbah* 7:28.
2. Here, following the call of Thomas Berry and others, I am expanding the meaning of *bri'ot* beyond its usual reference of "people" to the more literal "creatures." The way to God is through the world; this includes both the path of human love and a compassionate embrace of all Creation.
3. Here, I cannot help recall Rabbi Nahman's scatological image of the *tsaddik* who sits next to his own refuse heap, surely a prescient parody of our times if ever there was one! See Band's translation of *The Tales,* p. 274, and my brief treatment in *Tormented Master,* pp. 362 ff.
4. *Sources on Judaism and Vegetarianism* have been collected by Richard Schwartz (Marblehead, Mass.: Micah, 1988).
5. Deuteronomy 22:6.
6. Leviticus 22:28.

Evan Eisenberg,
"Wilderness in Time, Sabbath in Space

This essay is adapted from my book *The Ecology of Eden* (New York: Knopf, 1998). It is best read in conjunction with my essay in Volume 1 of this anthology, particularly the passage near the end about sabbath, sabbatical, and jubilee.

1. On Jackson, see *The Ecology of Eden,* chap. 25; Eisenberg, "Back to Eden," *The Atlantic Monthly,* November 1989, pp. 57–89.

2. Arthur Waskow, *Down-to-Earth Judaism* (New York: Morrow, 1995), chap. 19. Back in 1975, Waskow proposed a modern adaptation of the Jubilee, with radical economic implications; see *Godwrestling* (New York: Schocken, 1978), chap. 11). More recently, a similar proposal by the Dutch rabbi Awraham Soetendorp (voiced as well by the Dutch cleric Father Dominik Grania) has received serious attention from the Global Forum, the International Council of Churches, and the Vatican (Ruvik Rosenthal, "Jubilee for All," *The Jerusalem Report* 8, no. 11 [1997]:40–1). One of its key points, the write-off by creditor nations of developing nations' debts, could help the planet as well as the poor by slowing the mad scramble to exploit natural resources and export cash crops.

3. Abraham Joshua Heschel, *The Sabbath* (New York: Farrar, Straus, and Young, 1951).

4. On Earth Jazz, see *The Ecology of Eden,* chap. 23.

5. I am improvising here on remarks made by Arthur Green at the Jewish Community of Amherst, February 25, 1995.

6. See Scholem, *Major Trends in Jewish Mysticism,* 3rd ed. (New York: Schocken, 1954), lecture 7; *On the Kabbalah and Its Symbolism* (New York: Schocken, 1965), chap. 3; *On the Mystical Shape of the Godhead,* rev. ed. (New York: Schocken, 1991), lecture 2.

7. On "decoupling," see *The Ecology of Eden,* chap. 28.

8. Barry Commoner, *Making Peace With the Planet* (New York: Pantheon, 1990), pp. 147–48.

9. See Elizabeth Pennisi, "Conservation's Ecocentrics," *Science News* 144 (1993):168–70.

10. (Boston: Houghton Mifflin, 1993).

Ellen Bernstein,
"Land, Community, and Sprawl"

This article was based on a talk given on Tu B'Shvat 5760 (2000 CE) for the Women's Shabbat Congregation Adath Jeshurun on Old York Road in Elkins Park, Pennsylvania.

Irene Diamond and David Seidenberg, "Recovering the Sensuous through Jewish Ecofeminist Practice"

This article was originally prepared for the conference on "Ecofeminism: A Practical Environmental Philosophy for the 21st Century," April 2–4, 1998, at the University of Montana.

ABOUT THE
CONTRIBUTORS

Thaer Abu Diab is co-director of the Palestinian-Israeli Environmental Secretariat.

Leonard Yehudah Angel is a poet, playwright, philosopher, World Federalist activist, and Jewish meditation pacifist. His plays include *The Unveiling* and *Eleanor Marx* (Playwrights Union Canada). His philosophical books include *How to Build a Conscious Machine* (Westview) and *Enlightenment East and West* (SUNY).

Ellen Bernstein founded Shomrei Adamah/Keepers of the Earth and edited *Ecology & the Jewish Spirit: Where Nature and the Sacred Meet* (Jewish Lights). She is director of community building at the Jewish Federation of Greater Philadelphia. She was a member of Philadelphia's mayoral transition team in 2000, and is a member of the board of the Natural Lands Trust.

Dr. David B. Brooks works in a part of Canada's international aid program that supports research on natural resources and environmental management in developing countries. His most recent book is *Watershed: The Role of Fresh Water in the Israeli-Palestinian Conflict*.

Irene Diamond teaches in the political science department at the University of Oregon, where she is co-director of the Rockefeller Humanities Fellowship Program, "Ecological Conversations: Gender, Science, and the Sacred." She lives in Eugene, Oregon, with her nine-year-old daughter Maya Chaya Sarah.

Rabbi Fred Dobb was ordained in 1997 from Philadelphia's Reconstructionist Rabbinical College. Ever since an environmental education walk across the United States ten years ago, he has been writing, teaching, and organizing around ecology and Judaism. He serves on the board of trustees of COEJL and the Teva Learning Center and as rabbi of Adat Shalom Reconstructionist Congregation in Bethesda, Maryland.

Evan Eisenberg is the author of *The Ecology of Eden* and *The Recording Angel*. His writing on nature and culture has appeared in *The Atlantic Monthly, The New Republic, The Nation, Natural History,* and other publications. A sometime cantor and former gardener for the New York City parks department, he lives in Manhattan with his wife, an urban planner, and their daughter.

Erich Fromm (d. 1980) was best known for drawing on psychoanalytic theory and practice to analyze and heal societal ills, in such books as *Escape from Freedom, The Art of Loving,* and *The Forgotten Language.* He is the author of *You Shall Be as Gods,* a reinterpretation of the Hebrew Bible.

Rabbi Everett Gendler was born in Iowa and served congregations in Mexico, Brazil, and Princeton, New Jersey, before spending nearly twenty-five years as the rabbi at Temple Emanuel in Lowell, Massachusetts, and nearly twenty years as chaplain and instructor at Phillips Academy in Andover, Massachusetts. He is an organic gardener and an avid proponent for nonviolence, social justice, peace, and the environment.

Dr. Arthur Green is a professor at Brandeis University and former president of the Reconstructionist Rabbinical College. His books include *Seek My Face Speak My Name,* and *Tormented Master: The Life and Spiritual Quest of Rabbi Nahman of Bratslav* (Jewish Lights). He is also the translator/editor of the works of two major Hasidic rebbes.

Rabbi Abraham Joshua Heschel (d. 1972) grew up in the family tradition of great Hasidic rebbes and became known as a major theologian and then as a committed religious activist against racism and the Vietnam war while serving as professor of ethics and mysticism at the Jewish Theological Seminary. His books include *God in Search of Man, The Sabbath, The Insecurity of Freedom,* and *Moral Grandeur and Spiritual Audacity* (ed. Susannah Heschel).

Naomi Mara Hyman is the editor of *Biblical Women in the Midrash,* the co-editor (with Ari Elon and Arthur Waskow) of *Trees, Earth and Torah: A Tu B'Shvat Anthology* and a student in the professional development *(smicha)* program of ALEPH: Alliance for Jewish Renewal.

Rabbi Michael Lerner is the editor of *Tikkun* magazine and the author of *Surplus Powerlessness* and *The Politics of Meaning.* The ideas put forward in his essay for this volume are developed in his books *Jewish Renewal: A Path to Healing and Transformation* (HarperCollins) and in *Spirit Matters* (Hampton Roads).

Aurora Levins Morales is a Puerto Rican Jewish writer, historian, and activist. She grew up in the mountains of western Puerto Rico and learned ecology from her biologist father, her bird-watching, bromeliad-loving mother, and the children of coffee workers. She lives in Berkeley, California, with her daughter.

Judith Plaskow is a long-time Jewish feminist-activist and theologian of feminist Judaism who is a professor of religious studies at Manhattan College. She is the author of *Standing Again at Sinai.*

Yossi Sarid was minister for the environment in the Israeli government during the prime ministerships of Yitzchak Rabin and Shimon Peres, from 1992 to 1996. He is a leader of the Meretz party and in 1999 reentered the government coalition led by Ehud Barak.

David Schechter is a playwright and director based in New York City. His plays on Jewish themes include the award-winning *Hannah Senesh,* which has toured extensively throughout the United States and Israel.

Eilon Schwartz is director of the Heschel Center for Environmental Learning and Leadership and teaches at the Melton Center for Jewish Education of the Hebrew University. He is currently writing a doctoral dissertation on the connection between human nature and the natural world, and its implications for educational philosophy. He lives in Tel Aviv with family and friends.

Rabbi Jeremy Schwartz is a teacher, translator, and author who lives in the greater Boston area. He is a graduate of the Reconstructionist Rabbinical College and served as the first assistant director at Kolel: The Adult Centre for Liberal Jewish Learning, located in Toronto.

Rabbi David Seidenberg is completing work for a Ph.D. degree in ecology and Kabbalah at the Jewish Theological Seminary, where he was ordained in 1994. A founder of the Hasidic egalitarian minyanim in New York and Los Angeles, and former congregational rabbi in British Columbia, he works on peace and economic justice issues as well as ecology. He teaches and writes in Seattle.

Evi Seidman is a "stand-up philosopher" and poet, educator, and activist for environmental sanity and social justice. She now rabble-rouses in small-town politics in the Mid-Hudson Valley and is writing memoirs of personal adventures during the women's movement of the 1970s.

Paul Pesach Smith is co-director of the Palestinian-Israeli Environmental Secretariat.

Rabbi Margot L. Stein is an award-winning singer/songwriter whose musical play, *Guarding the Garden,* toured North America for four seasons and was seen by some twenty thousand people. She has produced five albums of Jewish music, both solo and in collaboration with the a cappella trio MIRAJ and the ensemble Shabbat Unplugged. Their current release, *A Night of Questions,* provides original and traditional music to accompany the new Reconstructionist Haggadah.

Dr. Alon Tal is the director of the Environmental Policy Research Center at the Arava Institute for Environmental Studies. He also teaches environmental law and environmental politics as an adjunct lecturer at Tel Aviv and Hebrew University. Dr. Tal serves as chairman of Life and Environment, the umbrella organization for Israel's environmental groups. He lives on Kibbutz Ketura with his wife and three daughters.

Robin Twite is a former director of the British Council in Israel. He has worked on conflict resolution at Hebrew University and coordinates work on environmental issues for the Israel-Palestine Center for Research and Information.

Rabbi Arthur Waskow founded and is director of The Shalom Center and is a Pathfinder of ALEPH: Alliance for Jewish Renewal. He wrote *The Freedom Seder; Godwrestling; Seasons of Our Joy; Down-to-Earth Judaism: Food, Money, Sex, and the Rest of Life;* and *Godwrestling—Round Two: Ancient Wisdom, Future Paths* (Jewish Lights), recipient of the Benjamin Franklin Award in 1996. He is a co-editor of *Trees, Earth, and Torah: A Tu B'Shvat Anthology.* He and his wife, Phyllis Ocean Berman, teach, lead Jewish renewal davvening, lecture, and do storytelling in many synagogues, campuses, retreat centers, and interreligious conferences. Together they wrote *Tales of Tikkun: New Jewish Stories to Heal the Wounded World.* They live in Philadelphia.

About JEWISH LIGHTS Publishing

People of all faiths and backgrounds yearn for books that attract, engage, educate and spiritually inspire.

Our principal goal is to stimulate thought and help all people learn about who the Jewish People are, where they come from, and what the future can be made to hold. While people of our diverse Jewish heritage are the primary audience, our books speak to people in the Christian world as well and will broaden their understanding of Judaism and the roots of their own faith.

We bring to you authors who are at the forefront of spiritual thought and experience. While each has something different to say, they all say it in a voice that you can hear.

Our books are designed to welcome you and then to engage, stimulate and inspire. We judge our success not only by whether or not our books are beautiful and commercially successful, but by whether or not they make a difference in your life.

We at Jewish Lights take great care to produce beautiful books that present meaningful spiritual content in a form that reflects the art of making high quality books. Therefore, we want to acknowledge those who contributed to the production of this book.

Stuart M. Matlins, Publisher

PRODUCTION
Marian B. Wallace & Bridgett Taylor

EDITORIAL
Sandra Korinchak, Emily Wichland,
Martha McKinney & Amanda Dupuis

COVER DESIGN
Casey Nuttall, Hingham, Massachusetts

TEXT DESIGN
Sans Serif, Inc., Saline, Michigan

COVER & TEXT PRINTING AND BINDING
Versa Press, East Peoria, Illinois

Spirituality

The Women's Torah Commentary: *New Insights from Women Rabbis on the 54 Weekly Torah Portions* Ed. by *Rabbi Elyse Goldstein*

For the first time, women rabbis provide a commentary on the entire Torah. More than 25 years after the first woman was ordained a rabbi in America, women have an impressive group of spiritual role models that they never had before. Here, in a week-by-week format, these inspiring teachers bring their rich perspectives to bear on the biblical text. A perfect gift for others, or for yourself. 6 x 9, 432 pp, HC, ISBN 1-58023-076-8 **$29.95**

Bringing the Psalms to Life
How to Understand and Use the Book of Psalms by *Rabbi Daniel F. Polish*

Here, the most beloved—and least understood—of the books in the Bible comes alive. This simultaneously insightful and practical guide shows how the psalms address a myriad of spiritual issues in our lives: feeling abandoned, overcoming illness, dealing with anger, and more. 6 x 9, 208 pp, HC, ISBN 1-58023-077-6 **$21.95**

Stepping Stones to Jewish Spiritual Living: *Walking the Path Morning, Noon, and Night* by *Rabbi James L. Mirel* & *Karen Bonnell Werth*

Transforms our daily routine into sacred acts of mindfulness. Chapters are arranged according to the cycle of each day. "A wonderful, practical, and inspiring guidebook to gently bring the riches of Jewish practice into our busy, everyday lives. Highly recommended." —*Rabbi David A. Cooper.* 6 x 9, 240 pp, Quality PB, ISBN 1-58023-074-1 **$16.95**; HC, ISBN 1-58023-003-2 **$21.95**

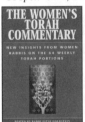 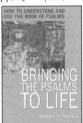  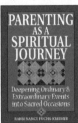 

Parenting As a Spiritual Journey:
Deepening Ordinary & Extraordinary Events into Sacred Occasions
by Rabbi Nancy Fuchs-Kreimer 6 x 9, 224 pp, Quality PB, ISBN 1-58023-016-4 **$16.95**

The Year Mom Got Religion: *One Woman's Midlife Journey into Judaism*
by Lee Meyerhoff Hendler 6 x 9, 208 pp, Quality PB, ISBN 1-58023-070-9 **$15.95**;
HC, ISBN 1-58023-000-8 **$19.95**

Moses—The Prince, the Prophet: *His Life, Legend & Message for Our Lives*
by Rabbi Levi Meier, Ph.D. 6 x 9, 224 pp, Quality PB, ISBN 1-58023-069-5 **$16.95**;
HC, ISBN 1-58023-013-X **$23.95**

Ancient Secrets: *Using the Stories of the Bible to Improve Our Everyday Lives*
by Rabbi Levi Meier, Ph.D. 5½ x 8½, 288 pp, Quality PB, ISBN 1-58023-064-4 **$16.95**

Or phone, fax or mail to: JEWISH LIGHTS Publishing
Sunset Farm Offices, Route 4 • P.O. Box 237 • Woodstock, Vermont 05091
Tel: (802) 457-4000 • Fax: (802) 457-4004 • www.jewishlights.com
Credit card orders: (800) 962-4544 (9AM–5PM ET Monday–Friday)
Generous discounts on quantity orders. SATISFACTION GUARANTEED. Prices subject to change.

Theology/Philosophy

Torah of the Earth: *Exploring 4,000 Years of Ecology in Jewish Thought*
In 2 Volumes   Ed. by *Rabbi Arthur Waskow*

Major new resource offering us an invaluable key to understanding the intersection of ecology and Judaism. Leading scholars provide us with a guided tour of ecological thought from four major Jewish viewpoints. Vol. 1: *Biblical Israel & Rabbinic Judaism*, 6 x 9, 272 pp, Quality PB, ISBN 1-58023-086-5 **$19.95**; Vol. 2: *Zionism & Eco-Judaism*, 6 x 9, 336 pp, Quality PB, ISBN 1-58023-087-3 **$19.95**

Broken Tablets: *Restoring the Ten Commandments and Ourselves*
Ed. by *Rabbi Rachel S. Mikva*; Intro. by *Rabbi Lawrence Kushner*;
Afterword by *Rabbi Arnold Jacob Wolf*   **AWARD WINNER!**

Twelve outstanding spiritual leaders each share profound and personal thoughts about these biblical commands and why they have such a special hold on us.
6 x 9, 192 pp, HC, ISBN 1-58023-066-0 **$21.95**

Evolving Halakhah: *A Progressive Approach to Traditional Jewish Law*
by *Rabbi Dr. Moshe Zemer*

Innovative and provocative, this book affirms the system of traditional Jewish law, *halakhah*, as flexible enough to accommodate the changing realities of each generation. It shows that the traditional framework for understanding the Torah's commandments can be the living heart of Jewish life for all Jews.   6 x 9, 480 pp, HC, ISBN 1-58023-002-4 **$40.00**

God & the Big Bang
Discovering Harmony Between Science & Spirituality   **AWARD WINNER!**
by Daniel C. Matt
6 x 9, 216 pp, Quality PB, ISBN 1-879045-89-3 **$16.95**; HC, ISBN 1-879045-48-6 **$21.95**

Israel—A Spiritual Travel Guide   **AWARD WINNER!**
A Companion for the Modern Jewish Pilgrim
by Rabbi Lawrence A. Hoffman   4¼ x 10, 256 pp, Quality PB, ISBN 1-879045-56-7 **$18.95**

Godwrestling—Round 2: *Ancient Wisdom, Future Paths*   **AWARD WINNER!**
by Rabbi Arthur Waskow
6 x 9, 352 pp, Quality PB, ISBN 1-879045-72-9 **$18.95**; HC, ISBN 1-879045-45-1 **$23.95**

Ecology & the Jewish Spirit: *Where Nature & the Sacred Meet*   Ed. and with Intros.
by Ellen Bernstein   6 x 9, 288 pp, Quality PB, ISBN 1-58023-082-2 **$16.95**;
HC, ISBN 1-879045-88-5 **$23.95**

Israel: *An Echo of Eternity*   by Abraham Joshua Heschel; New Intro. by
Dr. Susannah Heschel   5½ x 8, 272 pp, Quality PB, ISBN 1-879045-70-2 **$18.95**

The Earth Is the Lord's: *The Inner World of the Jew in Eastern Europe*
by Abraham Joshua Heschel   5½ x 8, 112 pp, Quality PB, ISBN 1-879045-42-7 **$13.95**

A Passion for Truth: *Despair and Hope in Hasidism*   by Abraham Joshua Heschel
5½ x 8, 352 pp, Quality PB, ISBN 1-879045-41-9 **$18.95**

Theology/Philosophy

A Heart of Many Rooms
Celebrating the Many Voices within Judaism
by *Dr. David Hartman* **AWARD WINNER!**

Named a *Publishers Weekly* "Best Book of the Year." Addresses the spiritual and theological questions that face all Jews and all people today. From the perspective of traditional Judaism, Hartman shows that commitment to both Jewish tradition and to pluralism can create understanding between people of different religious convictions.
6 x 9, 352 pp, HC, ISBN 1-58023-048-2 **$24.95**

A Living Covenant: *The Innovative Spirit in Traditional Judaism*
by *Dr. David Hartman* **AWARD WINNER!**

Winner, National Jewish Book Award. Hartman reveals a Judaism grounded in covenant—a relational framework—informed by the metaphor of marital love rather than that of parent-child dependency. 6 x 9, 368 pp, Quality PB, ISBN 1-58023-011-3 **$18.95**

The Death of Death: *Resurrection and Immortality in Jewish Thought*
by *Dr. Neil Gillman* **AWARD WINNER!**

Does death end life, or is it the passage from one stage of life to another? This National Jewish Book Award Finalist explores the original and compelling argument that Judaism, a religion often thought to pay little attention to the afterlife, not only offers us rich ideas on the subject—but delivers a deathblow to death itself. 6 x 9, 336 pp, Quality PB, ISBN 1-58023-081-4 **$18.95**; HC, ISBN 1-879045-61-3 **$23.95**

 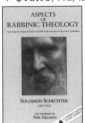   

Aspects of Rabbinic Theology by Solomon Schechter; New Intro. by Dr. Neil Gillman
6 x 9, 448 pp, Quality PB, ISBN 1-879045-24-9 **$19.95**

The Last Trial: *On the Legends and Lore of the Command to Abraham to Offer Isaac as a Sacrifice* by Shalom Spiegel; New Intro. by Judah Goldin
6 x 9, 208 pp, Quality PB, ISBN 1-879045-29-X **$17.95**

Judaism and Modern Man: *An Interpretation of Jewish Religion* by Will Herberg; New Intro. by Dr. Neil Gillman 5½ x 8½, 336 pp, Quality PB, ISBN 1-879045-87-7 **$18.95**

Seeking the Path to Life **AWARD WINNER!**
Theological Meditations on God and the Nature of People, Love, Life and Death
by Rabbi Ira F. Stone
6 x 9, 160 pp, Quality PB, ISBN 1-879045-47-8 **$14.95**; HC, ISBN 1-879045-17-6 **$19.95**

The Spirit of Renewal: *Finding Faith after the Holocaust* **AWARD WINNER!**
by Rabbi Edward Feld
6 x 9, 224 pp, Quality PB, ISBN 1-879045-40-0 **$16.95**

Tormented Master: *The Life and Spiritual Quest of Rabbi Nahman of Bratslav*
by Dr. Arthur Green
6 x 9, 416 pp, Quality PB, ISBN 1-879045-11-7 **$18.95**

Your Word Is Fire: *The Hasidic Masters on Contemplative Prayer*
Ed. and Trans. with a New Introduction by Dr. Arthur Green and Dr. Barry W. Holtz
6 x 9, 160 pp, Quality PB, ISBN 1-879045-25-7 **$14.95**

Spirituality

My People's Prayer Book: *Traditional Prayers, Modern Commentaries*

Ed. by *Dr. Lawrence A. Hoffman*

This momentous, critically-acclaimed series is truly a people's prayer book, one that provides a diverse and exciting commentary to the traditional liturgy. It will help modern men and women find new wisdom and guidance in Jewish prayer, and bring liturgy into their lives. Each book includes Hebrew text, modern translation, and commentaries *from all perspectives* of the Jewish world. Vol. 1—*The Sh'ma and Its Blessings*, 7 x 10, 168 pp, HC, ISBN 1-879045-79-6 **$23.95**
Vol. 2—*The Amidah*, 7 x 10, 240 pp, HC, ISBN 1-879045-80-X **$23.95**
Vol. 3—*P'sukei D'zimrah* (Morning Psalms), 7 x 10, 240 pp, HC, ISBN 1-879045-81-8 **$23.95**
Vol. 4—*Seder K'riyat Hatorah* (Shabbat Torah Service), 7 x 10, 240 pp, ISBN 1-879045-82-6 **$23.95**
(Avail. Sept. 2000)

Voices from Genesis: *Guiding Us through the Stages of Life*

by *Dr. Norman J. Cohen*

In a brilliant blending of modern *midrash* (finding contemporary meaning from biblical texts) and the life stages of Erik Erikson's developmental psychology, the characters of Genesis come alive to give us insights for our own journeys. 6 x 9, 192 pp, HC, ISBN 1-879045-75-3 **$21.95**

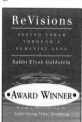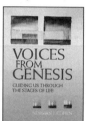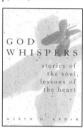

God Whispers: *Stories of the Soul, Lessons of the Heart*
by Rabbi Karyn D. Kedar 6 x 9, 176 pp, Quality PB, ISBN 1-58023-088-1 **$15.95**;
HC, ISBN 1-58023-023-7 **$19.95**

Being God's Partner: *How to Find the Hidden Link Between Spirituality and Your Work*
by Rabbi Jeffrey K. Salkin; Intro. by Norman Lear AWARD WINNER!
6 x 9, 192 pp, Quality PB, ISBN 1-879045-65-6 **$16.95**; HC, ISBN 1-879045-37-0 **$19.95**

ReVisions: *Seeing Torah through a Feminist Lens* AWARD WINNER!
by Rabbi Elyse Goldstein 5½ x 8½, 208 pp, HC, ISBN 1-58023-047-4 **$19.95**

Soul Judaism: *Dancing with God into a New Era*
by Rabbi Wayne Dosick 5½ x 8½, 304 pp, Quality PB, ISBN 1-58023-053-9 **$16.95**

Finding Joy: *A Practical Spiritual Guide to Happiness* AWARD WINNER!
by Rabbi Dannel I. Schwartz with Mark Hass
6 x 9, 192 pp, Quality PB, ISBN 1-58023-009-1 **$14.95**; HC, ISBN 1-879045-53-2 **$19.95**

The Empty Chair: *Finding Hope and Joy—*
Timeless Wisdom from a Hasidic Master, Rebbe Nachman of Breslov AWARD WINNER!
Adapted by Moshe Mykoff and the Breslov Research Institute
4 x 6, 128 pp, Deluxe PB, 2-color text, ISBN 1-879045-67-2 **$9.95**

The Gentle Weapon: *Prayers for Everyday and Not-So-Everyday Moments*
Adapted from the Wisdom of Rebbe Nachman of Breslov by Moshe Mykoff and
S. C. Mizrahi, with the Breslov Research Institute
4 x 6, 144 pp, Deluxe PB, 2-color text, ISBN 1-58023-022-9 **$9.95**

"Who Is a Jew?" *Conversations, Not Conclusions* by Meryl Hyman
6 x 9, 272 pp, Quality PB, ISBN 1-58023-052-0 **$16.95**; HC, ISBN 1-879045-76-1 **$23.95**

The Way Into... Series

A major 14-volume series to be completed over the next several years, *The Way Into...* provides an accessible and usable "guided tour" of the Jewish faith, its people, its history and beliefs—in total, an introduction to Judaism for adults that will permit them to understand and interact with sacred texts.

Each volume is written by a major modern scholar and teacher, and is organized around an important concept of Judaism.

The Way Into... will enable all readers to achieve a real sense of Jewish cultural literacy through guided study. Forthcoming volumes include:

  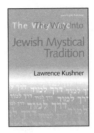 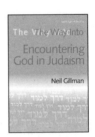

The Way Into Torah
by *Dr. Norman J. Cohen*

What is "Torah"? What are the different approaches to studying Torah? What are the different levels of understanding Torah? For whom is the study intended? Explores the origins and development of Torah, why it should be studied and how to do it. Addresses these and many other issues in this easy-to-use, easy-to-understand introduction to the ancient subject.

6 x 9, 160 pp, HC, ISBN 1-58023-028-8 **$21.95**

The Way Into Jewish Prayer
by *Dr. Lawrence A. Hoffman*

Explores the reasons for and the ways of Jewish prayer. Opens the door to 3,000 years of the Jewish way to God by making available all you need to feel at home in Jewish worship. Provides basic definitions of the terms you need to know as well as thoughtful analysis of the depth that lies beneath Jewish prayer.

6 x 9, 160 pp, HC, ISBN 1-58023-027-X **$21.95**

The Way Into Jewish Mystical Tradition
by *Rabbi Lawrence Kushner*

Explains the principles of Jewish mystical thinking, their religious and spiritual significance, and how they relate to our lives. A book that allows us to experience and understand the Jewish mystical approach to our place in the world.

6 x 9, 176 pp, HC, ISBN 1-58023-029-6 **$21.95** (Avail. Sept. 2000)

The Way Into Encountering God in Judaism
by *Dr. Neil Gillman*

Explains how Jews have encountered God throughout history—and today—by exploring the many metaphors for God in Jewish tradition. Explores the Jewish tradition's passionate but also conflicting ways of relating to God as Creator, relational partner, and a force in history and nature.

6 x 9, 176 pp, HC, ISBN 1-58023-025-3 **$21.95** (Avail. Sept. 2000)

Spirituality & More

These Are the Words: *A Vocabulary of Jewish Spiritual Life*

by *Arthur Green*

What are the most essential ideas, concepts and terms that an educated person needs to know about Judaism? From *Adonai* (My Lord) to *zekhut* (merit), this enlightening and entertaining journey through Judaism teaches us the 149 core Hebrew words that constitute the basic vocabulary of Jewish spiritual life. 6 x 9, 304 pp, HC, ISBN 1-58023-024-5 **$21.95**

The Enneagram and Kabbalah: *Reading Your Soul*

by *Rabbi Howard A. Addison*

Combines two of the most powerful maps of consciousness known to humanity—The Tree of Life (the *Sefirot*) from the Jewish mystical tradition of *Kabbalah*, and the nine-pointed Enneagram—and shows how, together, they can provide a powerful tool for self-knowledge, critique, and transformation. 6 x 9, 176 pp, Quality PB, ISBN 1-58023-001-6 **$15.95**

Embracing the Covenant
Converts to Judaism Talk About Why & How

Ed. and with Intros. by *Rabbi Allan L. Berkowitz* and *Patti Moskovitz*

Through personal experiences of 20 converts to Judaism, this book illuminates reasons for converting, the quest for a satisfying spirituality, the appeal of the Jewish tradition and how conversion has changed lives—the convert's, and the lives of those close to them. 6 x 9, 192 pp, Quality PB, ISBN 1-879045-50-8 **$15.95**

Shared Dreams: *Martin Luther King, Jr. and the Jewish Community*
by Rabbi Marc Schneier; Preface by Martin Luther King III
6 x 9, 240 pp, HC, ISBN 1-58023-062-8 **$24.95**

Mystery Midrash: *An Anthology of Jewish Mystery & Detective Fiction*
Ed. by Lawrence W. Raphael; Preface by Joel Siegel, ABC's *Good Morning America*
6 x 9, 304 pp, Quality PB, ISBN 1-58023-055-5 **$16.95**

The Jewish Gardening Cookbook: *Growing Plants & Cooking for Holidays & Festivals*
by Michael Brown 6 x 9, 224 pp, HC, Illus., ISBN 1-58023-004-0 **$21.95**

Wandering Stars: *An Anthology of Jewish Fantasy & Science Fiction* Ed. by Jack
Dann; Intro. by Isaac Asimov 6 x 9, 272 pp, Quality PB, ISBN 1-58023-005-9 **$16.95**

More Wandering Stars
An Anthology of Outstanding Stories of Jewish Fantasy and Science Fiction
Ed. by Jack Dann; Intro. by Isaac Asimov 6 x 9, 192 pp, Quality PB, ISBN 1-58023-063-6 **$16.95**

A Heart of Wisdom: *Making the Jewish Journey from Midlife through the Elder Years*
Ed. by Susan Berrin; Foreword by Harold Kushner
6 x 9, 384 pp, Quality PB, ISBN 1-58023-051-2 **$18.95**; HC, ISBN 1-879045-73-7 **$24.95**

Sacred Intentions: *Daily Inspiration to Strengthen the Spirit, Based on Jewish Wisdom*
by Rabbi Kerry M. Olitzky and Rabbi Lori Forman
4½ x 6½, 448 pp, Quality PB, ISBN 1-58023-061-X **$15.95**

   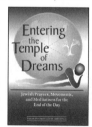 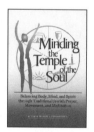